Dalits Issues

Dalit Issues

Caste and Class Interface

Edited by

T. Brahmanandam

RAWAT PUBLICATIONS

Jaipur • New Delhi • Bangalore • Guwahati • Kolkata

ISBN 978-81-316-0872-2

Published by
Prem Rawat for **Rawat Publications**
Satyam Apts, Sector 3, Jawahar Nagar, Jaipur 302 004 (India)
Phone: 0141 265 1748 / 7006 Fax: 0141 265 1748
E-mail: info@rawatbooks.com
Website: www.rawatbooks.com

New Delhi Office
4858/24, Ansari Road, Daryaganj, New Delhi 110 002
Phone: 011 2326 3290

Also at *Bangalore, Guwahati* and *Kolkata*

Typeset by Rawat Computers, Jaipur
Printed at Nice Printing Press, New Delhi

Contents

Preface

The present book is an outcome of the National Seminar organized by CMDR, Dharwad from 21 April to 22 April 2016 on 'Dalit Situation in India: After Economic Reforms'. The Seminar intended to deliberate the important aspects at the backdrop of the 125th Birth Anniversary of Dr B.R. Ambedkar for two days duration at CMDR. It was sponsored by the Indian Council of Social Science Research (ICSSR), New Delhi. The key architect of this Seminar was Dr T. Brahmanandam, Associate Professor at the Centre for Multi-Disciplinary Development Research (CMDR), Dharwad.

It is incumbent upon all of us to retrospect the legacy of Dr Ambedkar and the working of the Constitution as the foundation of a nation state. The century old syndromes of Dalit atrocity and discrimination are still continuing in spite of the special legislations like Protection of Civil Rights Act, 1955, and the Scheduled Castes and Tribes (Prevention of Atrocities) Act, 1989. Dr Ambedkar was fighting for the historic legacy of social justice, that seems to have lost or losing the ground in neo-liberalism which brings the old dictum back, 'survival of the fittest'.

The economic reforms post-1990s and waves of neo-liberalism failed to work within the framework of a constitutional scheme that gives right to education, right to life with dignity, right to be treated equally and the right of not to be exploited, etc. The Directive Principles of State Policy appeared to be less effective but still relevant enough to bring the ruling dispensation out of party politics. Feminism in India did not address the problems of downtrodden women. The so-called Left Movement got obsessed with the class struggle and gradually got lost in trade unions. The caste found a fertile ground in the resurgence of the Vedic culture. The caste-class dichotomy made the social equations more complex. The upper caste apparently became the ruling class. The politically privileged Dalits constituted a creamy layer, immune from atrocity and discriminations. Simultaneously, Dalits were pushed to vote bank politics in elections. The Human Rights Commission, supposed to be democracy's ombudsman was left with little statutory instruments. The judicial activism remains confined to Public Interest Litigation (PIL) taken in control by individuals and organizations. The text and texture of the Dalit discourse did not match with vocabulary of the ruling elite. The much needed social reform seemed merged into the social media from Una to United Nation. 'Injustice anywhere is threat to justice everywhere' (Martin Luther King Junior). Therefore, it was an academic imperative to put facts and figures into right perspectives to bring out what social sciences could contribute to this dialectics of democracy. When law fell apart and failed to protect its own subjects from being victims, what sense did it make for itself to take its own course so callously to prolong injustice by delaying justice? The 125th Birth Anniversary of Dr Ambedkar was thus a historic moment to be accountable to those who were left downtrodden.

There are two extremes growing unbound in the society. On one extreme (urban), we have IITs; and on the other extreme (rural), we have ITIs. On one extreme we have skyscrapers, on the other we have slum dwellers. On one extreme, there are farmers who are committing suicide for not being able to repay the paltry bank loans, and on the other, there are corporate giants who enjoy lavish lifestyle on huge bank loans. On one extreme, we have super-specialty hospitals, and on the other, the primary health centres of rural India run without basic amenities. The list is pretty long. Such growing disparity and discrimination has pushed the two segments into two different extremes. Rudyard Kipling's memorable lines, 'East is East, and West is West, and never the twine shall meet', stand as a challenge before us and blur the feasibility of building the bridge between the urban and rural. The smart city project, growing industrialization, shrinking agriculture, displacement of rural folk, all suggest the validity of Spencer's axiom of 'survival of the fittest'. Globalization, FDI, digital literacy, land acquisition, etc. will go against the rural India. The issue is more complex than it appears to be.

As we all know that the International Commission on Education for the 21st century has underlined the imperatives of education in terms of 'to know, to do, to be, to live together', and has drawn our attention to the tension between (a) the global and the local, (b) the universal and individual, (c) tradition and modernity, (d) long-term and short-term considerations, (e) need for competition and concern for equality of opportunity, (f) extraordinary expansion of knowledge and human beings' capacity to assimilate it, and (g) spiritual and the material. We are yet to deliberate on such tensions and construct a concord on each for all, and all for each. These are the challenges before us today. The CMDR has made a humble effort to understand different facets and interfaces for a paradigm shift to realize the goals of the Constitution drafted under the Chairmanship of Dr B.R. Ambedkar.

There have been 13 research papers presented and debated in the Seminar. Keeping in view the suggestions, the papers have been rephrased/edited wherever necessary. Publication of these papers in a book form will add value to the literature on Dalit studies and help understand the paradigm shift to realize the dreams of Babasaheb Ambedkar.

January 2017

T. Brahmanandam
CMDR, Dharwad

Acknowledgement

It gives me great pleasure and contentment to realize and witness the conference papers getting published in the form of a book. I give my good wishes to all contributing authors for their participation and giving their revised version to be published in the present book. On behalf of the Centre for Multi-Disciplinary Development Research (CMDR), I also express my heartfelt gratitude to all the contributors. The present book is a humble academic initiative towards realizing my dreams of working and bringing out relevant writings on various aspects of Dalits in India.

The following have their contributions with their papers as mentioned below:

Prof. Sanghmitra Acharya, Director of Indian Institute of Dalit Studies, New Delhi, presented her paper on 'Dalits in Conservancy and Sanitation Works: Exploring the Connects between Economic Reforms and their Health'. It is a comparative study of *Safai Karamcharis* and their conditions in across the country. It is a macro level study that brings the empirical data from selected states in order to give representational and rationale to the study. Prof. K.K. Bagchi, North Bengal University presented his paper on 'Affirmative Action Policies for Dalits in India: A Review of their Implementation'. It brings out the failure of affirmative actions with partial success. Dr T. Brahmanandam, CMDR, Dharwad presented a paper on '73rd Constitutional Amendment: An Impact Assessment' over the years, highlights the flaws in the system while including remedial measures. Dr A. Vadivelu of Periyar University presented a paper on 'Availability of Healthcare Services in PHCs of Salem District: Special Reference to Tamil Nadu'. The paper concludes that the country needs to make concerted efforts to improve the social and economic conditions of scheduled castes. Prof. Dandge of Shivaji University writes on 'Socio-Economic Deprivation of Scheduled Castes through Social Exclusion and Discrimination in India'. There are remedial measures for an egalitarian society. Suman Damare from the University of Hyderabad presented a paper on 'Scheduled Castes Sub Plan Act 2013 left to Vain'. This paper deals with data of undivided Andhra Pradesh. Prof. Kamble of Shivaji University presented his paper on 'Educational Participation of Marginalised Social Groups in Education of Maharashtra' on English language as the source of economic empowerment and social change. Dr K.M. Ziyauddin, Maulana Azad National Urdu University, Hyderabad, presented his paper on 'Manual Scavengers Far from Dignity and Inclusion'. It talks about the reality of the social construction of Muslim Mehtars who are working as scavengers, while comparing them with other manual scavengers amongst the Hindus. Prof. Gopinath Reddy of Centre for Economic and Social Studies, Hyderabad, presented a paper on 'Impact of Affirmative Action on Subaltern Castes: Evidence from the Recent Data'. The paper questions the effectiveness of Affirmative Action Policy. Dr Shiddalingaswami V. Hanagodimath of CMDR presented a paper on 'Dalits and Human Development Indices'. In this paper, he is trying to project Dalit development in education, health and their standard of living. Dr Subhankar Basu and Prof. Eliah, Metas Adventist College, Surat, presented a paper on 'Dalit, Discourse, and Democracy' from post-structuralism perspective. Dr Vinod Kumar Yadav, Centre for the Study of Discrimination and Exclusion, JNU presented his paper on 'Bonded Labour and its Implications: Sociological Reflections of a Mahadalit Community in Bihar'. This is an in-depth ethnographic study of bonded labourers with reference to the caste structure. Prof. Thangaraj, Former Head, Dept. of Economics, University of Madras, presented his paper on 'Different Constitutional Provisions and its Impact on Occupational Diversification among Social

Groups in India'. The paper projects the interfaces of law, economy, and society. I also express my sincere thanks and gratitude to Shri Bharat Bhusan IRTS (Rtd.) who has been the constant source of inspiration and guide.

I am thankful to ICSSR that has always been a great help in conducting research activities. Lastly, I extend my sincere thanks to Rawat Publications for their professionalism and cordial response in bringing out this volume.

T. Brahmanandam
CMDR, Dharwad

Contributors

A. Vadivelu is currently Assistant Professor, Department of Commerce, Salvaman Arts and Science College (Autonomous), Namakkal, Tamil Nadu.

K.M. Ziyauddin is Assistant Professor at Al-Beruni Centre for the Study of Social Exclusion and Inclusive Policy, Maulana Azad National Urdu University, Hyderabad.

Kanak Kanti Bagchi is Professor at North Bengal University, Siliguri (Dist. Darjeeling), West Bengal.

M. Gopinath Reddy is Professor at Centre for Economic and Social Studies (CESS), Nizamiah Observatory Campus, Begumpet, Hyderabad.

M. Thangaraj is former Professor and Head, Department of Economics, University of Madras, Chennai.

P.S. Kamble is Head, Department of Economics at Shivaji University, Kolhapur, Maharashtra.

Ramesh G. Dandge is former Professor at Department of Economics, Shivaji University, Kolhapur, Maharashtra.

Sanghmitra S. Acharya is currently Director for Indian Institute of Dalit Studies (IIDS), New Delhi and Professor at Centre of Social Medicine and Community Health, School of Social Sciences, Jawaharlal Nehru University, New Delhi.

Shiddalingaswami V. Hanagodimath is Assistant Professor at Centre for Multi-Disciplinary Development Research (CMDR), Dharwad.

Srikakolli Eliah, Principal, Metas Adventist College, Surat.

Subhankar Basu is a faculty at AljameaTus Saifiyah, Arabic Academy, Surat.

Suman Damre is pursuing his PhD from Department of Political Science, University of Hyderabad, Hyderabad.

T. Brahmanandam is Associate Professor at Centre for Multi-Disciplinary Development Research (CMDR), Dharwad.

Vinod Kumar Yadav is currently working as Assistant Professor, Department of Sociology, School of Social Sciences, Jamia Milia Islamia University, New Delhi.

1

Dalits in Conservancy and Sanitation Works

Exploring the Connects between Economic Reforms and their Health

SANGHMITRA S. ACHARYA

The 125th birth anniversary of Dr B.R. Ambedkar was on 14 April. While the nation pays tribute to the legend once again, it is ironical that his efforts to uplift the Dalits show little progress in the issue which was close to his heart. Dr Ambedkar rigorously campaigned against social discrimination and categorization of work based on caste. His untiring efforts against the practice of manual scavenging, a hideous practice of cleaning the human excreta from latrines manually, could be realized only as late as 2013 with the passage of the Act. While the legislative measure has been enacted, social efforts to execute it remain desirable.

The sanitation workers collect the human excreta with their brooms and tin-plate and carry it to a disposable ground. This work division has continued based upon the traditional Hindu social order, which allowed division of labour and assigned the Dalits the dirty and mean jobs, and the 2011 Census data confirms the continuation of the same. Dr Ambedkar, said: '… in India a man is not a scavenger because of his work. He is a scavenger because of his birth irrespective of the question whether he does scavenging or not'. In addition to facing apathy from the society, sanitation workers are at a risk of diseases such as dysentery, malaria, typhoid, skin infections, tuberculosis and exposure to toxic gases in sewers.

The data on house listing and housing in Census 2011 will continue to embarrass the government for its failure to eliminate manual scavenging. The Census data shows 8 lakh people engaged in clearing night soil by hand. It cannot be more shameful than this for the governments to remain in denial mode. 'Dignity Campaign-Action for Liberation of Dalit Manual Scavenger Women in India' is a study done by Jan Sahas with support from UN Women's Fund for Gender Equality. It studied 10,000 women manual scavengers in 15 districts of Bihar, Madhya Pradesh and Uttar Pradesh during 2013–2015 to understand their economic and political rights. The study reflected that 70 per cent women were into manual scavenging after marriage while 30 per cent were forced into it since childhood. Women were paid very less. The amount paid was not even fixed at many places. Most respondents earned less than ₹ 2,000 per month. Half of the manual scavenging families had no other source of income. The share of such families was as high as 83 per cent in Uttar Pradesh. Only 2 per cent of manual scavenging families had landholdings and only 1 per cent was involved in agriculture for additional income (Jan Sahas–Social Development Society and Fund for Gender Equality United Nations Entity for Gender Equality and the Empowerment of Women, UN Women).

At this point, when the country is boasting of fairly impressive growth, 'start ups' and 'stand up India', it is pitifully shameful to have the *Safai Karamcharis* (workers engaged in sewerage and allied works), engaged in conservancy work, most of whom are women, continue in their woeful state in the country. The nation has not been able to rid itself of considering 'cleaning' as polluting because there is an element of caste-based hierarchy entrenched in the mindsets of Indians, irrespective of religion. Contextualizing Dr B.R. Ambedkar to understand sanitation workers, especially women, is an endeavour through this presentation. Despite the Act banning Manual Scanvenging, the country still has more than 6,00,000 persons engaged in scavenging (Table 1).

Table 1

Manual Scanvenging

States	*No. of Manual Scavengers*
Uttar Pradesh	1,49,202
Madhya Pradesh	80,072
Maharashtra	64,785
India	6,76,009

Ministry of Social Justice and Empowerment of the Government of India.

Independent estimates 12,00,000 manual scavengers in the country.

Unlike us, other nations where caste does not exist, such caste-based entrenchment into unclean jobs is also absent. The West, although generates more garbage than us, treats their cleaners with dignity. Their cleaning brigade does not need to be freed from dehumanizing, obnoxious, abhorrent and disgusting practice of caste-based discrimination. They enjoy the dignity of being human as much the others do and therefore, the state also cares to provide them with safety equipments. By any standards of measurements, there are more accidents and deaths which have occurred in India among *Safai Karamcharis* (workers engaged in sewerage and allied works) while at work than anywhere else in the world.[1] In the last ten years, official deaths reported of manhole workers in Ahmedabad city alone is about 9 every year on an average. At least 22,327 Dalits die doing sanitation work every year. Safai Kamgar Vikas Sangh (SKVS), a body representing sanitation workers of the Brihhan Mumbai Municipal Corporation (BMC), sought data under the Right to Information Act in 2006. It revealed that 288 workers died in 2004–05, 316 in 2003–04 and 320 in 2002–03, in just 14 of the 24 wards of the BMC, that makes an average figure of about 25 deaths every month. These figures do not include civic hospital workers, gutter cleaners or sanitation workers on contract. Compare this with the 5,100 soldiers – army, police, paramilitaries – who have died between 1990 and 2007 combatting militancy in Jammu & Kashmir.

Remunerations of these workers are meagre and work guaranteed is nil. Municipal Corporation workers get ₹ 150 per day and those working as contract workers get between ₹ 40–50 a day. They are often employed for less than 8 hours and paid accordingly anything between ₹ 300–1,500 per month. This, when contrasted with our most compared neighbour China, suggests that the latter are better in terms of earnings and safety gears as compared to their counterparts in India. In most developed nations, workers are protected in bunny suits to avoid contact with contaminated water and sport a respiratory apparatus; sewers are well-lit, mechanically aerated with huge fans and therefore are not so oxygen deficient. In Hong Kong, a sewer worker, after adequate training, needs at least 15 licenses and permits to enter a manhole. The entry-level salary of a sanitation worker in New York is $30,000 per year. In the sixth year, he could earn $67,141 (₹ 2.18 lakh per month). In India your licences to become a sewer worker is ... the all-pervasive caste identity ... ! In India, the worker wears nothing more than a loincloth or half-pants. Permanent workers wear a 'safety belt' which helps haul them out when they faint or die inside the sewer. In India, a permanent sanitation worker with 20 years experience could make ₹ 12,000 a month.

Social inclusion of vulnerable populations who have been historically excluded has been the focus of the governments, affected communities, groups and individuals; the genesis of which began with the drafting of the Constitution with Dr Ambedkar in the Chair. Understanding the elements and processes which create a social divide has been a continuous intellectual pursuit despite the fact that subordination and marginalization of those engaged in scavenging and cleaning is fairly well recognized. Although, denial of access to resources and services to some individuals and groups is a universal phenomenon which has existed over time and space and varied from class, race, ethnicity, religion and gender, caste, however, is a unique determinant of social discrimination in the Indian Sub-continent – an evil against which Dr Ambedkar fought relentlessly throughout his lifetime, experienced the menace himself, but secured instruments to ensure safeguards for the others. The process of caste-based social discrimination is embedded in religion and history and thus, accentuates the deprivation and denial among those engaged in cleaning. The *Safai Karamcharis* (workers engaged in sewerage and allied works) are categorized as sewerage workers and sweepers. While sewerage workers are all men, sweepers are men and women both. They are employed as permanent, temporary, daily wage, and contract workers as sweepers, drain and manhole cleaners, night soil carriers and rag pickers. Those who complete 900 days of working are registered as permanent workers. Most of them are contractual and temporary workers who do not have any necessary claim to compensation in case of any accident during their work.[2]

In the present times, post reforms, during 2005–06, there are more poor among Dalits as compared to non-Dalits (Figure 1).

All *Safai Karamcharis* are from the Dalit communities. This is the reason why their vulnerability is exploited by people as well as the state. While environment and it conservation has caught everyone's attention and there is evident concern for the users of sewerage and allied work by way of provisioning of and access to toilets, reduction in open defecation, Total Sanitation Campaign (TSC) and other programmes like provisioning of safe drinking water and clean

Figure 1

Programmatic Initiatives towards Sanitation and the Workers

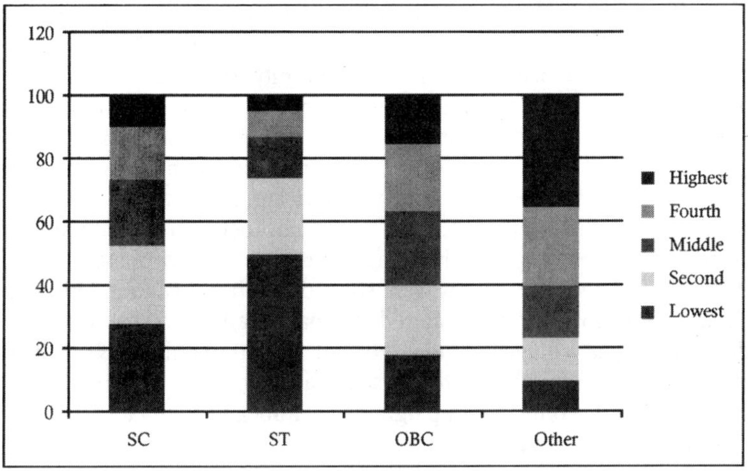

drains; the concern for sewerage and allied service providers is absent. The plight of these people has not drawn much attention from the required sectors. Perhaps because of the caste-ridden mind-set, India has not been able to do away with a practice that is admittedly 'a blot on humanity'. Unlike the other parts of the world, in India, sewerage and allied work is associated with caste. This work passes on to the progeny and is considered as guaranteed employment and source of regular income. It strengthens caste identity and consolidates entrenchment of youth in the 'polluted work'.

> I clean toilets in 20 houses every day. I use a tin plate and broom to remove the excrement that has collected in the toilet. I collect the excrement in a basket, and then I take it and throw it away. This work is so awful, I don't feel like eating.'
>
> – Manisha, Mainpuri district, Uttar Pradesh, January 2014.

> Gangashree walks through the village to manually clean human excrement from dry toilets in Kasela, Uttar Pradesh, which she will collect in her basket and carry to the outskirts of the village for disposal (Singh, 2014).

> (Manual scavenging) is the worst surviving symbol of untouchability.
>
> – National Advisory Council resolution, 23 October 2010

> (https://www.hrw.org/report/2014/08/25/cleaning-human-waste/manual-scavenging-caste-and-discrimination-india).

Swachchata Abhiyan

It is a cleanliness drive that will be implemented over a five-year period. Nearly, ₹ 62,009 crore is likely to be spent on this programme the Centre will pitch in ₹ 14,623 crore. The mission aims to cover 1.04 crore households, provide 2.5 lakh community toilets, 2.6 lakh public toilets and a solid waste management facility in each town. It started with Total Sanitation Campaign that is based on the principles of community-led total sanitation (CLTS) initiated by the Government of India in 1999. Its goal was to eradicate the practice of open defecation by 2017. However, CLTS did not focus on building infrastructure, but propagated changing cultural norms to prevent open defecation. The programmes were shaped as Nirmal Bharat Abhiyan during 1999 to 2012 and offered Nirmal Gram Puraskar to open defecation free villages. Under Nirmal Bharat Abhiyan, ₹ 10,000 were given to every family to construct a toilet. On 2 October 2014, Nirmal Bharat Abhiyan campaign was relaunched as Swachh Bharat Abhiyan (Clean India Mission).

Table 2

Department of Drinking Water and Sanitation

Components	*Total Cost (₹)*	*Centre's Share*	*State Share*	*Beneficiaries Share*
Individual Household Latrine for Below Poverty Line households	2,500 (3,000 for Hilly and difficult areas)	1,500 (2,000 for Hilly and difficult areas)	700	300
School toilet	35,000 (38,500 for Hilly and difficult areas)	24,500 (26,950 for Hilly and difficult areas	10,500 (11,550 for Hilly and difficult areas)	
Anganwadi toilet	8,000 (10,000 for Hilly and difficult areas	5,600 (7,000 for Hilly and difficult areas)	2,400 (3,000 for Hilly and difficult areas)	
Community Sanitary Complex	2,00,000	1,20,000	60,000	20,000
Rural Sanitary Mart	3,50,000	2,80,000	70,000	

India has made some progress in providing sanitation by building toilets to desist people from defecating in the open. Despite the efforts, India still has longest queues for toilets in the world WND.com-21–Nov-2015 (*The Huffington Post*, 20 November 2015).

Eradicating open defecation was the core objective of Swachh Bharat Mission (SBM). It aims to build 12 crore toilets in rural india at a cost of 1.96 lakh crore by 2019. More than one crore toilets were built as part of SBM since the launch of the Mission. However, as per the NSSO data, not even 50 per cent of them are being used. Despite newly constructed lavatories, people continue to use fields and use these toilets for storing grains or as general storage space. Undoubtedly, providing clean toilets is important. But in the absence of water availability, the questions arises of a choice between dirty, unusable, stinking toilets or open fields with fresh air. What will spark behavioural change towards Open Defecation Force (ODF) villages/spaces is important to be considered, especially in the context of who will clean them.

Government has been reluctant to publish the NSSO data because it does not reflect so well on the progress of SBM. It needs to be used for recalibrating the initiative of mushrooming toilets versus functional toilets in use; providing infrastructure which can be put to its intended use and thrust on reducing inequalities in access, based on wealth and location.

Millennium Development Goals (MDGs) on sanitation has emphasized on halving inequalities between richest and the poorest, rural and urban and slum and non-slum by 20 per cent. Technology and financing as constraints can be overcome, but the 'biggest barrier in sanitation is the unwillingness of ... political leaders to put excreta and its safe disposal on the international development agenda' (HDR, 2006; UNDP, 129).

Concern for Workers

Those who lend their lives for 'safe disposal' are not within the purview of the MDG. The Sustainable Development Goals (SDGs) strive for 'leaving no one behind ...'. The BBC, 25 August 2014, reported that the Human Rights Watch has called on the Indian government to end 'manual scavenging' – the practice of cleaning human waste by low-caste communities. The practice is banned by law in India. But this is rampant and activists say tens of thousands are involved in this demeaning work which opens them to prejudice and abuse. Unlike the other parts of the world, in India, sewerage and sanitation work is associated with caste. This work passes on to the progeny. It is considered a guaranteed employment and source of regular income, but it also works towards strengthening the caste identity. It consolidates entrenchment of workers, especially youth in the 'polluted work'. That is why even today India has more than 6,76,009 manual scavengers.

As part of the Swachh Bharat Campaign, many dignitaries and social figures from all walks of life wielded the broom to clean the filth. This, according to some, has provided dignity to sanitation workers (*TOIN/TOI*, 26 November 2015).

The apathy of the state and the other fellow human beings towards the work conditions, incentives, remunerations and their living conditions of these workers are appalling. Their labour for cleaning the filth and grime and hazardous pollution generated is not appreciated. On the contrary, we the very people of this sovereign republic which ensure equality in all spheres through its Constitution, label them as unclean and polluted, call them names, and treat them inhumanly. Considering them 'untouchables' is nothing short of that. The Nation is indebted to them – 'the lesser human beings' for keeping the cost of cleaning to the lowest possible. Had it been for mechanization for the work done by these workers, the state would be paying anything to the tune of at least 10 times more.[3]

The issue goes beyond poverty, indifference, lack of awareness, or reluctance to switch from this traditional work. Manual scavenging, what *Safai Karamcharis* do, 'is rooted in caste as surely as caste is rooted in Indian psyche'. Annie Zaidi in her article in *Frontline* dated 22 September 2006, has analysed it very accurately. Over the years, only the euphemistic change in the labels from *bhangis, mehtar* to *Safai Kamdars, Safai Karamchari, Safai Sainik* has happened. Shall we all look within ourselves and reconsider our perceptions of these people whose contribution towards the upkeep of the environment is second to none; and resolve to give them what is due to them since long? The dignity and social inclusion, to begin with, will gradually make way for access to resources.

Therefore, it is absolutely important to SAY NO to 'POLLUTED JOBS'. For this, few steps should be taken by the individuals and state. At the individual level, the important steps are: reconstruction of self-image, determination to completed education against all odds, looking for alternative to enhance skills, increase vocational propensity, and above all, avoid and overcome the trap of 'government job' in the name of sewerage cleaning and assured risk to life. The state's responsibility is towards mechanization of sewerage and sanitation work, adequate allocation of funds for safety and health of the current workers; and education of their children. Urban planners, public health specialists and civil engineers need to practice and evolve courses to sensitize human friendly management of waste. Poor access to resources has perpetuated low levels of development for a long time. Some subcastes among SCs engage in work which other caste persons do not do. Such work is detrimental to their health and paradoxically, is considered as 'polluted jobs'. There is a need for data on these specific groups engaged in 'polluted jobs' and for the access of subgroups to medical/para-medical/health education.

The government-delayed reaction against manual scavenging led to Employment of Manual Scavengers and Construction of Dry Latrines (Prohibition) Act in 1993. This act has a provision of punishment and fine on employment of scavengers or on the construction of dry toilets. However, manual scavengers continue to be employed even by some municipalities, Indian Railways and defence establishments and local authorities in rural areas. Manual scavenging is a disgrace, casting doubts on governments' claim to overcome caste barriers and projecting itself as an economic growth engine. The government's efforts to solve this problem has to be multidimensional.

First and foremost, expand the ambit of manual scavenging to include workers who clean the sewers, septic tanks and drains where human excreta is washed. Secondly, provide a rehabilitation programme for scavengers and their immediate family members. The purview of the programme could include training in other professions and technical education. Arm the sanitation workers of the state with the art of technology tools. Developed nations have tools and equipment which protect sanitation workers from direct exposure to sewerage water and waste. Also, extend the benefit of Rashtriya Swasthya Bima Yojna (RSBY) scheme to scavengers and their family members with provisions of free health check-up on regular basis. Finally, provide a financial safety net by extending subsidized loan for starting a new venture.

The true tribute to Dr Ambedkar would be to continue with his efforts of empowering the lives of the Scheduled Castes people and help them overcome the vicious cycle of caste and culture barrier, rather than offering flowers to his statue. Access to civic amenities and social facilities has always been a concern in the context of the Dalits. While much of the literature has explored social discrimination in general and partly in the field of education, not much seems to reflect on the experience of social discrimination and humiliation experienced by those engaged in scavenging and cleaning in their daily life and in rendering their services. Their access to health care, housing, education, basic infrastructure, provisions for work related safety, safeguards against health hazards, information on various schemes oriented towards their welfare and utilization of such schemes – all have largely remained confined as outcome figures. The process which precedes these outcomes has never or rarely been given any importance. It is for this reason that despite government measures towards affirmative action during the last few decades, the episodes of death due to humiliation and attack on dignity continue in the form of students committing suicide in premium institutions and girls and women being paraded unclothed in different parts of the country.

Dalit women constitute almost half of India's 160 million Dalits, comprise about 16 per cent of India's total female population and 8 per cent of the total population. Despite all this, they are isolated on various axes – economic, religious, political and ideological. It is also true of their experience in the mainstream women's movements, where most of them feel disconnected and alienated. In 2007, the report of the UN Committee Elimination of Discrimination against Women (CEDAW) addressed the issue of Dalit women in India. Most women do not report violence; only one per cent of the cases that are actually filed end in convictions. The 2009 Report of the UN Special Rapporteur on Violence against Women accounts that Dalit women in India are being raped and beaten by higher castes in the course of their daily lives, such as, while working in the field, going to the market or doing domestic work. Very often, women academicians and forerunners of the gender cause consider women as one homogenous group as far as the issues related to women are concerned. At the most, disparities are superfluously addressed by way of socio-economic hierarchies. Slightest of similarities drawn in terms of discrimination and exclusion from access to resources and services between women and Dalits is more likely than not to cause a furor. Both suffer subordination, both show poor social development indicators, both are considered impure and unclean, both have been excluded from decision-making processes at one or the other level and both have restrictions in expressing their voices. Thus Dalit women's experience of denial are doubly loaded.

Notes

1. Ramaswamy, G. (2005), *India Stinking*, Chennai: Navayana; UN Millennium Task Force on Water and Sanitation (2005), *Health, Dignity and Development: What will it Take?* United Nations, New York; CEC (2007), *Hole to Hell: A Study on Health and Safety of Sewage Workers in Delhi*, Centre for Education and Communication, New Delhi; http://www.thedailybeast.com/newsweek/2007/10/31/the-world-s-worst-job.html; Anand, S. (2007), 'Life Inside a Black Hole', *Tehelka Magazine*, Vol. 4, No. 47, 8 December 2007; Pepper, Daniel (2007), 'The World's Worst Job? India's Sewage Workers are Certainly in the Running', Newsweek Web Exclusive, 1 November 2007; Kumar, Alok (2010), *Squatting with Dignity: Lessons from India*, New Delhi: Sage.
2. Pepper, Daniel (2007), 'The World's Worst Job? India's Sewage Workers are Certainly in the Running', Newsweek Web Exclusive, 1 November 2007; Kumar, Alok (2010), *Squatting with Dignity: Lessons from India*, New Delhi: Sage.
3. Tam, Stephanie (2011), 'An Ecology of Vulnerability Sewerage in Ahmedabad, India', Harvard Graduate School of Design. This project was conducted with the support of HCP Design and Project Management and Urban Management Centre; Giri, Purushottam A., Abhiram M. Kasbe and Radha Y. Aras (2010), 'A Study on Morbidity Profile of Sewage Workers in Mumbai City', *International Journal of Collaborative Research on Internal Medicine and Public Health*, Vol. 2, No. 12, December, pp. 450–463, ISSN 1840–4529, http://www.iomcworld.com/ijcrimph/

2

Affirmative Action Policies for Dalits in India

A Review of their Implementation

KANAK KANTI BAGCHI

Provisions for Affirmative Action (AA) or positive discrimination or compensatory discrimination in favour of the Schedule Castes and Schedule Tribes (SCs and STs) or Dalits was made by the Constitution of independent India which largely followed the pattern of the Government of India Act, 1935. Besides reserving parliamentary seats for them they were given advantages in terms of admission to schools and colleges, jobs in the public sector and various pecuniary benefits for their overall development. Some of the constitutional provisions which aimed at providing affirmative action for SCs and STs are as follows. Article 17 makes abolition of 'untouchability' and its practice in any form a punishable offence. Article 46 intends to promote their educational and economic interest. Articles 16 and 335 permit preferential treatment in matters of employment in public services. Articles 330 and 332 provide for reservation of seats in Lok Sabha and State Assemblies. Later, the job related positive discrimination was extended to government-supported autonomous bodies.

Government's AA policies include many measures and programmes. In the political sphere, there is reservation of seats for SCs and STs according to population share both in Central and State legislatures, in public services of the State and Central Governments, in the case of admission in colleges and Universities, post-matric scholarship and hostel facilities for students, etc. It is expected that the SCs and STs, that is, Dalits would use such opportunities as springboards to achieve better and dignified lives and to integrate themselves fully to the mainstream of the society.

The AA measures for Dalits came into force since 1950 with the adoption of the Constitution. Thereafter, some more AA policies have been introduced from time to time. At the time of its first introduction as well as when their scopes were expanded and benefits were extended to more social groups, there was a debate on the justification of such expansion and extension. The debate is still continuing. In the present paper, we shall not enter into that debate. The main objective of this chapter is to trace out the achievements of AA policies of Dalits in India and to suggest measures regarding what more needs to be done for the success of such policies.

However, before we proceed further, we need to make it clear as to what do we mean by the term 'Dalit'. Originally, the term was used to mean those SCs who are the ex-untouchables. But gradually, all others SCs are also included in its ambit. Presently, the term is used to mean all SCs and STs. For the purpose of this paper we have accepted this latest use and connotation of the term.

The paper is based on secondary data and literature. It especially draws upon the works of Weisskopf (2004), Thorat (2005), Deshpande and Yadav (2006), Thorat and Senapati (2006, 2007), Deshpande (2006, 2012), Desai and Kulkarni (2008), Heyer and Jayal (2009), Desai and Dubey (2011), Deshpande and Weisskopf (2011), Thorat et al. (2016) and others. Secondary data has been collected mostly from the published works of these authors.

The paper is structured as follows: Section II delineates the achievements of AA policies in respect of fulfilment of quota of jobs in Central Government services, Public Sector Undertakings (PSUs), and Public Sector Banks (PSBs). Section III deals with the assessment of implementation and empirical tests of AA policies done by different researchers and concluding observations have been made in Section IV.

Achievements of AA Policies

In this section we shall make a review of the achievements of the AA policies as have been adopted by the Government of India from time to time.

Table 1

Number and Percentage Share in Central Government Employment, Decadal Point to Point

As on 1 January	SC		ST		Non SC/ST	
	Numbers	Percentage	Numbers	Percentage	Numbers	Percentage
1960	2,28,497	12.24	37,704	2.02	16,00,528	85.74
1970	2,91,374	11.66	60,325	2.41	21,47,584	85.93
1980	4,90,592	15.67	1,25,004	3.99	25,16,129	80.34
1990	5,90,108	16.97	1,85,245	5.33	27,01,700	77.70
2000	5,82,446	16.05	2,25,917	6.23	28,19,519	77.72
2003	5,40,220	16.52	2,11,345	6.46	25,17,780	77.01

Collected from Thorat and Senapati (2006): Sources mentioned therein: Annual Report, Ministry of Personnel, Public Grievances and Pensions, Government of India, New Delhi, 1985–1986, 1989–1990, and 2004–2005, p. 14.

Table 1 above shows the numbers and percentage share of SC, ST and non-SC, ST in Central Government employment (decadal point to point) since 1960 to 2003. It is revealed that there have been gradual improvements over the years for both SCs and STs as far as their recruitment in Central Government services is concerned. However, there has been more improvement for the SCs as compared to the STs. In 2003 (latest year for which data could be collected), the stipulated quota could be filled[1] for SCs, but in the case of STs, there is a shortfall of about one percentage point.

Table 2 below shows the employment data in a disaggregated way and is important to see the characteristic of empowerment of Dalits. It can be discerned from this table that though there have been improvements in the position of Dalits in all the four categories of services, it has not been equal across all categories, especially in B and C categories, the position of both SCs and STs falls short of the governmental provision of 15 per cent and 7.5 per cent respectively. In A category services the shortfall is above 3 percentage points both for SCs and STs. In B category services the shortfall is about 1–2 per cent for SCs and 3 per cent for STs. It may be hypothesized that the reasons are inherent, first in the flaws of implementation of reservation policies and secondly, in the unavailability of qualified candidates. However, these need to be proved by rigorous and dispassionate research. However, it is heartening to note that in both A and B category services, number of employees from Dalit categories is gradually increasing over the period under study.

Table 2

Percentage Share of the Social Groups to the Total Employees in Government Jobs by Categories (Excluding Sweepers)

Years	Group A				Group B				Group C				Group D			
	SC	ST	Non SC/ST	Total	SC	ST	Non SC/ST	Total	SC	ST	Non SC/ST	Total	SC	ST	Non SC/ST	Total
1965	1.64	0.27	97.59	100	2.82	0.34	96.56	100	8.88	1.14	89.71	100	17.75	3.50	78.82	100
1975	3.43	0.62	95.95	100	4.98	0.59	94.43	100	10.71	2.27	87.02	100	18.64	3.99	77.37	100
1985	7.65	1.73	90.62	100	10.04	1.58	88.39	100	14.88	4.20	80.92	100	20.81	5.70	73.49	100
1990	8.64	2.58	88.78	100	11.29	2.39	86.32	100	15.19	4.83	79.98	100	21.48	6.73	71.49	100
1995	10.15	2.89	86.96	100	12.67	2.68	84.65	100	16.15	5.69	78.16	100	20.53	6.48	72.99	100
2003	11.93	4.18	83.88	100	14.32	4.32	81.36	100	16.29	6.54	77.17	100	17.98	6.96	75.06	100

Collected from Thorat and Senapati (2006): Sources mentioned therein: Computed from the data provided in the Annual Report, Ministry of Personnel, Public Grievances and Pensions, Government of India, New Delhi, 1985–1986, 1989–1990, and 2004–2005, p. 18.

Table 3 below shows the composition of employment in public sector enterprise (PSEs)[2] according to social category. The quota of reservation applicable in PSEs are 15 per cent for SCs and 7.5 per cent for STs. It can be seen from Table 3 that over the period 1971 to 2004, share of SCs had increased from 7.42 per cent to 16.03 per cent, while that of STs had increased from 2.25 to 7.76 per cent. Thus, the share of Dalits in employment of PSEs appears to be in line with governmental provision. However, it is a matter of worry. A close look at Table 3 shows that while for Dalits an increasing trend of share in employment was visible up to 1990, it has started declining since then both for SCs and STs. But the share of non-SC/STs has been increasing since then, though their absolute number is decreasing. Thus, it is apparent that the effect of liberalization, privatization and globalization (LPG) has been more adverse on Dalits when compared to the non-Dalits. The other implication of this observed fact is that since Dalits are relatively backward as far as possession of skill or reskilling is concerned, they are suffering a setback in the exigent situation of acceleration of the degree of LPG.

Table 3

Numbers and Percentage of Employees in the Public Sector Enterprises – Decadal Point to Point

As on 1 January	*SC*		*ST*		*Non S January C/ST*	
	Numbers	*Percentage*	*Numbers*	*Percentage*	*Numbers*	*Percentage*
1971	40,640	7.42	12,309	2.25	4,94,680	90.33
1980	3,17,401	17.44	1,38,364	7.60	13,64,537	74.96
1990	4,28,491	19.58	2,16,355	9.88	15,43,989	70.54
2000	3,24,140	18.00	1,45,581	8.09	13,30,907	73.91
2004	2,36,618	16.03	1,14,481	7.76	11,24,990	76.21

Collected from Thorat and Senapati (2006): Sources mentioned therein: Public Enterprises Survey, Annual Report, Volume I, Ministry of Heavy Industries and Public Enterprises, 1978–1979, 1988–1989, 1989–1990, 1990–1991, and 1991–1993 to 2004–2005, New Delhi, p. 30.

Table 4 shows the distribution of percentage share of employees in public sector undertakings according to social groups and category of services. Like Central Government employment, in the case of PSEs also, the share of employment of Dalits is gradually increasing over the years both in pre- and post-liberalization periods. This indicates that the number of eligible persons among Dalits is increasing but perhaps, not to the extent required which is evidenced from the shortfall of the

Table 4

Percentage Share of the Social Groups to the Total Employees in Public Sector Undertakings by Categories (Excluding Sweepers)

As on 1 Jan	*Group A*				*Group B*				*Group C*				*Group D*			
	SC	*ST*	*Non SC/ST*	*Total*	*SC*	*ST*	*Non SC/ST*	*Total*	*SC*	*ST*	*Non SC/ST*	*Total*	*SC*	*ST*	*Non SC/ST*	*Total*
1971	0.52	0.17	99.31	100	1.54	0.16	98.30	100	5.49	1.29	93.22	100	15.96	5.94	78.09	100
1980	2.90	0.66	96.44	100	5.12	1.36	93.52	100	18.08	7.71	74.20	100	22.36	10.76	66.88	100
1990	5.95	1.43	92.61	100	8.73	2.51	88.76	100	19.20	8.95	71.85	100	31.39	19.82	48.79	100
2000	10.35	2.97	86.68	100	11.05	4.18	84.77	100	18.93	8.46	72.61	100	22.51	11.40	66.08	100
2004	11.48	3.46	85.06	100	11.72	5.31	82.97	100	17.07	8.14	74.79	100	18.20	10.53	71.27	100

Source: Public Enterprise Survey, Annual Report, Volume 1, Ministry of Heavy Industries and Public Enterprises, 1978–1979, 1988–189, 1989–1990, 1990–1991 and 1991–1993 to 2004–2005, New Delhi.

proportion in which they are supposed to be there. How far this shortfall is the result of discrimination and how far it is caused by the lack of availability of sufficient number of eligible candidates needs to be probed deeply.

In the case of Group C and Group D services the quota has been fulfilled with gradual improvement over the years. In Group C services, the number of SC employees has exceeded by nearly 2 per cent and for ST employees the excess is little less than one per cent point. But in the case of Group D services, the quota has been exceeded by more than 3 per cent both for SCs and STs. This is indicative of the adequate availability of eligible candidates for both C and D category of services from Dalits.

We have another important finding from Table 4 which is related to globalization. While in A and B category of services the increase in the number of SCs and STs has been consistent over the study period, in the case of C and D category services, there is an exception. It can be seen that in the case of C and D categories, percentage share of SCs and STs has gradually increased from 1971 and reached a peak in 1990, and thereafter, it has gradually declined in 2004. On the other hand, the share of non-SC/ST social group in C and D category services has gradually increased in 2004. The reasons for this trend need to be investigated for policy formulation. Prima facie, the trend indicates that while within Dalit groups people are losing their eligibility for group C and D services, their eligibility for group A and B services is gradually benefiting them more. It is likely that those who have technical and professional qualifications and education in private English medium schools and colleges are gradually forming a larger elite and well-off class. That is, inequality within Dalit groups is gradually increasing.

Table 5 shows the pattern of employment in public sector banks according to social category for a period of 26 years from 1978 to 2004. It shows a consistent trend in increase of employment of Dalits over the period in different categories of services. It is revealed that in the year 2004, representation of SCs (17.61%) has been higher than the governmental provision by more than 2 per cent. It falls short by nearly 2 per cent in the case of STs category, though in the case of STs also, there is a consistent rising trend. Liberalization seems to have some effect on this increasing trend, since a deceleration in the growth of employment of Dalits is visible after 1990.

Table 5

Employment in Public Sector Banks, Decadal Point to Point

Years	*SC*		*ST*		*Non SC/ST*	
	Numbers	*Percentage*	*Numbers*	*Percentage*	*Numbers*	*Percentage*
1978	55,976	10.19	8,571	1.56	4,84,784	88.25
1980	68,042	11.61	11,992	2.05	5,05,889	86.34
1990	1,26,974	14.39	37,362	4.23	7,17,921	81.37
2000	1,43,499	16.12	43,658	4.91	7,02,765	78.97
2004	1,33,685	17.61	43,454	5.72	5,81,910	76.66

Source: Annual Report, Ministry of Finance, Government of India, 1978 and 2004–2005.

Employment pattern in public sector banks disaggregated by grades of service and social category has been presented in Table 6. It is revealed that in officers grade the share of SC and ST employees is on the rise, but the share is still less than the quota prescribed by the government. This is more so in the case of ST category. In clerks grade also, the same trend is visible. Here, though the share of SC category has exceeded by more than one per cent in 2004, in the case of ST category there is a shortage of more than two per cent. In the grade of sub-staffs, the SC category is over represented by more than 10 per cent, while in the case of ST category there was a shortage of less than one per cent in 2004.

Thus, as far as employment in public sector banks is concerned, the SCs have fared better than the STs over the period from 1978 to 2004. The reasons for these are to be investigated for necessary policy formulation so that STs can catch up with the SCs.

Assessments and Empirical Tests of AA Policies

From the above analysis it is evident that over the years since 1960s, there has been some improvement in situation as far as representation of Dalits in government services are concerned. However, for many reasons the AA policies has not been able to deliver the desired results. Ghosh (1997) has made an assessment of implementation of the AA programme which is worthy to mention. According to him, '... The quotas earmarked for the SCs and STs are often not filled on account of the indifference of the heads of departments. According to the Chairman of the National Commission for Schedule Castes and Schedule Tribes, this is done systematically through a variety of subterfuges – from destroying

Table 6

Percentage Share of the Social Groups to the Total Employees in Public Sector Banks by Categories

Years	Officers				Clerks				Sub-Staffs			
	SC	ST	Non SC/ST	Total	SC	ST	Non SC/ST	Total	SC	ST	Non SC/ST	Total
1978	2.04	0.17	97.79	100	10.32	1.82	87.86	100	16.25	2.09	81.67	100
1980	3.09	0.65	96.26	100	11.93	2.24	85.82	100	20.06	3.09	76.85	100
1990	9.18	2.71	88.11	100	14.22	4.46	81.32	100	21.84	5.68	72.48	100
2000	12.51	4.22	83.27	100	14.88	4.76	80.36	100	24.47	6.25	69.28	100
2004	14.98	5.88	79.14	100	16.16	5.08	78.76	100	25.38	7.02	67.60	100

Source: Annual Report, Ministry of Finance, Government of India, 1978 to 2004–2005.

application forms from such persons, to filling up posts through ad hoc recruitment on the ground that there is a ban on new recruitment on a permanent basis ... they are also not filled owing to the non-availability of qualified people even at the standards specifically lowered for these groups. For example, in 1980, the upper caste Hindus who made up 25 per cent of the population held 89.63 per cent of the Central Government jobs while the SCs and STs who made up for almost the same percentage of population (23%) accounted for only 5.6 per cent of the jobs. The primary reason for this depressing situation is that caste feelings still persist in Indian society which does not permit an egalitarian approach to develop roots whatever the state might direct.' Though situations have now improved on all these fronts, but not yet they have not yet improved to the desired extent.

While making 'preliminary assessment' of compensatory discrimination in political representation, Galanter (1979) observed that: 'The general pattern of the past decades might crudely be summarized as development at the upper end and stagnation at the bottom. Compensatory discrimination means that a section of the Scheduled Castes and Scheduled Tribes has been incorporated into the modern class manning the organized sector. What does this portend for the bulk of untouchables and tribals who remain excluded and oppressed? Are they better or worse off by virtue of the fact that some members of their descent group have a share in the benefits of modern India? The meaning of reserved seats and of compensatory discriminatory policy ultimately depends on how one visualizes the relation of this new elite to the masses of Scheduled Castes and Scheduled Tribes'.

Assessing the comparative strengths and weaknesses of the AA programme in India and the USA, Deshpande (2006) observes that: 'the strength of the Indian program is that being constitutionally enshrined; it cannot be challenged legally and is practically irreversible. Also, its applicability to government seats has ensured SC/ST representation in the political sphere much more strongly than in the US. Several important political leaders, chief ministers of states, ministers in the Central government cabinet ... are Dalit. However, the implementation of the program in government jobs and educational institutions is mechanical and insincere. Most institutions get away by simply stipulating the mandatory quota; given the lack of a monitoring agency, there is neither the accountability to fill the quota nor penalties for loopholes used to circumvent quota restrictions. Follow-up support programs to enhance the performance of quota entrants are non-existent. Thus, mandating the requisite number of seats is often the beginning and end of the implementation of the Indian affirmative action program'.

Barker (2010) has done a study on the effects of reservation on caste persistence in India. The analytical results presented in the study support the argument of the proponents of reservation that benefits of reservations outweigh the drawbacks. That is, caste based reservation help members of historically depressed castes to advance socially and transcend their historic positions in society.

Deshpande and Weisskopf (2011) have tested the effects of AA policies on labour productivity in Indian railways. They have particularly studied whether the presence of SC and ST employees who have got entry through quotas has impacted productivity negatively or not. By analysing an extensive data set on the working of the largest employers in the public sector in India, they have found no evidence to support the claims of critics of affirmative action that increasing the proportion of SC and ST employees adversely affects productivity or productivity growth. On the other hand, some of the results suggest that the proportion of SC and ST employees in A and B categories of jobs is positively associated with productivity growth.

Commenting on the effects of AA policies on higher education of Dalits, Deshpande (2012) notes that: 'All available evidence indicates that a large majority of SC–ST candidates owe their presence in institution of higher education to reservation policies. While empirical studies on effects of AA in higher education are very few due to lack of data, the few studies that exist point towards the fact that SC-ST students find it hard to succeed in competitive entrance examination due to past handicaps (lack of good quality schooling, lack of access to special tutorial or coaching centres that prepare candidate for open competitive examinations and so forth)'. This statement establishes the fact that AA policies have been beneficial to Dalit students and it is required for at least some more years in future.

Weisskopf's study (2004) indicates that at least half the seats reserved for SC students and at least two – thirds of the seats reserved for ST students remain unfilled. He argues that this happens because of 'wastage' (dropping out) as well as stagnation (repeating courses because of failure or attendance gaps) at prior levels of education. In this context, it may be noted that there are remedial measures that could be applied to address these problems. The University Grants Commission has special funds allocated for such remedial measures, but these funds remain unutilized for the most part because of the lack of awareness about these funds, lack of motivators in the implementing college or University and lack of serious will to make the AA programme successful.

Desai and Kulkarni (2008) have examined the effects of AA policies focusing on results of such policies. They have particularly examined the question that whether educational inequalities between SCs and STs on the one hand and upper caste Hindus on the other have reduced by using data from successive NSS rounds between 1983 and 2000 or not. They have found that the educational inequalities between SC–STs on the one hand and upper caste Hindus on the other hand, have declined significantly at the primary education stage. There is also a decline for the middle and high school levels, but not significant. At the college levels, the inequalities between ST men and upper caste Hindus have declined, but for ST women, SC men and SC women, the inequalities have increased. They did not find evidence that the upper-income groups, the so-called creamy layer of Dalit and Adivasis, have got disproportionate benefit from the AA action programmes at the expense of their low-income counterparts.

The authors of the study have attributed these declines to the AA policies. This is supported by the fact that a parallel decline is not being observed for Muslims, who suffer similar disadvantages as the Dalits, but do not get any preferential treatment. They suggest that the decline in inequalities at the primary level might be due to AA measures in employment. But in college education, where AA is directly applicable, they find that inequalities have actually widened. This puts a question mark on the efficacy of AA policy. They have also found that after accounting for income and residence, SCs experience greater disadvantage in college education than STs. On this result, Deshpande (2012) observes that ' The reasons for AA in higher education not being able to successfully narrow the gaps is a cause of concern, but the gaps would, in all likelihood, have been even larger in the absence of AA.'

Concluding Observations

From the analysis of secondary data regarding fulfilling of quota in Central Government jobs, PSEs and PSBs, and the empirical tests done by several scholars on the working of AA policies in India we can conclude that they have achieved a partial success. There have been gradual improvements in the situation of Dalits over the years, though it is not to the desired extent.

From all available evidence, it appears that the main hurdle for achieving the desired goal of AA policies is their half-hearted implementation. Thus, it is imperative that the AA policies are implemented whole heartedly by people with whom the responsibility lies, and it is also needed that people for whom the AA policies are meant, become truly conscious about their rights.

Notes

1. 'Reservation for SCs, STs and OBCs is available for all groups of posts in the Central services, PSUs, public sector nationalized banks, and the public sector insurance companies in case of direct recruitment on all India basis by open competition at 15, 7.5, and 27 percentage points for SCs, STs and OBCs respectively. Further, in case recruitment is not by open competition, the applicable/stipulated quotas for reservation stand at 16.66 per cent for SCs, 7.5 per cent for STs, and 25.84 per cent for OBCs in that order (Thorat and Senapati, 2006), pp. 10–11.
2. PSEs include government departments as well as government companies whether in the centre or the state like irrigation and power projects, railways, posts and telegraphs, ordinance factories and other departmental undertakings.

References

Bhaskaran, P. Bala (ND), 'Towards an Effective Framework for Affirmative Action'. Retrieved from URL. Accessed on 10 April 2014.

Barker, Michael D. (2010), 'The Effects of Reservations on Caste Persistence in India', A Thesis submitted to the Faculty of the Georgetown Public Policy Institute of Georgetown University in partial fulfillment of the requirements for the degree of Master of Public Policy, 15 April, Washington DC, accessed on 10 April 14 though internet http://citeseerx.ist.psu.edu/viewdoc/download?doi=10.1.1.833.1505&rep=rep1&type=pdf.

Cassan, Guilhem (2011), 'The Impact of Positive Discrimination in India: Evidence from a Natural Experiment'. Retrieved from URL. Accessed 10 April 2014.

Chak, Dhananjaya (ND), 'Affirmative Action in Higher Education: Myths and Realities'. Retrieved from URL.

Chakrabarty, Gurupada (2000), 'Development of SCs and STs: The Success So Far', *Social Change*, Vol. 30, No. 374, pp. 143–162.

Chalam, K.S. (1990), 'Caste Reservation and Equality of Opportunity in Education', *Economic and Political Weekly*, Vol. 25, No. 41, pp. 2333–2339.

Chandidas, R. (1969), 'How Close to Equality are Scheduled Castes?', *Economic and Political Weekly*, Vol. 4, No. 24, pp. 975–979.

Deane, T. (2009), 'A Commentary on the Positive Discrimination Policy of India', *PER/PELJ*, Vol. 12, No. 1.

Department of Education (1987), *Dr. Babasaheb Ambedkar*, Vol. 3, Government of Maharashtra, Bombay.

Desai, Sonalde and Amaresh Dubey (2011), 'Caste in 21st Century India: Competing Narratives', *Economic and Political Weekly*, Vol. 46, No. 1, pp. 40–49.

Desai, Sonalde and Veena Kulkarni (2008), 'Changing Educational Inequalities in India in the Context of Affirmative Action', *Demography*, Vol. 45, No. 2, pp. 245–270.

Deshpande, Ashwini (2006), 'Affirmative Action in India and the United States', Equity and Development, *World Development Report 2006*. Retrieved from URL. accessed on 10-4-2017, pp. 1–223.

—— (2012), 'Social Justice through Affirmative Action in India: An Assessment', in Jeannette Wicks-Lim and Robert Pollin (eds), *Capitalism on Trial: Explorations in the Tradition of Thomas Weisskopf*, Northampton, MA: Edward Elgar Publishing Inc.

Deshpande, Ashwini and Thomas E. Weisskopf (2011), 'Do Reservation Policies Affect Productivity in the Indian Railways?', *Working Paper No. 185*, Centre for Development Economics.

Deshpande, Satish and Yogendra Yadav (2006), 'Redesigning Affirmative Action: Castes and Benefits in Higher Education', *Economic and Political Weekly*, Vol. 25, No. 1, June 17, pp. 2419–2424. Accessed through Internet. accessed on 10-4-2017.

Galanter, Marc (1979), 'Compensatory Discrimination in Political Representation: A Preliminary Assessment of India's Thirty-Year Experience with Reserved Seats in Legislatures', *Economic and Political Weekly*, Vol. 14, No. 7/8, Annual Number, pp. 437–454.

—— (1986), 'Compensatory Discrimination: Theme in the Indian Commitment to Human Rights', *India International Centre Quarterly*, Vol. 13, No. 3/4, December, pp. 77–94.

Ghosh, Partha S. (1997), 'Positive Discrimination in India: A Political Analysis', *Ethnic Studies Report*, Vol. 15, No. 2, July, pp. 135–172.

Gill, Manmohan S. (2002), 'Reservation: An Affirmative Action of Social Justice?', *Social Change*, Vol. 32, Nos. 1 and 2, March–June, pp. 27–38.

Hasan, Rana and Aashish Mehta (2006), 'Under-representation of Disadvantaged Classes in Colleges: What Do the Data Tell Us?', *Economic and Political Weekly*, Vol. 41, No. 35, September 2, pp. 3791–3796.

Heyer, Judith and Niraja Gopal Jayal (2009), 'The Challenge of Positive Discrimination in India', *CRISE Working Paper No. 55*, Centre for Research on Inequality, Human Security and Ethnicity, University of Oxford, February. Accessed through Internet on 6 April 2014.

Kirpal, Viney et al. (1985), 'Scheduled Caste and Tribe Students in Higher Education: A Study of an IIT', *Economic and Political Weekly*, Vol. 20, No. 29, Annual Number, pp. 290–302.

Kumar, Dharma (1992), 'The Affirmative Action Debate in India', *Asian Survey*, Vol. 32, No. 3, March, pp. 290–302.

Moes, Michele S. (ND), 'Understanding Instrumental and Moral Justification for Affirmative Action'. Accessed through Internet on 6 April 2014.

Mohanty, Mritiunjoy (2006), 'Social Inequality, Labour Market Dynamics and Reservation', *Economic and Political Weekly*, September 2, pp. 3777–3789.

Naik, J.P. (1979), 'Quality and Quantity: The Elusive Triangle in Indian Education', *International Review of Education*, Vol. 25, No. 2/3, Jubilee Number, pp. 167–185.

Premi, Kusum K. (1974), 'Educational Opportunities for the Scheduled Castes: Role of Protective Discrimination in Equalization', *Economic and Political Weekly*, Vol. 9, Nos. 45 and 46, November 9, pp. 1902–1910.

Thorat, Sukhadeo (2005), 'Why Reservation is Necessary?', *Seminar*, Vol. 549, May. Paper presented at Redressing Disadvantage: A Symposium on Reservation and the Private Sector. Accessed through Internet. http://ww.india-seminar.com/2005/549/549%sukhadeo%20thorat.htm. on 6 April 2014.

Thorat, Sukhadeo and Chittaranjan Senapati (2006), 'Reservation Policy in India: Dimensions and Issues', *Working Paper Series*, Vol. 1, No. 2, Indian Institute of Dalit Studies, New Delhi. Accessed through Internet on 6 April 2014.

—— (2007), 'Reservation in Employment, Education and Legislature: Status and Emerging Issues', *Working Paper Series*, Vol. 2, No. 5, Indian Institute of Dalit Studies, New Delhi. Accessed through Internet on 7 April 2014.

Thorat, Sukhadeo et al. (2016), 'Prejudice against Reservation Policies: How and Why?', *Economic Political Weekly*, Vol. 51, No. 8, February 20, pp. 61–69.

Webster, C.B. John (2001), 'The Dalit Situation in India Today', *International Journal of Frontier Missions*, Vol. 18, No. 1, Spring, pp. 15–17.

Weisskopf, Thomas E. (2004), 'Impact of Reservation on Admission to Higher Education in India', *Economic and Political Weekly*, Vol. 39, No. 27, September 25, pp. 4339–4348.

Xaxa, Virginius (2001), 'Protective Discrimination: Why Scheduled Tribes Lag Behind Scheduled Castes?', *Economic and Political Weekly*, Vol. 36, No. 29, pp. 2765–2772.

Zachariah, Mathew (1972), 'Positive Discrimination in Education for India's Scheduled Castes: A Review of the Problems 1950–1970', *Comparative Education Review*, Vol. 16, No. 1, February, pp. 16–29.

Zwart, Frank de (2000), 'The Logic of Affirmative Action: Caste, Class and Quotas in India', *Acta Sociologica*, Vol. 43, No. 3, pp. 235–249.

3

73rd Constitutional Amendment

An Impact Assessment Down the Line

T. BRAHMANANDAM

The idea of decentralization is, to a certain extent, embedded in the democratic practice of the political organizations. Democracy as a form of political institution may be viewed as an opportunity to ensure people's participation not only in the sovereign power of the state but also in the day-to-day functioning of government. J.S. Mill argues that the only government which can fully satisfy all the exigencies of the state is one in which all people participate (Datta, 2009, p. 1).

The formal, i.e. legitimate panchayat system was introduced by the British in the later part of the 19th century. However, the practice is believed to be ancient especially in places where the villages were not covered under the emperor's rule. In such places, the village elders or religious leaders used to discuss and sort out their problems. In fact, Kautilya mentioned about 'Panchayats' in his book *Arthashastra* (http://www.arthapedia.in/index.php). Not only was this referred to in Kautilya's *Arthashastra*, there were inferences of the existence of panchayats even in the *Rig Veda*. Within the modern federal set-up and also in hierarchical governance structure, Panchayati Raj is the lowest and closest to the community.

In hierarchical representative system of democracy, especially in the federal structure, the (village) panchayat system has direct interface with the villagers. Being the local self-government, it deals not with the administration of law and order but the development of villagers through their participation. It is the best citation of the practice of participatory democracy. Therefore, the interface between villagers and panchayat is densely interactive and reciprocal. There is little scope or space for alienation. The true spirit of participatory democracy gets reflected in the working of the Panchayat system. That is why, this system is also known as self-governance, self-management, mutual cooperation, etc. It fosters fraternity 'assuring the dignity of the individual and unity and integrity of the nation' (http://shodhganga.inflibnet.ac.in/bitstream/10603/354/11/09_chapter2.pdf, pp. 26–27) as envisaged in the Preamble to the Constitution of India. In this background, the proposed paper on '73rd Constitutional Amendment: An Impact assessment Down the Line', would critically examine the following objectives:

- To apprise whether the former Prime Minister, Rajiv Gandhi's vision of the Panchayati Raj has been fulfilled.
- To explore the transferability, and to what extent, of the subjects mentioned in the XI Schedule of the Constitution to Panchayati Raj Institutions (PRIs) in letter and spirit.

The paper has been divided into two parts. The first part deals with the panchayati raj system in India before the 73rd Constitution Amendment Act, 1993, and the second part deals with the post-73rd Constitution Amendment period. The paper is mostly based on secondary data consisting of research literature including the government reports and studies.

A Brief Review of Literature

The Greek philosopher Aristotle hailed from the Greek city-states known for having the best possible system of governance and administration. However, J.S. Mill is considered to be the best exponent of participatory and direct democracy which is very much relevant to the local self-government in Indian context. The Mayo Resolution of 1870, no doubt, added strength to the local self-government (http://shodhganga.inflibnet.ac.in/bitstream/10603/354/11/09_chapter1.pdf, p. 7). Thereafter, the Lord Rippon Resolution emerged as a landmark in the history and evolution of the local governments. This resolution is still considered to be the 'Magna Carta' of local democracy in India (Mathew, 2013, p. 4). Socialists such as Jayaprakash Narayan (J.P.) also advocated 'direct democracy' at village level and stated that the Gram Sabha signifies democracy at the village level. He also argued for the direct government (direct democracy) at least in one place. He further said that the relationship between panchayat and gram sabha should be that of the cabinet and assembly (Bandyopadhyay, Ghosh, Saila and Ghosh et al., 2003, p. 3986). The principal focus of the panchayat has to be the dispensation of social justice and resolution of local disputes. There are several studies which have highlighted the importance, status and functions of the panchayati raj. Within these, some of them are trying to understand the working of new PRI system. Singh (2009) suggests that the Drafting Committee of the Constitution had paid lip service to the local self-government institutions.

Whatever may be the half-baked approach of the Drafting Committee, the 73rd Constitution Amendment Act, 1993 also failed to have significant impacts on the local administration as the political elites in most of the states were not willing to share power with the PRIs. Lele (2001) has mentioned Rai (2000), arguing that the 73rd and 74th Constitution Amendment Acts have augmented/opened the democratic process of these deliberative bodies. Moreover, Constitution Amendment Acts have opened a larger debate of democratization where the marginalized groups get easy access to the decision-making process quite legitimately. However, in reality, even participation in the decision-making process as well as statutory provisions fail to provide guarantee to their empowerment. In majority cases, the marginalized groups that get elected to these bodies are facing open confrontations with traditional bodies like *Gavaki* in Maharashtra, *Khap Panchayats* in Haryana, and *Customary Village Council* (CVC) in Karnataka. Narayan in 2007, highlighted that the 73rd Constitution Amendment Act has forced the states to create panchayati bodies. The inadequacy of the Panchayati Raj resources falls short of its much needed demands for development expenditure. In 2002, the Government of Andhra Pradesh had diverted most of the funds of Swarna Jayanti Gram Samriddhi Yojana under the Gram Panchayat to the construction of individual household latrines and school toilets. Had the PRI functioned effectively, adequate and regular funds would have been provided. Singh and Kumar (2005) observe that the state control always reduces the PRIs to subordinate status. The paper provides details of different types of state control, such as institutional control, administrative control and financial control over the PRIs. With the institutional control, the ruling party at the state level has always tried to gain its own political interests. For example, in Haryana, the Chautala government tried to dissolve the panchayats much before the stipulated time in order to score advantages in the assembly elections year (ibid.). However, it could not succeed because of the stay order issued by the Punjab and Haryana High Court. The inadequate resource of PRIs with the financial control of state government has put PRIs in dilemma between autonomy and dependency. Such practices of the state government undermine the very purpose for which PRIs have been instituted.

Aiyar (2002), amongst others, has stressed the need for reforms in the following areas: (i) devolution of functions and finances to panchayat bodies, (ii) training of panchayat officials, (iii) formula-based grants to village panchayats and development of their capacity to raise local revenues, (iv) checks and balances over operation of village panchayats, audit by government, involvement of NGOs and disclosure of accounts, (v) conduct of elections electoral reforms and (vi) encouragement of local planning based on popular participation. To translate the intentions of the previous amendments into reality, perhaps another amendment is necessary.

Singh (2005) study on Gram Sabha and Social Audit in Schedule V Areas of Rajasthan, Maharashtra and Madhya Pradesh focuses on the role of 'social audit' by the Gram Sabha under the provisions of PESA in the Schedule V Areas. The study shows that a large majority of the members of Gram Sabha are not aware of the powers of Gram Sabha in all the three states and more so, in Madhya Pradesh. The study also notes that neither the official functionaries nor the members of Gram Sabha have any knowledge of the concept of 'social audit'. Ghatak and Ghatak (2002) study in West Bengal states that the average attendance in Gram Sansad is as low as 12 per cent; however, the quorum for the same is 10 per cent. This also shows the participation level of participation the villagers across states.

While searching for Dalit identity and equality in Karnataka, Pinto (2013) states that the dominant community is not really interested in Dalits taking part in the local administration. He further argues that once the political office is held by them, Dalit representatives behave more like the general representatives. Dinesha (2014) has come out of the political reservations at the local level. The 73rd Constitutional Amendment has, no doubt, created space for Dalit women in PRIs. However, in reality, they are not able to get fully involved in the decision-making process owing to a number of impediments such as caste and gender discrimination. The study also noticed that they failed to take independent decisions on many issues owing to lack of education. Another important point is that wherever Dalit women function effectively, they are subjected to vulgar and abusive comments and sometimes allegations from their opponents.

Panchayati Raj in Independent India

Immediately after independence, many leaders including Mahatma Gandhi thought of establishing Panchayati Raj Institutions (PRIs) at grassroots level for democratic decentralization. On the other hand, Dr B.R. Ambedkar strongly opposed village panchayats because the villages represent the regressive India, a source of oppression (Buch, 2012, p. 1). He further argued that the empowerment of village institutions would mean perpetual dominance of the upper caste people, who would continue to exploit lower castes and the poor. Dr B.R. Ambedkar, Chairman of the Drafting Committee of the Constitution, was a powerful voice representing the Dalit community of the country. He himself had experienced caste discrimination and exploitative practices of the upper castes. In such circumstances, village panchayats did not figure in the draft Constitution as Dr Ambedkar argued them as nothing 'but a sink of localism, den of ignorance and narrow-mindedness' (Lele, 2001: p. 4703; Mathur, 2013, pp. 8–9).

According to Rathi, Gandhiji, however, severely criticized this attitude because village communities based on a communitarian principle have been the units wherein individual happiness, freedom and independence have been realized since ancient times. Shubhangi (http://www.mkgandhi.org/articles/village_development.html). However, Dr Ambedkar opposed the concept of communitarian principle because deprived sections were not part of the community. All these circumstances forced Dr Ambedkar not to include village panchayats in the beginning but later included it as a limited measure in the Directive Principles of State Policy. Article 40 of the Directive Principles of State Policy states that the state should take all steps to organize village panchayats and endow them with such powers and authority as may be necessary to enable them to function as units of self-governments.

Initially, all the developmental plans were prepared without giving much importance to the village panchayats. When these programmes 'failed to generate popular interest and enthusiasm'

(Bhalerao, 1964, p. 804) in development work, the Planning Commission appointed a committee headed by Balwant Rai Mehta in 1956. The committee viewed that 'only grassroots level agencies can establish a link between the local leadership that enjoys the confidence of local people, and translate the policies of the government into action' (Singh, 1994, pp. 818–819). It also recommended a three-tier Panchayati Raj system in the country (Bandyopadhyay, Ghosh, Saila and Ghosh et al., 2003, p. 3987). While inaugurating the Panchayati Raj system at Nagaur in Rajasthan on 2 October 1959, Nehru hailed this as 'the most revolutionary and historical step in the context of new India' (Mathew, 2013, p. 6).

By mid-1960s, the Panchayati Raj had reached to almost all parts of the country. However, within two years of its accomplishments, it failed to keep on strengthening owing to a number of crises like food crisis and war with China. Achieving adequate food grain production was a major cause of concern for the policy makers, and in that direction many agricultural schemes were launched by the government, relying mostly on bureaucracy (Datta, 2009, p. 2). In the absence of constitutional sanction and clarity, most of the panchayats functioned as government agents rather than self-governing institutes. According to Mathur, these institutions were not seen as institutions of peoples' participation that played a role in deepening democracy, but rather seen as instruments to facilitate the implementation of national policies (Mathur, 2013, p. 13).

As soon as the Janata Party came to power at the centre, it showed interests in reviving panchayati raj system for planning and implementation at the local level. With this backdrop, Janata government appointed the Ashok Mehta Committee to review and suggest suitable measures for strengthening of panchayati raj in 1978. The committee had recommended a two-tier system of panchayati raj consisting of zilla parishad at the district level as the unit of administration and planning and mandal panchayats as the base. It also recommended compulsory taxation by/to zilla parishad to generate its own resources (ibid., p. 28), and all the developmental activities/functions should be in its/their control (Hirway, 1989, p. 1663; Singh, 1994, p. 819).

During Rajiv Gandhi's tenure, two more committees (G.V.K. Rao Committee and L.M. Singhvi Committee) were appointed to study the existing administrative system at local level and also to regenerate the PRI system. The G.V.K. Rao Committee had recommended the activation of the Panchayati Raj bodies. The L.M. Singhvi Committee had recommended the constitutional sanctions for panchayat institutions (Venkatraman, 1989, p. 403); it also recommended that 'Gram Sabha' should be the base for decentralized democracy (Alok, 2011, p. 13).

73rd Constitutional Amendment and Its Operational Level

Based on the recommendations of these two committees, Rajiv Gandhi, the then Prime Minister of India, introduced the 64th Constitutional Amendment Bill on local self-government in 1989. The sole idea behind the 64th Constitutional Amendment Act was to restructure the Panchayati Raj bodies and to bring uniformity, efficiency, and responsiveness in public services. While introducing the 64th Amendment Bill in the Lok Sabha, the Prime Minister said, 'This Bill seeks to enshrine democracy at grassroots level' as it intended 'to give power to people', and it will 'end corruption, fight to finish power brokers and middlemen' in politics. The Prime Minister claimed this Bill would be a 'historic and revolutionary Bill' (Hirway, 1989, p. 1663). However, the Bill got defeated in the Rajya Sabha with a small margin, and subsequently during the Narasimha Rao's government, the bill was passed with near unanimity by the Lok Sabha on 22 December 1992 and by the Rajya Sabha on 23 December 1992. It became the 73rd Constitutional Amendment Act (CAA) on 24 April 1993. The CAA has incorporated all the recommendations of L.M. Singhvi Committee and urged all states to commensurate with the Act. However, the CAA has exempted the small states with a population less than 20 lacs from constituting the intermediate bodies.

Mathew points out that certain essential prerequisites are necessary to make PRIs function as local self-government institutions: (a) a clear-cut demarcation should be drawn between the state and panchayati raj bodies and also among the three local bodies, (b) adequate financial power and authority commensurate with the development responsibility and (c) functional autonomy within the federal structure. The need was felt to set up the boundaries of PRI bodies so that they can function without any crisscross of responsibilities. Since the constitutional amendment opens possibilities for fulfilling these conditions, the new Panchayati Raj Institution must be seen as the third tier of governance (Mathew and Mathew, 2003, pp. 18–19).

Operational Aspect and an Impact Assessment

Reservation of seats and posts of chairpersons to SCs, STs and women in panchayati bodies: Article 243D of CAA made mandatory reservation for the SCs and STs in proportion to their population in both seats and posts of chairpersons at all levels of PRI. On this point, Mathur made a significant observation that Article 243D says about the reservation of seats and posts for the SCs in proportion to their population. According to the Constitution, only 15 per cent of reservation is provided to SCs in educational and other services. In India, more than 53.6 per cent of the SCs population is concentrated in Punjab, Uttar Pradesh, West Bengal, Tamil Nadu, Andhra Pradesh and Bihar. However, all these states have adopted what the Constitution of India has mandated for the SCs, i.e. 15 per cent rather than the proportion to their population in the districts and villages. This is also the blatant violation of article 243D in actual practice (Mathur, 2013, p. 95). The CAA also says that not less than one-third of seats and posts of chairperson should be reserved for women including SCs and STs women. All these provisions have helped them to get elected to PRIs on one hand, and on the other, it has also facilitated them to be decision makers. Due to this, more than 21 lakh representatives stand elected to the three levels of panchayats. Of these, more than 40 per cent are women, 16 per cent belong to SCs and 11 per cent belong to STs (Raghunandan, 2007, p. 29). For details, see Table 1. It brought a virtual democratic revolution with 30 lakh representatives getting elected at the local level every five years, out of whom 10 lakh are women and more than six and a half lakh are Dalits. Among six and a half lakh, Dalit women are also getting elected as presidents and ward members (Mathur, 2013, p. 37).

Table 1

Composition of Panchayats in 2006

Panchayat Level	*Number*	*Elected Representatives*	*Women %*	*SC%*	*ST%*
District Panchayat	602	11,825	41	18	11
Intermediate Panchayat	6,097	1,10,070	43	22	13
Village or Gram Panchayat	2,34,676	20,73,715	40	16	11

Source: Ministry of Panchayati Raj (2006). (Also see Raghunandan, 2007, p. 29).

Mandated reservation of one-third of panchayat positions for women had been successfully implemented by 2000 (except in Punjab and UP). While for SCs/STs it has been somewhat less than their demographic weight in some states, the ratio was below 70 per cent in Gujarat, Odisha and UP (Chaudhuri, 2006). Many people thought that the CAA would certainly make these local bodies active. However, there has been a prolonged delay by the state governments in transferring these constitutionally mandated powers and functions to the local bodies. There are a number of reasons which have been spelt out below for the delay in transferring these powers.

Delay or Irregular Election to PRIs: In spite of the mandatory provisions mentioned in Part XI of the Constitution on the creation of panchayats, the Constitutional bodies fail to prepare electoral rolls, and conducting regular elections to these bodies has never been considered as the constitutional breakdown in the state. For indefinite delaying of elections, an observation has been made with reference to Andhra Pradesh where the Congress government had delayed the conducting of elections of the PRI bodies for more than 2 years because of lack of clarity on Backward Class (BC) reservations. Elections were conducted to these bodies only in 2014 because of the High Court interventions (*The Hindu*, 2014). Another example is Bihar for not conducting elections to PRI bodies until 2001. Even after the 73rd Amendment Act, the Government of Bihar did not conduct elections to local bodies and kept delaying because of litigations pertaining to the reservation of leadership positions in Panchayats. Finally, it conducted elections to these bodies in 2001 without reservations being provided for leadership positions in Panchayats (http://www.nrcddp.org/file_upload/Status%20of%20Panchayati%20Raj,%20Bihar.pdf).

Based on these facts, the working group on Decentralized Planning and Panchayati Raj of the Tenth Plan observed that 'most of the court cases, grievances of aggrieved parties related to reservation of seats for SCs/STs/OBCs/women, delimitation of constituencies, percentage of reservation for chairpersons of lower tier to higher tier, etc. and in most of the cases, the state governments have not pursued these pending court cases vigorously for their early hearing so that a final decision of the court becomes available as early as possible' (Pal, 2004, p. 139). This reflects that the political elites at the state level are not interested to incorporate women and marginalized groups in the developmental process.

Structural Constraints for Reserved Seats: Article 243D also specifies the mandatory rotation, i.e. the structural constraints of reservation of seats among constituencies from one election to the next election in three-tier panchayati system. As per this Act, if a seat or constituency is reserved for a particular category, he or she is eligible to contest for that particular term only and they cannot contest for second term from the same constituency. It implies that women and other marginalized groups cannot contest from the same constituency once their five-year term expires. This has denied them the right to contest from the same constituency. The states such as Andhra Pradesh, Haryana, Himachal Pradesh, Madhya Pradesh, Odisha, Chhattisgarh Maharashtra, and Rajasthan have also introduced the two-child norm as an eligibility criteria for contesting elections. Though this norm goes against both men and women, it is more detrimental to women especially to the scheduled castes and scheduled tribes community because majority of the families follow the norm of big and joint family. To assess the impact of this norm, a study was conducted by the Mahila Chetna Manch, Bhopal-based NGO and it observed that unless and until proper information of 'two-child norm' is disseminated to the rural areas, it is impossible to empower the economically and socially vulnerable sections of the society (Datta, 2009, p. 23).

Conflict of Interest between Traditional Bodies and Constitutionally Elected Bodies: The traditional bodies like 'collectives' or 'gavaki' in Maharashtra and 'customary village councils' (CVCs) in Karnataka are functioning parallel to the village panchayats. In fact, in Maharashtra they are called as 'collectives' or 'gavaki'. In Maharashtra, 'gavaki' is dominated by the upper caste and elite landlords. It does not have any legal sanctity in the state. Despite having no legal sanctity, these bodies are powerful than elected representatives at the village level. Gavaki is very active in the Konkan region of Satara, Ahmad Nagar, Nandurburg, Raigad and several other districts. These gavakis (kangaroo courts) deliver illegal judgments like social boycott, cleaning of public latrines, donating blood or arranging social functions. In 2013, a pregnant girl from the Gosavi community, who got married to a Dalit boy, was killed by her father. This act of cruelty was committed by girl's father due to the pressure and high handedness of the community members. A similar diktat was issued in Raigad district by which Santosh Jadhav was ostracized by the Kunbi community in 2005 for defying the diktat against contesting for the sarpanch's post at Harihareshwar in Raigad. These unlawful judgments of the kangaroo courts have motivated the incumbent Chief Minister Devendra Fadnavis to propose a law on the Prevention of Social Boycott Act of 2015. 'The main aim is to crack down on the parallel justice system in Maharashtra, which frowns at inter-caste marriages, change in social practices or even people's choice of clothes.' (https://sjsa.maharashtra.gov.in/en/maharashtra-cm-devendra-fadnavis-pushes-social-boycott-law-against-parallel-justic e-system). This shows the strength of the *'Gavaki'* in Maharashtra. They are very effective in areas where women or Dalits are in power. Based on the above observations, Lele rightly said that 'reservations which intended to empower marginalised sections in rural governance are being made ineffective by these established traditional bodies in the rural areas' (Lele, 2001, p. 4703). Even today, in many parts of India, the *traditional bodies* are part and parcel of the village culture, and the law makers should give a chance to these traditional bodies to play some sort of conciliatory role on local issues. This would certainly promote the cooperation between elected representatives and traditional bodies and avoid confrontation between them which may again defeat the purpose of the Constitutional Amendment Act (CAA).

The Khap Panchayats (KP) are another example of the traditional body that exercises powers parallel to the village panchayats, especially in Jat dominated areas of North India, i.e. Haryana, Panjab and the Meerut region of Uttar Pradesh. In this region, the Khap Panchayats emerged as an extra judicial body that pronounces harsh punishments as retribution based on the age-old customs and traditions. In Haryana, when a Dalit girl was gang raped by four youths, instead of condemning the incident, the KP directed that girls should be married off early so that rapes can be avoided. Later, the same Dalit girl committed suicide. When the girl committed suicide, the Congress President Smt Sonia Gandhi visited the girl's family, and she just condemned the incident and never uttered a word against the KP's extra judicial power (*The Indian Express*, 2012). Even the former Chief Minister Bhupender Singh Hooda said that 'Khaps are social institutions and steps taken in a hurry to curb them would have dangerous impacts on the law and order situation in the state' (Mathur, 2013). The appeasement policy taken by the political leaders would certainly encourage the KP to act more vigorously.

Obstructive or Discriminatory Laws against Weaker Sections by the Political Elite: One of the main objectives of the 73rd Constitution Amendment Act is to empower the weaker sections by offering constitutional status to the PRI bodies. However, in reality, certain state governments are passing more and more obstructive laws against these sections of the society. For example, the Rajasthan government has issued an ordinance stating that if a person wants to contest the post of village sarpanch, then he/she has to have the minimum qualification of std. VIII. In case of reserved constituency for scheduled caste, one should have the qualification of std. V. In states like Rajasthan where the women literacy is 46 per cent, much below the national average, it severely affects the prospects of SC and ST women candidates who mostly fail to satisfy the educational criteria for contesting elections as their educational status is much lower than that of general women. It may look good to suggest educational qualifications for the candidates across communities, provided 100 per cent literacy is achieved. If not so, it is intended to create hurdles among weaker section. Another discriminatory law against the marginalized sections is the Haryana Panchayati Raj (Amendment) Bill, 2015 (*The Hindu*, 2015). Recently, the government of Haryana has passed this Act fixing the educational qualifications for the contest of local body elections. In addition to this, the candidates have to provide proof of having household toilets. In a country where educational qualification is not fixed for the Lok Sabha and State Assembly elections, how can one fix educational qualification as a criteria for eligibility to local body elections? This kind of legislations will certainly hinder women, OBCs, and Dalits who are forced to give up education because of their socio-economic backwardness and gender discrimination.

Proxy Rule: In addition to these, there are certain negative facets observed by women and Dalit representatives while discharging their duties. Wherever women and Dalits are elected to the PR bodies, the elected persons would be the de jure representative, whereas the de facto representative would be someone else. In the case of women representatives, the de jure would be women and de facto would be the eldest male member of the family. This is also known as 'proxy rule'. In this situation, a woman would be placed nominally, and the role of the president would really be done by her husband/male member of the family, who would act as the de facto president. The sole aim of the CAA is to empower the weaker sections like women and Dalits. But in reality, it is defeating the purpose of empowering women and Dalits (Reddy, 2003, p. 1290).

When former Prime Minister Rajiv Gandhi introduced the 64th Constitutional Amendment Bill in the Lok Sabha, he wanted the grassroot institutions to be made more efficient, responsive, empowering people and ending corruption. However, in practice, everything went on as usual contrary to the vision and ideas of Rajiv Gandhi. Even in 1989, the non-Congress opposition created pressure on the government to withdraw the Panchayati Raj Constitutional Amendment Bill on ground of anomalies in the preamble to the proposed Bill (Hewitt and Rai, 2010, p. 36).

Conclusion

When India got independence, Gandhi wanted that villages should be made as self-governing units so that they can serve the local needs at local level. However, this idea was not considered by the Drafting Committee of the Constitution. To fulfil Gandhi's Gram Swaraj, an amendment was introduced to the Constitution in 1993. This Amendment Act has brought drastic changes in the PRI bodies, introducing reservation in presidents/sarpanch and ward members for SCs and STs according to the size of their population. It was also suggested that not less than one-third of the seats would also be reserved for women in the entire three-tier system of panchayati raj. Due to the 73rd Constitution Amendment, the much needed changes have been introduced to the PRI bodies. However, in reality it failed because of the powers and functions of PRIs have not been clearly stated and demarcated from that of the state administration. In some cases, the political leadership of the state is not very favourable to empower the marginalized groups and also the PRI. In this connection, the same leadership is framing new laws with regard to education, households, toilets and local bank clearance.

Dr Ambedkar did not want to include the panchayats in the Constitution because it was nothing 'but a sink of localism, den of ignorance and narrow-mindedness and a source of oppression. While countering his arguments, Madhava Rau of Mysore said, 'It is true some villages are faction ridden and remain the stronghold of untouchability'. Looking at this worst situation, Mr Rau insisted that even if 30 per cent of the population could be classified as good, it could not be ignored. Taking all these into consideration, certain changes were brought into the PRI system through the 73rd Constitutional Amendment. Despite these changes, a large section of the marginalized groups feels that it does not come close to Gandhian wisdom because of the paucity of its powers and very limited financial resources. Very often, the elections of these bodies are not conducted regularly. In many states, the traditional bodies are functioning parallel to panchayats, even today. Under these circumstances, the policy makers should review it and make necessary changes to transfer the 29 subjects (for List of Subjects see Annexure) to the village panchayats, conduct elections to these bodies regularly, to give power and resources to Gram Sabha/Ward Sabha to implement the schemes/works. Only then, it can serve the purpose of people at grassroot level both to strengthen democracy and to help build Gandhi's Gram Swaraj.

References

Aiyar, M. (2002), 'Panchayati Raj: The Way Forward', *Economic and Political Weekly*, Vol. 37, No. 31, pp. 3239–3297.

Alok, V.N. (2011), 'Role of Panchayat Bodies in Rural Development since 1959', Theme Paper for the Fifty-Fifth Members' Annual Conference, Indian Institute of Public Administration, New Delhi.

Bandyopadhyay, D., S.K. Ghosh and B. Ghosh (2003), 'Dependency versus Autonomy-identity Crisis of India's Panchayats', *Economic and Political Weekly*, Vol. 38, No. 38, pp. 3984–3999.

Bhalerao, C.N. (1964), 'Some Social, Political and Administrative Consequences of Panchayati Raj', *Asian Survey*, Vol. 4, No. 4, pp. 804–811.

Buch, N. (2012), 'Gram Sabha and Panchayati Raj', *Social Action*, Vol. 62, No. 1, pp. 1–15.

Chaudhuri, S. (2006), 'What Difference Does a Constitutional Amendment Make? The 1994 Panchayati Raj Act and the Attempt to Revitalize Rural Local Government in India', in P. Bardhan and D. Mookherjee (eds), *Decentralization and Local Governance in Developing Countries: A Comparative Perspective*, Cambridge, MA: MIT Press.

Datta, P. (2009), 'Democratic Decentralization through Panchayati Raj in Contemporary India: The Changes and Challenges', *Working Paper No.*

49, South Asia Institute, Department of Political Science, Heidelberg University.

Dinesha, P.T. (2014), 'Dalit Women Panchayat Representatives and Social Exclusion', *KILA Journal of Local Governance*, Vol. 1, No. 1, pp. 15–22.

Ghatak, M. and Maitreya Ghatak (2002), 'Recent Reforms in the Panchayat System in West Bengal', *Economic and Political Weekly*, Vol. 37, No. 1, pp. 45–58.

Government of Maharashtra. Social Justice and Special Assistance Department. Retrieved from http://sjsa.maharashtra.gov.in/en/maharashtra-cm-devendra-fadnavis-pushes-social-boycott-law-against-parallel-justice-system. Accessed on 18 September 2016.

Hewitt, V. and S.M. Rai (2010), 'Parliament', in Nirja G. Jayal and Pratap B. Mehta (eds), *Politics*, New Delhi: Oxford University Press.

Hirway, Indira (1989), 'Panchayati Raj at Crossroads', *Economic and Political Weekly*, Vol. 24, No. 29, pp. 1663–1667.

Historical Development of Panchayati Raj and Gram Sabha in India. Retrieved from http://shodhganga.inflibnet.ac.in/bitstream/10603/354/11/09_chapter2.pdf.26–74. Accessed on 18 September 2016.

Lele, M.K. (2001), 'Local Government: Conflicts of Interests and Issues of Legitimisation', *Economic and Political Weekly*, Vol. 36, No. 51, pp. 4702–4704.

Local Governance System in Rural India. Retrieved from http://www.arthapedia.in/index.php. Accessed on 18 September 2016.

Mathew, G. (2013), *Status of Panchayati Raj in the States and Union Territories of India*, New Delhi: Institute of Social Sciences and Concept Publishing Company.

Mathew, G. and A. Mathew (2003), 'India: Decentralization and Local Governance: How Clientelism and Accountability Work?', in Axel Hadenius (ed.), *Decentralization and Democratic Governance: Experiences from India, Bolivia and South Africa*, Stockholm: Elanders Gotab.

Mathur, K. (2013), *Panchayati Raj*, New Delhi: Oxford University Press.

Ministry of Panchayati Raj (2006), *Annual Reports of the Ministry of Panchayati Raj 2005–06*, Government of India, New Delhi.

Narayana, E.A. (2007), 'Panchayati Raj in Andhra Pradesh: An Appraisal of its Working since 73rd Constitutional Amendment', *The Indian Journal of Political Science*, Vol. 68, No. 4, pp. 809–814.

Pal, M. (2004), 'Panchayati Raj and Rural Governance: Experiences of a Decade', *Economic and Political Weekly*, Vol. 39, No. 2, pp. 137–143.

Pinto, Ambrose (2013), *Dalits in Karnataka in Search of Identity and Equality*, New Delhi: Manak Publications Pvt. Ltd.

Raghunandan, T.R. (2007), *Rural Infrastructure, Panchayati Raj, and Governance: India Infrastructure Report*, New Delhi: Oxford University Press.

Rai, Shirin M. (2000), 'Looking to the Future: Panchayats, Women's Representation and Deliberative Politics'. Paper presented at the conference on Women and Panchayat Raj Institutions, 8–27 April.

Rathi, Shubhangi (ND), 'Gandhian Concept of Village Development and India's Development Policy' (special reference to Panchayati Raj). Retrieved from http://www.mkgandhi.org/articles/village_development.html. Accessed on 18 July 2016.

Reddy, M.G. (2003), 'Status of Decentralised Local Bodies: Post–73rd Amendment Scenario', *Economic and Political Weekly*, Vol. 38, No. 12/13, pp. 1284–1292.

Singh, H. (1994), 'Constitutional Base for Panchayati Raj in India: The 73rd Amendment Act', *Asian Survey*, Vol. 34, No. 9, pp. 818–827.

Singh, M. and V. Kumar (2005), 'State Control Over Panchayati Raj Institutions', *The Indian Journal of Political Science*, Vol. 66, No. 2, pp. 221–232.

Singh, R. (2009), 'Unfinished Agenda of Gandhi's Gram Swaraj: Fifty Years of Panchayati Raj', *Mainstream*, Vol. 42, No. 43. Retrieved from http://www.mainstreamweekly.net/article1690.html. Accessed on 10 November 2016.

Singh, S.K. (ed.) (2005), *Empowering of Gram Sabha and Social Audit*, Volume IV of series on Self-governance for Tribals, Hyderabad: NIRD.

State of Panchayats State Profile – Bihar. Retrieved from http://www.nrcddp.org/file_upload/status%20of%20panchayati%20raj,%20bihar.pdf. Accessed on 18 July 2016.

Venkatraman, A. (1989), 'Proposed Constitutional Amendment on Panchayati Raj: Some Reflections', *The Indian Journal of Political Science*, Vol. 50, No. 3, pp. 405–406.

Newspaper Clippings

Khaps Say Marry Them Young, Cong. Sees Conspiracy (8 October 2012), *The Indian Express* (Chandigarh).

Supreme Court Upholds Haryana Panchayat Law (10 December 2015), *The Hindu* (New Delhi).

Zilla Parishad Territorial Constituency (ZPTC) and Mandal Parishad Territorial Constituency (MPTC) Elections on 6 April (11 March 2014), *The Hindu* (Hyderabad).

Annexure

All the 29 subjects

1. Agriculture, including agricultural extension
2. Land improvement, implementation of land reforms, land consolidation and soil conservation
3. Minor irrigation, water management and watershed development
4. Animal husbandry, dairying and poultry
5. Fisheries
6. Social forestry and farm forestry
7. Minor forest produce
8. Small-scale industries, including food processing industries
9. Khadi, village and cottage industries
10. Rural housing
11. Drinking water
12. Fuel and fodder
13. Roads, culverts, bridges, ferries, waterways and other means of communication
14. Rural electrification, including distribution of electricity
15. Non-conventional energy sources
16. Poverty alleviation programme
17. Education including primary and secondary schools
18. Technical training and vocational education
19. Adult and non-formal education
20. Libraries
21. Cultural activities
22. Market and fairs
23. Health and sanitation, including hospitals, primary health centres and dispensaries
24. Family welfare
25. Women and child development
26. Social welfare, including welfare of the handicapped and mentally retarded
27. Welfare of the weaker sections, and in particular, of the Scheduled Castes and Scheduled Tribes
28. Public distribution system
29. Maintenance of community assets.

4

Availability of Healthcare Services in PHCs of Salem District

Special Reference to Tamil Nadu

A. VADIVELU

The Statement of Problem

The notion of pollution-purity pervades over all aspects of social life, including food, cloth, metals, occupations, etc. Thus, not only are persons and castes pure and impure or less pure or more impure, but everything in Hindu society is seen in terms of purity-pollution. Gold is pure and silver is less pure; silk is pure and cotton is impure, etc. The inhuman and exploitative conditions in which these people were forced to live for centuries made them conscious of their deplorable condition in the Hindu society. Besides their own realization, factors external to the caste system also contributed to the weakening of the caste system.

The Constitution of India has listed the 'untouchable' castes as 'Scheduled Castes' with a view to provide them protection against discrimination, exploitation and degradation. It provides for their social, economic, political, cultural and educational upliftment. A policy for reservation of jobs, positions, educational facilities and constituencies for state assemblies and the Lok Sabha and for nomination to local bodies has been adopted by the governments of independent India. Today, 15 per cent reservation is available to SCs in government jobs and in educational institutions for studies. Provisions have been made against social discrimination and untouchability with a view to attain equality of SCs with the caste Hindus. However, ascriptive status cannot be changed simply by constitutional provisions. The processes of social change and modernization of traditional values alone can bring about a change in due course of time. The Constitution of India makes provisions for the upliftment of SCs in economic, political and educational fields.

Since these provisions have made a tangible impact and have generated a certain level of consciousness among SCs, the upper and intermediate castes have begun to feel uncomfortable. Clashes between the caste Hindus and SCs have been frequently reported from different states. SCs are emerging as a force to reckon with representing secular values, egalitarianism and the quest for equality. However, some sections of SCs, who have derived considerable benefits from the constitutional provisions, have attained an elite status among them. These sections continue to enjoy the special provisions despite enormous improvement in their socio-economic condition. Such beneficiaries from amongst SCs are known as 'creamy layer'.

In some areas, SCs are still not allowed access to temples, tea stalls and public wells or water taps. However, today, demands are rarely of a religious and ritual nature. What the Harijans demand today is to be treated as persons. They should not be driven from their land, should no longer be bonded labourers and should be given fair wages. Their children should be educated and considered equal to children of other communities. They should be allowed to have their say in all democratic institutions. However, the fact remains that SCs continue to be inferior to the caste Hindus in all secular or mundane matters. SC leaders are subordinate to the caste leaders. SC votes have generally been controlled by different political groups and parties. Many of the leaders of these castes do not wish to be identified with SCs. They, in fact, desire to be identified with the upper caste leadership.

Nearly 90 per cent of SCs live in villages and they continue to suffer because they work under the command of dominant castes and landlords. They continue to be economically dependent on the upper caste and class groups. Constitutional provisions have been availed by the poor SCs in a marginal way. Since they continue to be poor, they are subjected to exploitation. It has been noted that today, there is an increasing possibility for upward mobility for SCs. Mobility is possible through two processes: by corporate mobility and by competition between castes and within castes. There is intercaste variability in regard to social mobility and also, there are sacred and secular channels for status emulation. Migration, education and white-collar jobs (like those held by the caste Hindus) have been the main source of social mobility among SCs.

One serious consequence of the first pattern is creation of socio-economic unevenness between different SCs and among members of the same SC. The benefits of constitutional provisions and uniformity to other changes have not reached different SCs and individuals. As a result of the second pattern, 'caste wars' or hostilities of the SCs against the upper castes have also increased. It is now accepted that SCs suffer today not so much because of social and cultural disabilities, as the imbalances created by structural differentiation in their ranks have become pronounced. This unevenness is a result of the faulty execution of policies and plans. The atrocities committed on SCs and their exploitation by the dominant caste Hindus should be analysed in view of these distinctions and their relations with the caste Hindus.

Review of Literature

Van de Poel E. and Speybroeck (2009) examined decomposes the gap in child malnutrition between ST/SC and the remaining Indian population, looking at both ST/SC's disadvantageous distribution of health determinants and possible discriminatory or behavioural differences. Blinder-Oaxaca was applied to decompose the gap in children's average height-for-age z scores, using data from the 1998/1999 Indian Demographic Health Survey. The gap was found to be primarily caused by ST/SC's lower wealth, education and use of healthcare services, but differences in the effects of health determinants also played an important role in the same. It was found that within rural areas, ST/SC are not necessarily located further from educational and healthcare facilities.

Rajendra P. Mamgain (2014) examined the nature, forms and consequences of social exclusion in the Indian society. It argues how social exclusion resulted in low development outcomes for SCs as compared to other social groups even having comprehensive constitutional safeguards. The paper attempts to analyse the underlying causes of atrocities on SCs in the framework of social exclusion, discrimination, vulnerability and rising assertiveness among SCs about their rights and dignity. It argues for new thinking and related actions altogether which could accelerate the economic well-being of SCs at a faster pace, embolden the social reforms and intensify cultural movements to change societal mindsets.

Pushpendra Kumar and Abha Gupta (2015) examined the utilization of maternal healthcare services within and across social groups among married women in India using data from third round of District Level Household and Facility Survey conducted during 2007–08. Maternal healthcare utilization is measured through full antenatal care, safe delivery and postnatal care. Besides, selected socio-economic and demographic factors have been included as predictor variables. Bivariate, logistic regression and concentration curve have been employed to understand the intercaste differences, net effect of the predictor variables on selected outcomes and intra-caste differentials respectively. The findings show significant difference in the utilization of maternal healthcare services by caste, women's age at first birth, educational attainment, place of residence, economic status and region. Besides, high inequality is found among poor and non-poor in 'Other Caste' followed by Other Backward Classes.

Zulufkar Ahmad Khanday and Mohammad Akram (2012) studied to highlight the discrimination and exploitation of these marginalized groups, especially in terms of their health. Further, a study is carried out about how the rights of these marginalized groups are violated within the society. In India, there are multiple socio-economic disadvantages that members of particular groups experience, which limits their access to health and healthcare. Some of the prominent factors on the basis of which individuals belonging to marginalized groups are discriminated in India are structural factors, age, disability, mobility and stigma that act as barriers to health and healthcare. Sometimes, each group faces multiple barriers due to their multiple identities. Finally, it can be said that the health status of these marginalized groups in India is very poor as compared to the other sections of population.

Anek Lal Barman (2013) studied that Indian society is based on a caste system with vast inequalities in social, political, economic and educational spheres. The present study has been conducted on a purposive sampling of 100 scheduled caste people. The data has been collected through field survey. The results revealed that the socio-economic status of scheduled caste people is low. Their backwardness is caused by financial problems. Because of this problem, they failed to achieve the education of their children. The Constitution of India has specific provision to bring scheduled caste into the mainstream of national life. It is not merely a matter of compassion or charity to see that they should be helped to develop.

P.R. Rejoice and A.K. Ravishankar (2011) examined assess to the utilization of antenatal care services among currently married scheduled caste women in India. The data have been extracted from National Family Health Survey–3 (NFHS–3) conducted during 2005–06 all over India. A total of 6,212 currently married scheduled caste women in the age group of 15–49 were taken as sample for the study. Cross tabulation and binary logistic regression methods were applied for determining the influencing factors. Concluded age, education and wealth index were significantly associated for getting full antenatal care service among scheduled caste women.

Objective of the Study

- To study the socio-economic background of sample respondents.
- To examine the community based on healthcare services in PHCs.

Methodology

The researcher selected the area in Salem District for the study. The study is based on primary and secondary data. PHCs were selected in villages Veerapandy, Gangavalli, Mecheri, Tharmanalam and Yercaud, with the criteria of size of population, different community people, literacy rate, different occupational status as well as health indicators like availability of healthcare facilities, mortality rate and life expectancy of the people. From these villages, 125 sample respondents were selected by using random sampling method. Both quantitative and qualitative informations were collected from the respondents, those who have suffered from any disease or illness. The researcher has processed, tabulated and analysed the received informations by using simple statistical and econometric tools like percentage distribution scaling technique analysis.

Summary and Conclusion

Socio-Economic Background of the Sample Respondents

Along with the general information of the sample households, individual characters are also important while discussing the socio-economic status (SES) of the sample household members. The individual information namely, sex, age, marital status, educational attainment, occupational status and earnings of members per month are also given in the following Table 1.

Table 1

Socio-Economic Background of the Sample Respondents

Socio-economic Variable	*No. of Sample Respondents*	*Per cent*
Religious		
Hindu	86	68.8
Gender		
Female	76	60.8
Age group (in years)		
25–35	57	45.6
Social status		
MBC	54	43.2
Type of the household		
Nuclear household	69	55.2
Marital status		
Married	57	45.6
Educational attainment		
Secondary	48	38.4
Occupational status		
Agriculture labourers	43	34.4
Earnings of the member (₹ per month)		
₹ 3,001–5,000	49	39.2
Total	125	100.0

Source: Primary Data.

It is found that more than nine tenth (68.8%) belongs to Hindu religion. From this survey, with respect to sex of the sample household members, more than six tenth (60.8%) are females. More than four-tenth (42.4%) were in the productive age group of 25 to 35 years. From this, the researcher infers that 43.2 per cent of them are Most Backward Community (MBC). This shows that mostly Salem District is dominated by these set of people and they belong to the following communities, viz., MBC, BC and SC/ST. We infer that half (55.2%) are in nuclear household system. From the total members, more than four-tenth (45.6%) were married.

The educational attainment has also been categorized into five categories, viz., primary, secondary, higher secondary, higher education and illiterates respectively out of which three-tenth (38.4%) were secondary. It is evidenced that when the level of education goes on higher side, then there is small percentage in the distribution of sample household members. We have categorized the received occupational pattern of members into seven, namely agriculturists, agricultural labours, non-agricultural labourers, self-employed, salaried, pensioners and non-workers like the classification of National Sample Survey Organization (NSSO). Amongst these, three-tenth (34.4%) were agricultural labourers. It is necessary to study the income of the sample household members when we discuss it against the socio-economic background. Nearly four-tenth out of the total (39.2%) were income group (₹ 3,001–5,000).

Community Based on PHCs Services

The fairness and impartiality of doctors, along with services of operation theatre, lab technician, pharmacist, room, ambulance services and bed facilities, fan facilities, entertainment, water/toilet facilities in giving treatment to the rural people, all these assume significance in the context of caste domination in rural areas. So the caste group wise respondents were recorded and analysed here.

Table 2

Community Based Variables on PHCs Services

Variables	*SC*	*ST*	*MBC*	*BC*	*Total*
Doctor's services	47 (37.6)	38 (30.4)	23 (20.0)	17 (13.6)	125 (100)
Staff nurse's treatment	34 (27.2)	43 (34.4)	30 (24.0)	18 (14.4)	125 (100)
Village health nurses' services	28 (22.4)	19 (15.2)	51 (40.8)	27 (21.6)	125 (100)
Operation theatre services	24 (19.2)	13 (10.4)	43 (34.4)	45 (36.0)	125 (100)
Lab Technician services	43 (34.4)	28 (22.4)	31 (24.8)	23 (18.4)	125 (100)
Bed facilities	34 (27.2)	14 (11.2)	41 (32.8)	36 (28.8)	125 (100)
Fan facilities	27 (21.6)	25 (20.0)	30 (24.0)	43 (34.4)	125 (100)
Pharmacist services	23 (18.4)	18 (14.4)	52 (41.6)	37 (29.6)	125 (100)

Cont'd...

...Cont'd

Water / Toilet facilities	36 (28.8)	24 (19.2)	38 (30.4)	27 (21.6)	125 (100)
Room services	22 (17.6)	19 (15.2)	54 (43.2)	25 (20.0)	125 (100)
Entertainment facilities	28 (22.4)	23 (18.4)	43 (34.4)	31 (24.8)	125 (100)
Ambulance services	31 (24.8)	28 (22.4)	43 (34.4)	23 (18.4)	125 (100)

Source: Primary Data.

Note: Figures in Parentheses are per cent.

Services of Doctors

It was found that majority of the SC and ST respondents opined that there is fairness and impartiality in the services of doctors at PHCs. However, the respondents from the MBC and BC category were gives equal treatment by the doctor at PHCs in the selected sample areas. More than 37 per cent of SC respondents have expressed satisfaction over their treatment and also handling their cases at Primary Health Centre (PHC). This indicates that their much satisfied than the remaining other (ST, MBC and BC) category of people. It not only suggests the satisfaction of SC category and it indirectly conveys the impression that more number of people belonging to this depend on the PHC services for their ailments.

Services of Staff Nurses

The researcher had an interest to know the services of staff nurses of the sample household members. From the total members, majority of the (34.4%) of the sample respondents (ST category) opined that there is fairness in the services of staff nurses at PHCs.

Services of Village Health Nurses

The village health nurses go to the doorstep of every pregnant woman in the village and offer them treatment and advice. Village health nurses have given the home delivery treatment and other services for money. Majority of the (40.8%) MBC respondents are beneficiaries from assistant nurses' services. However, the respondents from the SC/ST category of the socially backward community face some problem that prevails in the PHCs due to unequal services of village health nurses. Moreover, the Village Health Nurses (VHNs) are not interested in attending to those patients who belong to SC/ST community and do not go to the SC/ST people's houses.

Services of Operation Theatre

With respect to availability of the facility of operation theatre services, it is available only in the general hospital and is not available in PHCs. The patients are sent to the nearby general hospital. More than three-tenth (36.0%) of the respondents (BC category) are beneficiaries of the services of operation theatre. Most of the SC and ST category are given treatment at PHCs operation theatre services which is not available to tribal and rural areas. The patients are therefore, going to private and general hospitals.

Services of Lab Technician

As the services of lab technician are not available in some PHCs, they have to go to private hospitals for their needs, which cost them much. Overall, PHCs' lab technician services are unfair owing to the large numbers of in-patient and out-patients, due to which it becomes critical to provide these. The SC category said that only four-tenth (34.4%) of the respondents utilized these lab technician services.

Services of Beds

With regard to the availability of bed facility, all the category respondents said that they were comfortable and clean. These services are available only in upgraded PHCs. Three-tenth (32.8%) of the respondents said that the availability of bed services is for the beneficiaries from the MBC category. The availability of bed services during delivery, antenatal and emergency cases is unequal to the socially backward groups, viz. SC and ST.

Fan Facilities

With regard to the availability of fan facility, all the respondents of all category comfortable. More than (34.4%) of the sample respondents from the BC category have utilized these fan facilities.

Services of Pharmacist

All the respondents are taking services of pharmacist in PHCs. The medicines that are given by these pharmacists is very useful in diseases such as BP, diabetes, cold, fever, headache and also during delivery and antenatal checkup. Four-tenth (41.6%) of the respondents farming the MBC category said that the services of pharmacists were satisfactory for them.

Water/Toilet Facilities

Toilet facility is a basic essential facility for the PHC. It is necessary not only for the in-patients but also for the out patients, especially for pregnant ladies. Three-tenth (30.4%) of the sample respondents from the MBC category are beneficiaries of the water/toilet facilities.

Entertainment Facilities

Television is provided to PHCs for the entertainment of patients. Both in-patients and out-patients need such type of entertainment in order to relax and watch movies during waiting time. Around 34.4 per cent of respondents of the MBC category have utilized these entertainment facilities.

Room Services

All the patients, whether they are in-patients or out-patients should have an attendant with them to look after them. These attendants need a rest room. More than four-tenth (43.2%) of the room services are available for the MBC community.

Ambulance Services

Ambulance service is one of the life-saving services. The life of a person in emergency depends on the availability or non-availability of this service. Reasonable availability of ambulance services is available in only upgraded PHCs in rural and urban areas. In tribal area, ambulance service is not available at PHCs. Three-tenth (34.4%) of the sample respondents from the MBC category are beneficiaries of the ambulance services. Most of the SC and ST category are given treatment at PHCs' ambulance services, and it is not available in tribal and partially available in rural areas.

Overall Performance Weightages of PHCs Services

Along with this, the available infrastructure facilities are also captured, such as operation theatre, bed, fan, pharmacist, water and toilet facilities, attender's rest room and ambulance services. The variables which have been taken for the performance analysis are qualitative in nature. Hence, three-point scaling technique has been adopted viz. Poor, Moderate and Good for each and every service with respect to hospital services. The following table gives the details of the variables and weightage is assigned to each variable.

Table 3

Overall Performance Weightages of PHCs Services

Categories	*Poor*	*Moderate*	*Good*
SC	11 (8.8)	13 (10.4)	7 (5.6)
ST	13 (10.4)	12 (9.6)	10 (8.0)
MBC	9 (7.2)	14 (11.2)	6 (4.8)
BC	8 (6.4)	10 (8.0)	12 (9.6)
Total	41 (32.8)	49 (39.2)	35 (28.0)

Source: Primary Data.

The above Table 3 shows the overall performance of PHCs' services in the study areas. Nearly four-tenth (39.2%) of the sample respondents said that it is moderate in performance and remaining three-tenth (32.8%) said that the level of performances was poor for the services. Two-tenth (28.0%) of sample respondents said that the services provided were good.

Conclusion

Apart from the provision of the basic needs for their survival, the country needs to make concerted efforts to improve the social and economic conditions of scheduled caste by increasing the level of literacy among them, giving alternative job opportunities and making improved farm technologies accessible to those primarily engaged in agrarian occupations. To further improve the overall well-being and quality of life of this disadvantaged group, the reach of various health services, especially for women and children, needs to be increased. Primary health care centres (PHCs) are also able to address the problems of poor coverage of basic healthcare and lack of equipments by communities in health systems, not only by improving their economic status and accessibility of health services, but also by lowering down health inequality among SCs and STs.

References

Barman, Anek Lal (2013), 'Socio-Economic Status of Scheduled Caste People in Kamrup District of Assam', *Scholarly Research Journal for Interdisciplinary Studies*, Vol. 2, No. 15.

Khanday, Zulufkar Ahmad and Mohammad Akram (2012), 'Health Status of Marginalized Groups in India', *International Journal of Applied Sociology*, Vol. 2, No. 6, pp. 60–70.

Kumar, Pushpendra and Abha Gupta (2015), 'Determinants of Inter and Intra Caste Differences in Utilization of Maternal Health Care Services in India: Evidence from DLHS–3 Survey', *International Research Journal of Social Sciences*, Vol. 4, No. 1, pp. 27–36.

Mamgain, Rajendra P. (2014), 'Social Exclusion, Discrimination and Atrocities on Scheduled Castes in India: The Worrying Spots and Future Challenges', *Journal of Economic and Social Development*, Vol. 10, No. 1.

Rejoice, P.R. and A.K. Ravishankar (2011), 'Utilization of Antenatal Care Services among Scheduled Caste Women in India', *International Journal of Current Research*, Vol. 33, No. 6, pp. 202–207.

Van de Poel, E. and N. Speybroeck (2009), 'Decomposing Malnutrition Inequalities between Scheduled Castes and Tribes and the Remaining Indian Population', *Ethnicity and Health*, Vol. 14, No. 3, pp. 271–287.

5

Socio-Economic Deprivation of Scheduled Castes through Social Exclusion and Discrimination in India

R.G. DANDGE

Scheduled Castes are those castes which have been enlisted in the Article 341 of our Constitution. Some specific provisions have been incorporated in the Constitution to provide social justice to the members of these castes through the policy of protective discrimination. The basic purpose of incorporating these developmental provisions was to change the traditional social structure of our society, which is based upon socio-economic and political inequalities. These special provisions have played an important role in improving the socio-economic conditions and achieving a respectful position to the members of the scheduled caste communities in the society. Economic growth with social justice has been the major objective of planning process and rural development programmes in India. In spite of these constitutional provisions, scheduled caste community has been experiencing social exclusion and discrimination consequently, resulting in socio-economic deprivation of this community which constitutes around 16 per cent of the total population. In this paper, an attempt has been made to examine the socio-economic deprivation of scheduled castes and its linkages to social exclusion and discrimination.

Generally, economic deprivations of scheduled castes is examined through level of poverty across social groups. It is found that the poverty level of SCs is much higher than the poverty level of any other social groups in rural and urban areas. Majority of scheduled caste households do not get sufficient income to meet minimum subsistence needs. Moreover, high poverty among Dalits has been chronic and inter-generational. During 1993–94 poverty level of SCs was 60.5 per cent, as against 45.7 per cent for non-SC groups, which reduced to 29.4 per cent in 2011–12 for SC community and 22.0 per cent for others. Sector-wise position revealed that in rural area it was 62.4 per cent among SC community and 50.3 per cent for others. The position during 2011–12 showed that it was 31.5 per cent among SC community and 25.4 per cent for other social groups. In urban areas it was 51.7 per cent among SC community during 1993–94 and 31.9 per cent among other social groups. The position during 2011–12 showed that it was 21.7 per cent among SC community and 13.7 per cent for other social groups. Thus, when all are taken into account, it is revealed that the level of poverty among scheduled caste community was much higher as compared to other social groups.

Moreover, there has been social deprivation of this community. In fact, as per the Article 15(4) 45 and 46 of the constitution, government is committed to promote education among socially and economically backward communities particularly SCs and STs. It is considered that education is one of universal rights and not a privilege meant for some class/castes of the society. Indian constitution has stressed universal access to education and enrolment of children of school-going age, irrespective of their castes. Nevertheless there is no equal access to education across social groups. SCs are one of the most backward in terms of education. The level of literates is lower among the peoples belonging to SC community. The reason for the lower level of literacy among the scheduled castes is that they were deprived of education facilities from generation to generation. In fact, inequality in education between various social groups has continued and even widened in spite of educational growth. Moreover, discrimination is also practised in accessing housing and health facilities and other social amenities. The root cause behind socio-economic deprivation is social exclusion and discrimination that is being practised in the society. In fact, they are closely linked with each other. Social exclusion is the denial of equal opportunities imposed by certain section of society on the others, which ultimately leads to the inability of an individual to participate in the basic social, political and economic functioning of society. The process of social exclusion is being operated in various forms, such as (i) the denial of ownership, access and control over natural resources and access to capital, (ii) the denial of opportunities for healthcare, education, housing, public amenities and other basic needs, (iii) the denial of the rights to participate in social, economic, political and cultural life is denial of interaction with the society, and (iv) the denial of human rights, human dignity and constitutional rights. Thus, it is a process of segregating group of the people/communities from social, political, economic, cultural, educational and religious domains of societal life. Consequently, SC community gets excluded from livelihood opportunities, employment, earning assets, housing, minimum consumption required for survival. Thus, it reveals the fact that social exclusion and discrimination result in economic deprivation of the marginalized communities in terms of high magnitude of poverty, unemployment, low standard of living and social deprivation in term of low educational status, lack of access of housing, medical facilities and other amenities.

In India, social discrimination revolves around the existing caste system that excludes, discriminates, isolates and deprives some groups on the basis of group identities like caste, race, etc. Historically, in India the caste system has regulated the social and economic life of people which is based on the division of people into social groups or castes in which the civil, cultural and economic life of people is predetermined or ascribed by birth and made hereditary, which in turn, put restriction on change and mobility. Thus, social exclusion has historical roots which led to a stratification of society and resulted in socio-economic inequalities in society. There are excluded and discriminated communities such as scheduled castes, tribes, women, minorities, children, transgender and other marginalized groups. Among these groups, Scheduled Castes are the most disadvantaged group due to the notion of untouchability and low social strata.

In rural areas, land has been a significant asset and the main source of income to the majority of households. It determines the socio-economic status and credit worthiness of these households. Hence, the nature of distribution of land resources among the cultivating households determines the pattern of distribution of income, wealth and social status. In India, the distribution of land and caste system are closely linked with each other. Higher castes enjoy special rights and privileges over the ownership of land resources, while the scheduled castes who are placed at the bottom of social hierarchy are deprived from such rights through the process of social exclusion and discrimination.

The share of SC households in possession of land resources has been negligible, i.e. less than 4 per cent as compared to their share in the total population. Moreover, of the total SC households in rural areas who owned land, only 19 per cent SC households own economic holdings (i.e. more than five acres) as compared to other social groups (42.0%). It means that the majority of SC households are concentrated in the categories of marginal holdings (owning land less than one acre) and up to some extent in small holdings (owning land between 2.20 acres to 5 acres), which is not very suitable for scientific and efficient production of crops. Thus, nearly 70 per cent SC households were either landless or near landless. Moreover, dalits also suffer from discrimination in the land lease market. They do not get land for cultivation on lease even if they are ready to pay a higher rent. Similarly, they face discrimination in the labour market also. The discrimination in labour markets refers to the situation of unequal treatment given to the workers possessing same skills and efficiency, but belonging to different race, caste and gender in hiring labour and wage payment. It is observed in the labour market that labourers belonging to SC category having equal capability, efficiency and skills are excluded from labour market, and those who are engaged in labour markets are subject to the practice of discrimination either in terms of promotion, wage payment or working conditions. Moreover, employment opportunities are denied in labour market particularly in unorganized and private sectors on the grounds of the caste and notion of untouchability even if they are found to be equally competent and efficient. Moreover, there is compulsory and forced inclusion of SCs in low graded and unskilled labour markets. It is found that nearly 70 per cent SC households are labourers on wage employment for their subsistence. This has been caused due to low accessibility in land resources, capital and other productive assets.

Similarly, SC households which are engaged as self-employed households either in agriculture and non-farm activities in rural areas and in various economic enterprises in urban areas have to face caste discrimination in various types of markets such as credit market, input market, product market, etc. They do not get adequate credit inputs in proper time and in adequate quantity because financial institutions and other input supplying agencies are controlled by higher castes. Even in the product market, Dalit entrepreneurs have to face discrimination in selling their products even if they keep good quality of products for marketing, due to the notion of untouchability. Generally, higher caste consumers are reluctant to purchase goods from SC sellers which ultimately has adverse affect on the growth prospect of business. Therefore, their participation in industrial sector as self-employed/entrepreneurs is found to be low.

Moreover, SC communities face social exclusion and discrimination in accessing social infrastructures like education, housing, health, etc. provided by government public institutions or private institutions. In civil and culture spheres, social exclusion occurs in public services like entry into temple, public distribution scheme and common property resources. In the political sphere, SCs/STs face discrimination in the use of political rights and participation in the decision-making process.

Conclusion

The lack of access to land and other productive assets, low level of self-employment, high level of unemployment and low involvement in business activities, together ultimately result in higher magnitude of poverty among scheduled castes both in rural and urban areas, which in turn is caused by social exclusion and discrimination. As it has been observed that economic deprivation has been mainly concentrated in landless labourers and small farmers and workers engaged in unorganized sector. There is a need to rethink about reorganization of the agrarian structure, in which reallocation of land resources should be made on the basis of the relative share of each social groups (SC, ST, etc.) to the total population and the relative socio-economic backwardness of the each caste.

This strategy will be useful in breaking up the monopoly of higher castes over the ownership of land resources in rural areas. Moreover, cultivable land, government land and land occupied by various institutions should be transferred to marginalized communities. Training in agri-business with adequate government support is required to promote agriculture for their livelihood. Business enterprises on co-operative or group basis should be promoted with adequate support from Government and from foreign countries. Special measures are required to reduce labour market discrimination. Moreover, the global labour market should be integrated and so that employment opportunities based on efficiency and skill are made available to the workers belonging to scheduled caste community and other marginalized communities. Moreover, there is also a need to promote social development of this community and reduce the existing gap between social groups.

References

GoI, NSS Reports. 2004–05.

Planning Commission Reports. 2012.

Thorat, S.K. and Katherine Newman (eds) (2010), *Economic Discrimination in Modern India*, New Delhi: OUP.

Thorat, S.K. and Narendra Kumar (eds) (2008), *Dr B.R. Ambedkar: Perspectives on Social Exclusion and Inclusive Policies*, New Delhi: OUP.

6

Scheduled Castes Sub-Plan Act 2013

Lift to Vain

SUMAN DAMRE

The empowerment of Dalits has been the top priority for which the State has initiated number of welfare measures to these sections after independence and the Scheduled Cast Sub-Plan is one among them. For the effective implementation of this Sub-Plan, certain states have enacted special legislations in their states. Consequently, the Legislative Assembly of Andhra Pradesh on 2nd December 2012 had passed the historic Andhra Pradesh SC/ST Sub-Plan (Planning allocation and utilization of financial resources) Act, 2013. With the passing of this bill, Andhra Pradesh became the first state to make such legislation by giving statutory status by ensuring allocation of funds to these sections in proportion to their population. The law would facilitate comprehensive development of Dalits and ensure social security, provide them protection, equality and also bridge the gap between Dalits and other sections of society.

This paper aims to study the historical background of the Scheduled Castes Sub-Plan (SCSP). As a part of historical recollection, this paper addresses issues related to the evolution of SCSP as a strategy through planning process and also explores different guidelines, supportive mechanisms for effective implementation of SCSP. It also focuses on the implementation of SCSP in Andhra Pradesh and how the allocated fund is being diverted to other programmes by the state government.

Historical Background of Scheduled Castes (SCs)

The Scheduled Castes (SCs) occupy the lowest rung of the socio-economic ladder of our society. Even after five decades of independence there is no change in the socio-economic status of SCs. A number of development programmes were initiated for the upliftment of their status over a period of more than 50 years but their status is more or less unchanged. The SCs earn their livelihood mostly through labour or low occupations like scavenging, leather tanning, etc. which reflects their social and economic dependence and subjugation. The SCs have been the victims of social, economic, religious and political atrocities. They were treated as untouchables in the past for several centuries and were not given access to education, public gathering, right to own property and freedom to choose an occupation of their choice. High levels of poverty, illiteracy, hunger and starvation and sickness continue to devastate the lives of Dalits across the country.[1]

Constitutional Safeguards

After independence, the policy of government was guided by protective discrimination towards the weaker sections of society. As such, to safeguard the interests of weaker sections, the Constitution provides special concessions to enable them to catch up with rest of Indian society in the development. In this regard, certain castes and tribes have been included in the schedule, based on social and economic disabilities for special treatment in developmental planning.

Table 1

Constitutional Provisions for SCs

S. No	*Constitutional Provision*	*Contents*
1.	Article14	The State shall not deny to any person equality before the law or the equal protection of the laws within the territory of India.
2.	Article15 [4]	The State to make special provisions for the advancement of any socially and educationally backward class or for SCs.
3.	Article16 [4]	Nothing in this article shall prevent the State from making any provision for the reservation of appointments or posts in favour of any backward class of citizens which, in the opinion of the State, is not adequately represented in the services under the State.
4.	Article 17	Untouchability is abolished and its practice in any form is forbidden The enforcement of any disability arising out of Untouchability shall be an offence punishable in accordance with law.

Cont'd...

...Cont'd

5.	Article 46	Promotion of educational and economic interests of Scheduled Castes, Scheduled Tribes and other weaker sections. The State shall promote with special care the educational and economic interests of the weaker sections of the people, and, in particular, of the Scheduled Castes and the Scheduled Tribes and shall protect them from social injustice and all forms of exploitation.
6.	Article 330	Reservation of seats for Scheduled Castes and Scheduled Tribes in the House of the People.
7.	Article 335	Claims of Scheduled Castes and Scheduled Tribes to services and posts. The claims of the members of the Scheduled Castes and the Scheduled Tribes shall be taken into consideration, consistently with the maintenance of efficiency of administration, in the making of appointments to services and posts in connection with the affairs of the Union or of a State.
8.	Article 340	State to appoint a commission to investigate the conditions of the socially and educationally backward classes.
9.	Article 341	To specify the castes to be deemed as SCs.

Genesis of Scheduled Castes Sub-Plan (SCSP)

The Scheduled Castes Sub-Plan (SCSP) [earlier known as Special Component Plan (SCP)] was first put forward in the year 1978. The SCSP aims at identifying schemes in each sector which can benefit Scheduled Castes (SCs) should merely be equivalent to their proportion of population. This strategy is based on the philosophy that the effort for the development of SCs has to be made in every sector of the plan and by every departmental agency implementing the plan programmes. The SCSP includes modification of policy as well as new policy orientations intended to achieve a rapid development of SCs. The need based programmes to be formulated for SCs would keep in focus the targets groups in the occupational categories. The core programme for economic development would lay emphasis on land development and agricultural productions, animal husbandry, leather work, weaving, and other cottage and village industries, fisheries and small scale and tiny industries. The SCSP was introduced in the Sixth Five-Year Plan (1980–85). Its plan states that the Central, State and Union Territories (UT) should exclusively allocate budget in the annual and five-year plan outlay in proportion to their population. The prime objective of the SCSP was to ensure adequate funds to implement schemes that would benefit SCs to reduce the gap between SCs and the rest of the society and speed up the process of integrating them with the mainstream. The idea was to ensure their total development through educational empowerment, capacity building, employment and income generating devices, asset building and other initiatives.

Prior to the Sixth Five-Year Plan the availability of funds for the development of SCs was provided under the welfare of Backward Classes sector in the annual plans of the states which was inadequate to address the concerns of SCs. The Backward Classes sector was supposed to supplement the benefits expected to accrue to SCs from general development programmes. But, despite repeated instructions from the Government of India, it was not possible to assess the benefits accruing to general development programmes of SCs. By the end of the Fifth Five-Year Plan, it was realized that the strategy for the development of SCs would have to be based on a comprehensive economic and human resource development efforts, so that they could participate in terms of equality and receive a reasonable share in the fruits of general economic development.

The then Prime Minister, Indira Gandhi while addressing the conference of Chief Ministers and Governors of all the States and ministers of Backward Classes Welfare in April 1975,[2] emphasized on the responsibility of Government in executing the programmes relevant to SCs, who were suffering from dual disabilities of severe economic exploitation and social discrimination. The conference of Chief Ministers and Governors adopted a resolution calling for the quantification of efforts made for each sector, and of benefits from schemes in each general sector for the development of SCs, declaring that the accepted strategy of the SCSP for SCs has to be implemented from the Sixth Five-Year Plan. The main thrust of development will be provided by general sectors and the states will be assigned the role of examining the benefits of Dalits in every general sector. The Special Component Plan as a strategy for development of SCs, can thus be traced to a resolution adopted by the conference of State Ministers for Backward Classes held in April in 1975.[3] To achieve this objective, the strategy of the Special Component Plan was evolved during the Sixth Five-Year plan with emphasis on family and beneficiary oriented development schemes. The SCSP is to be financed from the following sources: (i) flow from state plan, (ii) flow from central sector and centrally sponsored schemes, (iii) Special Central Assistance (SCA) and (iv) Institutional Finance.

However, the conference of State Ministers in charge of Backward Classes Welfare (1975) adopted certain policy options for the welfare of SCs. The conference recommended that each Department should analyse the schemes in the general sector and quantify the benefits which should be available to SCs. It was also recommended that a sub-committee of the cabinet and committee of secretaries under the chairmanship of Chief Secretary should oversee and direct the flow of sectoral allocation in favour of SCs. In accordance to these recommendations for the identification of schemes in various sectors, the ministry also laid down guidelines for onward transformation of all states and union territories vide Do. No. BC 110013/4/75 SC/ST–11 dated the 29 March 1976.[4] In the formulation of the Draft Plan 1978–83, the Planning Commission has issued the following guidelines:

1. Review of each of these sectoral programmes both at the Centre and the state with reference to the eligibility conditions to be adopted in favour of SCs.
2. Formulation of sub-committee of the cabinet and a committee of secretaries under the chairmanship of chief secretaries to oversee and direct the flow of sectoral allocation in favour of SCs.
3. Creation of cells in the planning/finance departments to ensure flow of resources.
4. Department in charge of Social Welfare to watch the progress of quantification by the various departments and also evaluate at the district level whether the benefits as earmarked have reached to the beneficiaries.
5. Launching of a massive programme of economic development including provisions of inputs for agriculture, minor irrigation annual husbandry, cottage industries for landless labourers.
6. The State Education Department to shoulder the responsibilities for providing pre-matric education to the entire SC population. Scholarships, stipends, books, mid-day meals, uniforms, residential schools, especially for the most backward sections among SCs all to be provided out of the Education Budget.[5]

Thus, a beginning was made in the preparation of the SCSP for SCs in 1979–80 and subsequent discussions helped the Government of India to refine their concept of SCSP in the Annual Plan 1980–81. In March 1980, Prime Minister Indira Gandhi wrote to all the Central Ministries and State Governments that 'this Special Component Plan, already prepared by the State Governments should not only be improved quantitatively and qualitatively, but should also be implemented satisfactorily. Its satisfactory implementation does not only require due attention to the programmes, but also a clear cut personnel policy consisting inter alia of the orientation of officers of various departments concerned with development towards the needs of SCs and their careful selection, training and continuity of tenure.

Salient Features of SCSP

1. Earmarking funds for SCSP projects from the total outlay for the Plan Outlay, both at the Central and State levels, at least in proportion to Dalit's proportion in the population.
2. Making the Social Welfare Department or the department concerned with the welfare and development of Dalits as nodal department for the SCSP.
3. Placing the funds earmarked for the SCSP at the disposal of nodal department, which in turn will reallocate the funds to sectorial departments.
4. Placing SCSP funds under separate budget heads or sub-heads for each department implementing the SCSP.
5. Appointing monitoring committees at the block, district and state levels with elected representatives, among others, as members.

Planning Commission Guidelines for SCSP

In pursuance of the then Prime Minister's letter, Manmohan Singh, the then Member Secretary, Planning Commission, issued the guidelines for preparing Special Component Plan to all state/union territory governments on 27th June 1980.

1. The Special Component Plan should clearly indicate the member of targeted SC families below the poverty line, which would be assisted to access the poverty line at the end of 10980–85 plan.
2. The SCSP should enable SCs families in states to cross the poverty line within a short and specified period, if possible, at least half of them in this Plan period itself.

3. While the major outlays would come from the beneficiary oriented dividable schemes under various sectors, in order to optimize the need, careful analysis and adaption should be done to ensure that larger benefits flow to SCs. It may be noted that the SCA for the development of SCs would be substantially linked to the size of the SCSP.
4. Need based programmes for occupational category of SCs may be formulated, particularly in sectors like agriculture and land development, animal husbandry, horticulture, fisheries, village and small industries. Cooperation and economic viability of the schemes formulated should also be ensured through linkages with credit on marketing structure.
5. Programmes to be undertaken by the SC Finance Development Corporation may be separately indicated with financial and physical targets.
6. Schemes for training SCs should be through skill formation at institutions like Krishi Vigyan Kendras, Udyog Vigyan Kendras and Trysem. These training programmes should necessarily be linked with institutional finance so as to enable the beneficiaries to become self-employed or wage employed.
7. Educational and social service programmes like health, housing, water supply and nutrition may be carefully drawn up by indicating necessary targets of SC beneficiaries under each of these schemes.
8. Special Programmes for SC women and sweepers and scavengers can also be drawn separately.
9. A monitoring and evaluation system should be evolved to review and reformulate the schemes as necessary, to achieve the desired results. All development departments should be made aware of their special responsibility in respect of programmes, which benefit SCs.[6]

Despite the fact that the Government of India introduced a number of welfare schemes aimed at helping the SCs, it is apparent that the main objective of the SCSP did not reach the expectations of people even after 25 years from its introduction in the year 1980. The Planning Commission of India has reviewed the strategy of SCSP and its implementation. Chandrapal, Principal Adviser, Planning Commission, observes that 'the strategy of SCSP has been in operation for more than 20 years, yet they could not influence all the concerned in its right perspective. Further, there is lack of effective monitoring to ensure that all the ministries a both the central and state levels earmark funds received under the SCA'. Finally, the Planning Commission of India reiterated the existing guidelines in the year 2006.

Further Planning Commission Guidelines (2006)

1. SCSP should be an integral part of Annual Plans as well as Five-Year Plans, therein making non-divertible and non-lapsable provisions with the clear objective of bridging the gap in socio-economic conditions of SCs within a period of 10 years. It is reiterated that only those schemes should be included under SCSP that ensure direct benefits to individuals or families belonging to SCs.
2. Information regarding the flow of funds to SCSP of your State (Budget, Allocation, Sanction and Expenditure) during 9th Plan and the first four years of Tenth Five-Year Plan (2002–06) and the details of the schemes/programmes covered for the development and welfare of SCs and STs along with their physical and financial performance may be sent to Planning Commission.
3. Be ensured that the state allocates SCSP funds in proportion to the SC population in the state.
4. Secretary, Social Welfare, should be the Nodal Officer in the designing of schemes/programmes of SCSP and allocation of funds to the implementing departments/agencies. If it is not feasible, a dedicated unit of SCSP may be constituted in the Planning Department of the State with the Secretary, Social Welfare as Nodal officer for designing, implementing and monitoring of SCP schemes/programmes in the State.[7]

Supportive Mechanism for SCSP

Special Central Assistance (SCA) is envisaged as an additional to the states SCSP and was not tied up to any specific schemes. Being supplementary its aim is to motivate the state governments to provide larger outlays in their SCSP. It is meant for the totality of the state's efforts for the development of SCs and the only condition that is laid down is that this fund needs to be used by the states for income generating development schemes. SCA is distributed among the states/union territories on the basis of factors like population of SCs, backwardness of the states and the efforts of state governments as reflected in their annual SCSP (Planning Commission, 2006: p. 18).

Monitoring Mechanisms for SCSP

In 2006, the Planning Commission of India reviewed the monitoring mechanisms for effective implementation of SCSP. They are:

1. To constitute state and district/block level monitoring committees to monitor the implementation of various schemes under SCSP of various development departments. The district/block level committees should review the progress of implementation of schemes and utilization of funds on monthly basis, and the State level Committee may review the progress on quarterly basis.
2. Members of Parliament, a State Legislative Assembly in the concerned Zilla Parishad/Block Panchayat area, prominent SC personnel/social worker, who are well acquainted with the problems of SCs, representative of NGOs working for the welfare of SCs and SC members of Village Panchayats may also be included in the State/District/Block level Monitoring Committees.
3. The district/block level monitoring committees may be made responsible for identifying the developmental needs of SCs living in various Panchayat areas falling under the jurisdiction of concerned District/Block and suggest suitable schemes for their development. This process may be completed by the end of the third quarter of the financial year and reported to the nodal department concerned with SC welfare and development, which will, in consultation with the concerned development departments, formulate suitable schemes with financial and physical targets for implementation during the next financial year.
4. The Nodal Department may ensure timely release of funds to the concerned Development department and the development departments may ensure immediate release of funds, soon after the receipt of funds from Nodal department, to their field level implementing agencies. Any lapse on the part of field level implementing agencies in timely utilization of funds and proper implementation of schemes may be viewed seriously.
5. Evaluation to assess the impact of economic development of schemes implemented under the SCSP on the socio-economic conditions of SCs may be conducted by the Nodal department on regular basis. Dissemination of information to SCs all over the State/UT about the schemes/programmes available for

their development may be the responsibility of the Nodal department. The Nodal department may also ensure the follow up of the schemes implemented and maintenance of proper records on assets created under SCSP in the District/Block.[8]

Scheduled Castes Sub-Plan (SCSP) in Andhra Pradesh

In March 1980, Prime Minister Indira Gandhi wrote to all the Union Ministries and State Governments stating that this Special Component Plan, already prepared by the State Governments should not only improved quantitatively and qualitatively but should also be implemented satisfactorily.

This was communicated to the State Government through a letter dated 30th October 1978 from P.S. Krishnan, Joint Secretary, Ministry of Home Affairs. While the Ministry of Home Affairs was urging various state governments and union ministries to prepare a Special Component Plan for SCs, Ajith Mozoomdar, Secretary, Planning Commission, wrote to all secretaries of the states and central ministries on 19 May 1979 on the preparation of centrally sponsored scheme of Scheduled Castes' Special Component Plan. (Letter No.D.O.No.PC/SW/11–2 (5)/77, dated 5 May 1979) (Veer and Singh, 2004).

Additional Guidelines under the SCSP by State Governments

It is emphasized that there is a need to implement schemes relating to the welfare of SCs under the SCSP. The details of some of the schemes suggested for implementation by the State Government are as under:

1. The State Government should prepare Special Component Plan (SCP) as per the proportion of SC population of the State.
2. The villages with 50 per cent and above SC population may be saturated first and provided with all the development activities under Bharat Nirman, schools, education, skill development, trainings for self-employment, etc.
3. A group of 5–10 SC farmers may be constituted for skill development by the State Agriculture Department/Extension Agency. This group may be provided a package of small tractors with accessories and tube wells in the electrified villages and pump sets in non-electrified villages may be provided with other agricultural inputs like quality seeds,

pesticides, fertilizers, etc. This farmers group may also be given training for cultivation of suitable crops and undertaking activities in the sectors of fisheries, animal husbandry, horticulture, etc.

4. An educational complex in the name of educational institute may be set up in each district. The facilities relating to sports, multipurpose hall and intermediate college with sports education may be provided in this institute on the pattern of NavodayaVidyala and KendriyaVidyala. This educational institute will also have classes from 1 to 12 with hostel facilities for 70 per cent SC boys and girls and 30 per cent boys and girls from general population. Around 70 per cent expenditure of this institute will be provided from the SCSP earmarked funds and 30 per cent will come from the General Plan.
5. In every Divisional Headquarters, a polytechnic may be set up. Further, one or two training colleges for nursing and paramedical training courses, Auxiliary Nurse Midwife (ANMs), physiotherapists, technicians and radiologists may be provided exclusively for SCs. The nursing colleges, exclusively for SC girls, may be attached to the provided medical colleges. A 70 per cent expenditure of this institute will be provided from the SCSP earmarked funds and 30 per cent will come from the General Plan. The expenditure for running these courses will be made out of the Special Component Plan outlay earmarked in the State.
6. In each district, coaching-cum-guidance centres may be opened in Universities/Colleges appearing for various competitions. The expenditure of these coaching-cum-guidance centres may be borne out of SCSP funds.
7. Good quality ITIs may be established in each district for imparting employable skill exclusively for the unemployed SC youth in order to provide employment opportunities within and outside the State. To tackle the problem of unemployment, training courses (not routine training courses) should be started in a big way in the State. These capsule training courses may consist of 4–5 months theoretical training on personnel management, material management, financial management, marketing management alongwith and 6–7 months practical training. Such trained personnel should be provided loans at cheaper interest rates from banks/SC Development

Corporation to start production ventures in clusters in those areas where infrastructural facilities already exist. There should be a commercial complex in the main market of District Head-quarter and shops/outlets to be allotted to these trained SC entrepreneurs to sell their products/manufactured goods.

8. The candidates, preparing for various competitive exams like admission in Engineering colleges and medical colleges and other services, may be allowed to take admission in any reputed private training centre, and their full fees should be reimbursed by the Government from SCSP funds.
9. Government may also think of providing one time financial support of say ₹ 25 to ₹ 40 lakh to the recognized social institutions for starting intermediate/degree colleges in each block, exclusively for SC boys and girls for admitting 70 per cent SC boys and girls and 30 per cent boys and girls from general population as is being done in UP.
10. It was suggested that residential schools for SC boys and girls should be set up in all the districts where the percentage of SC concentration is high. The residential schools should have facilities of vocational training, coaching-cum-guidance centre, sports centre and cultural centre. Under vocational training, training related to trades like electrician, electronics, fitter, draftsman, mechanic, plumber, fashion designer, computer operator, data entry operator, etc. need to be given by starting IITs in SC dominated areas. Technical education should be given due importance so as to provide self-employment to SCs.
11. The tuition fee of the SC students studying in private colleges and institutions should be fully reimbursed by the Social Welfare Department under SCSP funds.
12. The State Government should provide scholarships to SC students for all income groups studying in classes 1st to 10th as in UP, and the rate of stipend may be worked out realistically by the State.
13. Road and connectivity is another important sector which affect transport and communication of villagers. All the villages having more than 50–60 per cent of SCs concentration need to be saturated first with road connectivity. The programmes under Bharat Nirman may be targeted especially to SC village development.

14. In those villages where no land is available, especially in SC dominated areas, land should be purchased and allotted to homeless for construction of houses under Indira Awas Yojana.
15. The forest villages in the State need to be converted into revenue villages where basic minimum services have to be provided like education, housing, drinking water, health facilities, road connectivity, etc.
16. Conversion of dry-toilets to wet toilets may also be taken out of these funds in a big way so that scavenging colonies should be developed with rehabilitation programme.
17. There is always food scarcity in SC dominated areas and the State Government is suggested to select Self-Help Groups of 5–10 SCs who may be allotted ration shops for distribution of essential commodities. Subsidy/loan could also be provided to them on recoverable terms up to ₹ 5 lakh.
18. Training may also be imparted in the existing Police Training Centres or Home Guards training centres to SC youth (18–21 years who have passed Matriculation) for Constables and Home Guards. While the Home Guards will look after the security of the villages as Village Defence Committee, the later may be recruited as Constables in the State Government. Similarly training may also be given to at least 5,000 SCs for Conductor and Driver jobs through State Transport Corporation.
19. The State Government was suggested to provide ₹ 25,000 towards *Kanyadhan* for SC girls who passed Intermediate Examination.
20. In urban slum areas, a multipurpose community hall need to be provided to cater to the needs of the SC families.[9]

Budget Allocation and Implementation of SCSP in Andhra Pradesh

Despite the fact that the strategy of SCSP has been in operation for more than thirty years, they could not influence all those concerned towards the right perspective. Further, lack of effective monitoring to ensure that all these concerned earmark funds, received under the SCSP and SCA to SCSP, are utilized both effectively and purposefully is another area of concern in this regard. Despite the Planning Commission guidelines, the earmarking of funds under SCSP brings certain issues while some Ministries/Departments being regulatory in nature are not able to earmark funds for SCSP. Some others having activities which are non-divisible in nature, are also finding it difficult to earmark funds under SCSP. In respect of Special Central Assistance (SCA) to the SCSP, it was observed that non-release of SCA funds on time by the State finance departments to the state/nodal departments of welfare has been adversely affecting the smooth running of various income generating programmes that are undertaken for SC families living below the poverty line. Such delays are not only affecting the beneficiary families but also causing predicament to the nodal department, as they are not able to make full use of the allocated funds and finally resulting in unspent funds. Often, such unspent SCA funds as reported, are getting diverted to other purposes leaving the earmarked/intended purposes unattended to. The following Table 2 gives the clear picture of SCSP implementation in Andhra Pradesh.

The Table 2 shows that, from 1980–81, the Government of Andhra Pradesh should have allocated the budget proportionate to the population of SCs where the population of SCs is 15 per cent, but the allocation of budget under SCSP since its adoption never took place according to the proportion to the population. Despite the fact, the required budget allocation in the year 1980–81 was 69.30 crore where the state government allocated 49.99 crore, i.e. 9.30 per cent. Out of 49.99 crore, the state government had spent 36.7 crore where the allocated budget was also not utilized properly for the betterment of SCs. In addition to this indifference towards Dalits, 32 crore rupees were diverted or remained unspent from the budget. It is a case of improper allocation and the allocated budget remained unspent. Sometimes the budget was diverted to some government organized programmes or it lapsed completely.

It is apparent from the Table 2 that from 1986 to 1989 and 1991–92, the Government of Andhra Pradesh did not allocate the budget under SCSP.[10] From 1992–93 to 2006–07, the allocations did not cross 12 per cent; it has allocated less than what is required, and the expenditure is much more less. In the years 2007–08 and 2009–10, again the allocation is less than the percentage of population, though it has become mandatory to allocate 16.2 per cent. For the 2003–04 financial year, the then ruling Telugu Desam Party (TDP) Government allocated some more funds as compared to previous years, and the expenditure was more than actually

Table 2

Scheduled Castes Sub-Plan (SCSP) Allocations During 1980–81 to 2013–14. (rupees in crores)

S. No. I	Years II	Total State Plan Outlay III	Required Allocation (% SCs) IV	Total Outlay Under SCSP V	% SCSP Allocation to State Outlay VI	Total Expenditure Under SCSP VII	% Expenditure VIII	Diversion/Unspent/Not Allocated (IV–V)+(V–VII)=IX
1.	1980–81	462.05	69.30[1]	42.99	9.30	36.71	8.41	32.59
2.	1984–85	978.31	146.74	127.47	13.03	102.40	8.33	44.34
3.	1985–86	1,044.00	156.6	120.56	11.55	109.43	9.76	47.17
4.[2]	1986–89	–	–	–	–	–	–	–
5.	1989–90	1,251.22	187.68	154.35	12.34	129.26	8.74	58.42
6.	1990–91	1,445.00	216.75	137.20	9.49	–	–	79.55
7.	1991–92	–	–	–	–	–	–	–
8.	1992–93	1,996.94	299.54	170.84	8.56	182.78	9.15	117.60
9.	1993–94	2,075.55	311.33	207.66	10.01	214.99	10.36	96.67
10.	1994–95	2,170.00	325.50	256.07	11.83	216.97	10.00	108.53
11.	1995–96	2,719.78	407.97	300.57	11.05	267.46	9.83	140.51
12.	1996–97	2,773.13	415.97	232.82	8.40	227.95	8.22	188.02
13.	1997–98	3,585.05	537.76	339.72	9.48	213.92	5.97	323.84
14.	1998–99	4,678.95	701.84	510.83	10.92	532.61	11.38	169.23
15.	1999–00	5,479.5	821.93	545.21	9.95	189.42	3.46	632.51
16.	2000–01	8,228.12	1,234.21	450.51	5.48	344.38	4.19	889.84
17.	2001–02	8,319.02	1,347.68[3]	424.52	5.10	225.29	2.71	1,022.56
18.	2002–03	8,553.19	1,385.61	903.91	10.57	873.84	10.51	409.14

Cont'd…

...Cont'd

19.	2003–04	10,970.45	1,777.21	1,113.19	10.15	1,374.41	12.77	271.16
20.	2004–05	13,291.20	2,153.17	1,181.03	8.89	1,341.5	11.71	811.63
21.	2005–06	15,650.77	2,535.42	1,332.12	8.51	1,333.54	9.92	1,201.88
22.	2006–07	20,000.00	3,240.00	1,557.65	7.79	2,369.37	13.01	870.63
23.	2007–08	30,500.00	4,941.00	4,355.09	14.28	3,830.16	14.10	1,109.93
24.	2008–09	44,000.00	7,128.00	7,630.42	17.34	3,611.44	11.80	3,516.98
25.	2009–10	36,635.58	5,934.96	5,609.03	15.31	2,764.8	9.41	6,454.95
26.	2010–11	36,727.97	5,949.93	6,132.55	16.70	2,521.83	11.60	3,428.72
27.	2011–12	43,000.00	6,966.00	7,233.35	16.85	4,915.21	13.06	2,318.14
28.	2012–13	54,030.00	8,752.86	7,487.00	13.86	–	–	1,265.86
29.	2013–14	52,955.28	8,578.75	8,578.75	16.2	–	–	0
Grand Total		**4,13,521.1**	**66,523.71**	**57,135.41**	**11.22**	**27,929.67**	**9.51**	**25,610.4**
2014–15[4]		48,637.90	7,509.6[5]	7,579.4[6]	15.58	1,500[7]	19.79[8]	6,009.6
2015–16		52374.55	8086.63	8,089.24	15.44	3,500		4,586.63

**Sources:* AP social welfare, Directorate of Economics and Statistics Hyderabad, KVPS, CDS.

1. Allocation of budget proportion to the population of SCs, i.e. 15 per cent.
2. No allocations were shown.
3. Allocation of budget under SCSP increased to 16.2 per cent according to 2001 population census.
4. Budget allocation in separate Telangana state from 2014–15 onwards.
5. According to 2011 census the SC population is 15.44 per cent (Source: http://finance.telangana.gov.in/uploads/budget–2014–15).
6. Budget allocation is 15.58 per cent (Source: http://finance.telangana. gov.in/uploads/budget–2014–15-books).
7. Source: Kula Nirmulana Porata Samithi (KNPS), Hyderabad.
8. About 19.79 per cent is utilised from the allocated amount, i.e. 7,579.4 crore (Allocation) and 1,500 crore (Utilization).

allocated, i.e. the actual allocation was 10.15 per cent but the expenditure was 12.77 per cent. It clearly shows the political interest of TDP in raising the allocation suddenly, just before the 2004 elections. After 2004 general elections, the process of improper allocation of budget continued by the Congress Government. In the financial years 2007–08 and 2009–10, again the allocation was less than the percentage of population. The ruling Congress party suddenly raised the percentage of allocation and expenditure under the SCSP before the general elections in 2009. The Congress Government followed the footsteps of TDP in raising the budget for vote-bank politics. For the first time in the year 2010–11 and 2011–12, the allocation of SCSP budget was more than what it was supposed to be, i.e. the actual allocation of budget was 16.2 per cent but the allocation of budget was 16.70 per cent and 16.85 per cent respectively but the allocation of budget remained on records only because the expenditure was 11.60 per cent for the annual year 2010–11 and 13.06 per cent for the year 2011–12. It is to observed that ₹ 3,428.72 crore (2010–11) and ₹ 2,318.14 crore (2011–12) had been diverted to some other government organized programmes. The overall budget under the SCSP, as much as ₹ 25,610.4 crore, remained not allocated/unspent/diverted. It is also noteworthy that the Cabinet Sub-Committee (CSC) admitted the fact that the funds which were specially meant for the development of SCs have been diverted to some other programmes. It is also highlighted by the TDP in the AP Legislative Assembly that at least ₹ 21,000.00 crore have been deliberately not allocated/unspent/ diverted for over the period of 8 years.[11]

The newly formed Telangana State Government stated that the State Government has attached the topmost priority for the development of Scheduled Castes population in the State, which accounts for 15.44 per cent of the total population as per the 2011 census. But these things remained on paper only. The SC Sub-Plan Act also could not prevent the diversion of funds when the Telangana State did not allocate/utilize/divert the funds and lapsed the amount. In 2014–15 annual year, the allocated amount was ₹ 7,579.4 crore, but only ₹ 1,500 crore was utilized. In 2015–16 annual year, the allocation was ₹ 8,089.24 crore, but the state government utilized only ₹ 3,500 crore. In fact, in 2014–15, there was about ₹ 6,009.6 crore and in 2015–16 there was about ₹ 4,586.63 core which was misused/diverted or lapsed.

Table 3

Diversion of SCSP Funds

	Funds Diverted to non-SC Works	*Rupee in Crores*
S. No.	*Different Schemes*	*SCSP*
1.	Jalayagnam (Irrigation)	2,430.00
2.	Outer Ring Road	107.00
3.	Cleaning of Hussain Sagar Lake	91.00
4.	Metro Rail Project	81.00
5.	Beautification of Towns	397.00
6.	District Roads	396.00
7.	Village Roads	67.00
8.	Arogyasri Scheme	225.00
9.	Public Health	20.00
10.	YuvaKiranalu	25.00
	Total	3,839.00

Source: KVPS, Cabinet Sub-Committee (CSC) report, AP Assembly Debates on SC/ST Sub-Plan.

Table 3 shows the diversion of SCSP allocated funds to other government organized programmes like cleaning of Hussain Sagar Lake, Metro Rail Project, Outer Ring Road, Arogyasri Scheme, etc. the diverted amount is as much ₹ 3,839 crore. The diversion shows the prejudices of state government towards the empowerment of SCs. There are majority of Dalits who are deprived of education, health and basic facilities and still these communities do not avail the basic facilities. It is to be understood that much of the fund was spent in Hyderabad towards the cleaning of Hussain Sagar, Metro Rail Project and beatification of cities, and Outer Ring Road is nowhere related to the development of Dalits. Certainly, the state government always gives some focused attention towards the maintenance of cities and other programmes during the budget. The facilities provided by the state is for everyone, but why has the state government diverted the funds of the SCSP which aims at empowering the SCs. Is it only that the Dalits are making use of the facilities like roads, hospitals, etc.? Majority of SCs are poverty stricken and are below the poverty line and they are away from all walks of life.

Need of Legislation for SCSP

The need for a separate legislation was felt as funds allocated for the SCSP were not utilized fully and effectively and have been used for other purposes including infrastructural development by almost all the parties in power. The government failed to allocate funds in the budget in proportion to the population of Dalits. Despite the Planning Commission's guidelines in 2006, the state governments continued diverting funds allocated for the SCSP to various developmental programmes in the state. The objectives of the Sub-Plan were never fulfilled at bringing socio-economic equality to SCs on par with advanced sections of people in the state. The erstwhile Andhra Pradesh Government consistently turned a blind eye to the development of Dalits in the state by allocating a low budget against the proposed guidelines of Planning Commission of India. The Centre for Dalit Studies (CDS), Kulavivaksha Vyathireka Porata Samithi (KVPS) and other political parties have protested to the diversion of allocated funds for the SC Sub-Plan in the state.

Protests by Dalit Associations, NGO's, elected representatives and retired civil servants from time to time on the poor implementation of the SCSP, have vehemently opposed the diversion of SCSP funds to other activities and also pressurized the state government to provide a statutory status for sub-plans. Consequently, a Cabinet sub-committee was constituted by the Government of AP, in April 2012, to study the concept of SCSP. The Cabinet sub-committee in pursuance of its objectives held a series of stakeholder consultations with the officials and elected representatives, particularly with Dalit MPs, MLAs, representatives of civil society and all political parties. The Cabinet sub-committee, in its report, recommended the state government to address these deficiencies by enacting a law mandating certain key principles, processes and institutions which are critical for the effective implementation of Scheduled Castes Sub-Plan (SCSP). Consequently, the Legislative Assembly of Andhra Pradesh on 2nd December 2012, had passed the historic Andhra Pradesh SC/ST Sub-Plan (Planning allocation and utilization of financial resources) Act, 2013.

Conclusion

The misuse (diversion, lapse) of earmarked funds has been a major reason for the lack of social and economic development of Dalits. But, most of the schemes and the infrastructure (i.e. roads, drinking water, houses and irrigation, etc.) development programmes are not reaching remote habitations, and most of them are not even direct beneficiaries. Moreover, the funds allocated under the SCSP have been diverted indiscriminately. Though there is a Nodal Agency at state level headed by the Social Welfare Ministry and the Collectors at the district level are to ensure the proper allocation and implementation of the SCSP, the State government is blatantly misguiding the Planning Commission on one hand, and Dalit community on the other. In addition to it, as the privatization of services like health and education is taking place in a big way, it has become difficult for Dalits to access services and livelihood opportunities with shrinking resource base. Moreover, the undivided Andhra Pradesh Government has consistently failed in implementing the Planning Commission guidelines. It has been diverting the SCSP allocated funds to various developmental programmes in the State, which has no connection with SCs.

The continued backwardness of Dalits and an unenthusiastic response by political parties in governments galvanized Dalit groups, Civil Society Organizations and the political parties to fight for a better deal. The long struggle by different groups forced the Government of erstwhile Andhra Pradesh to enact a special legislation to prevent the diversion of funds.

It is found that the prime objective in making a legislation with necessary safeguards is not only to ensure to allocate sufficient funds for the welfare of Dalits, but also to utilize these funds properly in the effective implementation of the schemes or programmes which directly benefit Dalits.

The state which enacts more and more new laws, also violates the existing laws if there is no strong political commitment. Erstwhile Andhra Pradesh has failed to implement the SCSP which consequently led to the demand for the SCSP Act. But, still the commitment of the government is quite essential in the implementation of SCSP. The very idea of developing SCs in India is to emancipate them from the clutches of poverty, discrimination and atrocities committed by the caste driven society. Moreover, such facilities might benefit the educated class in the Dalit community but not the rural masses. In order to make the state assistance accessible to the rural masses along with the middle-class urban Dalit families, the SCSP can take the necessary and commensurable steps that are aptly designed programmes for them, as the SCSP Act contains the legal safeguards which can be secured by appealing to the court if needed. But once again, it is evident that the acts cannot prevent the state from the misuse/abuse of the funds because the Telangana

State Government has followed the footsteps of previous governments in diverting the SCSP funds.

Notes

1. Pathak and Pandey (2005).
2. Paswan and Jaideva (eds) (2003), p. 151.
3. Veer and Singh (2004), p. 223.
4. Ibid.
5. Ibid., p. 224.
6. Planning Commission (2006), p. 41.
7. Ibid., p. 50
8. Ibid., pp. 25–28.
9. Ibid., p. 51.
10. No allocations were shown by the government.
11. Cabinet Sub-Committee Report, 2012.

References

CPI (M) (2012), *In the Cause of Dalits*, Hyderabad: Prajashakti Publications.

Jaideva, P. (2002), *Encyclopaedia of Dalits in India* (Vol. 7), New Delhi: Gyan Publishing House.

Kannappan, P. (2008), *Scheduled Caste Welfare*, New Delhi: APH Publishing.

Paswan, S. and P. Jaideva (eds) (2002), *Encyclopaedia of Dalits in India: Reservation* (Vol. 5), New Delhi: Gyan Publishing House.

—— (2003), *Encyclopaedia of Dalits in India: New Dimensions in Dalit Problems* (Vol. 14), New Delhi: Gyan Publishing House.

Pathak, S.N. and S.P. Pandey (2005), *Scheduled Castes Development: A Study of Special Component Plan*, New Delhi: Serials Publications.

Planning Commission (2006), *Scheduled Castes Sub Plan: Guidelines for Implementation*, New Delhi: Government of India.

Qureshi, M.U. (2006), *Encyclopaedia of Social Problems and Social Welfare* (Set of 10 Vols.), New Delhi: Anmol Publications Pvt. Ltd.

Rajawat, M. (ed.) (2004), *Encyclopaedia of Dalits in India: History of Dalits* (Vol. 1), New Delhi: Anmol Publications Pvt. Ltd.

Veer, U. and B. Singh (2004), *Encyclopaedia of Dalits*, New Delhi: Kalpaz Publications.

7

Educational Participation of Marginalized Social Groups of Maharashtra

P.S. KAMBLE

The researchers have suggested some alternative criterions, which is that growth reduces poverty, increased income benefits the poor more than the non-poor proportionately by benefiting the very poor and not just the poor, and that poverty reduction in the current period is higher than the past benchmark, such that the current share of the poor in incremental income exceeds their share in the past, exceeds their population share and meets international norms and this kind of growth is non-discriminatory and reduces the disadvantages. With these criterias, pro-poor growth requires that the pattern of growth should have an inbuilt bias in its strategies which brings relatively higher gains to the poor from income growth. The growth process itself needs to have elements embedded in it, which will bring substantial incremental income gains for the poor (Thorat and Dubey, 2013, p. 6). Maharashtra is one of the economically developed states in India. It is a popular state on various grounds. It is a historical, pro-social reforms state, politically strong with a number of social, environmental, political movements, and so forth. Hence, it is expected that along with the economic development, its social development through the social sector is of much importance. Therefore, here an attempt is made to examine the actual development of social sector in the state of Maharashtra by taking into account its sectors and subsectors, especially in physical terms with emphasis on social stratification of involvement. Human resource is very much important on various grounds. It is an important part of social sector. Hence, human resource development is an indicator of the development of the social sector in the economy. Education plays a very important role in the development of human resources development of a country in general, and the state in particular. We are discussing the issue of inclusive growth in general and inclusive education in particular. Hence, this study is an attempt to examine the participation of marginalized social groups like SCs and STs in education with reference to Maharashtra, which is a developed state in our country.

Review of Research Studies

A review of some of the important research studies relating to the topic of the research project has been taken and are as follows:

Kundu and Varghese (2010) in their study titled 'Regional Inequality and Inclusive Growth in India under Globalization' analyse the trends and patterns of economic inequality across Indian states since the early 1990s. The basic objective of the study is to understand the dynamics of growth in the country resulting in regional imbalances and propose measures for alleviating the problem. The interstate inequality in per capita income and consumption expenditure shows a clear increasing trend during the first and second phase of structural reforms. But, the strategy of inclusive growth and balanced regional development launched since 2003–04 has led to the accelerated average growth in the less developed states, including those in the North-East. This has made only a marginal impact in stalling the trend towards accentuation of regional imbalances. According to authors, reduction to poverty has been relatively less in the less developed countries as compared to the developed states, resulting in the concentration of poverty in a few backward states. The study concludes that correlation of economic development with amenities, although statistically significant, is relatively low, which suggests that the problems pertaining to health, education, and access to other amenities cannot be effectively addressed just by focusing on economic development, strategic Intervention or regional inequality. AIMA (All India Management Association) (2011) in its study titled 'Inclusive Growth a Challenging Opportunity', argues that in order to achieve an inclusive growth, holistic and integrated solutions are needed so as to facilitate the rapid and sustainable growth. According to this study, the task of building an inclusive India for its 1.2 billion people is so large and complex that it cannot be accomplished by either the government or the private sector working in isolation. Achieving inclusive growth is not only to be seen as a priority in the Planning Commission's Five-Year Plans, but also as an equally significant opportunity for every enterprise in the public and private sector. 'Inclusion' for India is not a mere buzzword that individuals and enterprises talk about, but an imperative that calls for concerted action towards bringing inclusion in every aspect of how individuals, public and private enterprises as well as the government operate and envisage to grow. There is a crucial need for the government to focus on better and more efficient delivery mechanisms to improve access to currently backward regions. It is a fact that majority of the low-income states have rich geographic resources. But, due to their poor infrastructure, these regions are often caught in a vicious circle of poverty from which they find difficult to breakout. If these regions can take a leaf out of experiences in countries such as Australia and tailor it for local needs, they present a greater opportunity for its people. It is argued that the demographic dividend played a role in the economic miracles of the four East Asian Tigers – Hong Kong, Singapore, Korea, and Taiwan. Nayak et al. (2010) in his paper titled 'Inclusive Growth and its Regional Dimension' states that Indian economy is elevated to a path of high growth triggered mainly by macroeconomic reforms and expansion of economic activities across the sectors. But, there are some serious concerns about a number of imbalances, inter-sectoral, interregional and interstate in the growth scenario. These imbalances have definitely a serious impact on the goal of 'inclusive growth' as envisaged in the Eleventh Five-Year Plan. The present study concludes that poverty ratio is still very high in the economy despite high growth. No significant increase in employment in the unorganized sector of the economy is observed. According to the authors of the study, while contribution of the agriculture sector in the real GDP has declined fairly fast, the share of employment in the agriculture sector has not declined to that extent. It is therefore that the average productivity in this sector has remained very low as compared to the other developing countries. As a large section of the population continues to be dependent on the agriculture sector, directly or indirectly, this has serious implications for inclusiveness on the dynamics of growth. The present study emphasizes the role of finance in the growth and analyses the regional dimension of financial inclusion in terms of state-wise and sector-wise allocation of credit over the years. The study observes that the distribution of bank credit across sectors and regions is not equitable. Shankar Acharya (2007) in his research study titled 'India's Growth: Past and Future', reviews India's growth performance since 1950 and indicates a few salient features and turning points and major drivers of India's current growth momentum, while pointing to some of the risks and vulnerabilities that could stall the current dynamism if corrective action is not taken. It appraises the country's medium term growth prospects and assesses some implications of India's rise for the world economy. According to the author, India's growth at an average rate of almost 6 per cent a year over the past quarter of a century (with per capita growth of nearly 4% a year) is both remarkable and commendable. In 1980, there was almost no respectable scholar or institution predicting such sustained development of this poverty-ridden populous country. Likewise, the prevailing fashion of bracketing India's rise with China's exceptionally dynamic development under rubrics like 'China and India Rising' may mask more than it reveals. The study concludes that if India's development in the last 25 years has been good, China's has been extraordinary. While India has been a gradual 'globalizer', China's surging development has been far more intensively based on global trade and capital flows. As a result, the global economic impact of China's rise has been much more dramatic in terms of the usual matrix of international economic relations, trade, capital flows and energy as well. Daniel Lederman (2010) in his research study titled 'International Trade and Inclusive Growth' provides two analytical frameworks for understanding the role of trade in promoting inclusive growth in developing economies. A working definition of inclusive growth emphasizes on long-term sustained growth associated with productivity growth and employment opportunities for broad portions of households and firms within countries. According to the author, international integration can promote inclusive growth when workers and firms are able to adjust to enter into growing economic activities and adopt technologies availed through international trade. The frameworks in this paper are built on simple household and firm choice models which require only basic knowledge of development economics. The study highlights how these frameworks can help analysts to focus on research and policy questions related to the impacts of international trade across the distribution of households and firms within countries. The study also discusses publicly available data sets that can be used to explore some aspects of inclusive growth. M.H. Suryanarayana (2008) in a study titled 'Inclusive Growth: What is so exclusive about it?' argues that in the wake of the economic reform programme undertaken since 1991, distributional issues have received considerable attention and policy concern. Therefore, the government has worked out an approach to the Eleventh Five-Year Plan, which lays emphasis on a strategy of inclusive growth. It is a fact that the inclusive growth has become virtually a universal concern with even the UNDP harping on it; what it calls a 'million dollar question – what inclusive growth is and how to achieve it?' The author defines inclusion/exclusion for an outcome scenario on broad based growth from three different perspectives, viz., production, income and consumption distribution. This study also provides some illustrations based on the National Accounts Statistics and the National Sample Survey consumer expenditure distributions for the year 2004–05. But, for the want of detailed information on the production and income dimensions, the study examines their covariation. Within the methodological inadequacies of verifying a broad based growth process in terms of mean-based averages of income and absolute-norm based measures of deprivation, the study proposes averages based on orders for verifying broad based growth and extent of inclusion of the poor in terms of consumer expenditure distribution. The study reveals the conclusion that mean-based estimates exaggerate disparities across social groups in India.

The foregoing review of some important research studies relating to research topics adequately reveals that the development of social sector for inclusive growth is a much missing aspect in the research studies relating to inclusive growth, even though it is an important element of inclusive growth. Social sector development is a missing aspect in research studies carried out relating to India, and same is the situation relating to Maharashtra State. There are only few studies about the inclusive growth of India, very exceptionally of the individual states and states as a whole. The absence of any research study on inclusive growth of the state of Maharashtra is a salient feature of the studies reviewed till now. More importantly, the role of social sector in the inclusive growth of the economy is a neglected aspect of those researches that have been carried out in this area. Likewise, not a single attempt is found directed towards the examination of social sector development in the context of inclusive growth at national level, as well as state level.

Research Methodology

The present research study is an analytical and empirical type of research in the sense that, it examines the state of the social sector development with a single criterion, i.e. education in the state of Maharashtra. In the representation of different social groups, such as SCs, STs, OBCs, NTs and Open in the social sector development adequate care is taken in the analysis. No doubt, it is an empirical research because it is based on the secondary data. This research study adopts a combination of research methods such as analysis of documents/data, interview and questionnaire as well.

The present research study covers the total period of 10 years from 2002 to 2012, which is a period of two five-year plans namely 10th FYP and 11th FYP at national level, which is expected to be adopted in the states as well. The strategy of inclusive growth has been accepted in India at national level; consequently in the states in the 11th FYP, hence the present study assesses the social sector development with a single indicator – education of Maharashtra for achieving its inclusive growth during the period of 11th FYP from 2007 to 2012. But the picture of social sector development especially the education of Maharashtra, has been depicted by examining it during the 10th FYP from 2002 to 2007, which enables us to arrive at the actual social sector development for inclusive growth during the 11th FYP period. The comparison of social sector development of the State of Maharashtra during the period of 10th FYP and 11th FYP enables us to arrive at the net inclusive social sector development with focus on education materialized for the inclusive growth of the state. The method of before and after is used to examine the net social sector development in the state for its inclusive growth.

Social sector is an important sector of the economy in any country on various counts. It is a broad sector comprising the subsectors like Education, Public Health, Women and Child Welfare, Employment and Poverty, Housing, Water Supply and Sanitation and Social Justice. All these subsectors of the social sector have not been taken into consideration, but only education has been taken into account by the present research study. The present study depends on secondary data only, which has been collected from sources such as Economic Survey of Maharashtra, Annual Reports of Education, Public Health, Women and Child Welfare, Employment and Poverty, Housing, Water Supply and Sanitation, Social Justice Ministries of Government of India and the Government of Maharashtra, Reserve Bank of India Publications like Annual Reports, Report on Currency and Finance, Economic Survey of Government of India and Government of Maharashtra, Reports of the various Ministries of Government of India and Government of Maharashtra and Plan documents of both the Central plan as well as the plans of Maharashtra for the period under study have been taken into consideration. The processing of the collected data, comprising scrutiny, editing, coding, classification and tabulation has been carried out by using the softwares Excel and SPSS. The analysis of the data has been carried out by applying simple but appropriate statistical tools such as Compound Growth Rate (CGR), Ratio Analysis, Frequency distribution, Mean, Range, and Coefficient of Variation (CV).

Participation of Marginalized Social Groups in Education of Maharashtra

Education is a very important social service and part of social sector of the economy. Teacher is a means of providing educational facilities in the state. Hence, the social stratification of the teacher community in the state of Maharashtra is examined below to identify its social inclusiveness.

Table 1

Social Group (Caste)-wise Teachers in Maharashtra, 2012–13

S. No.	*Caste*	*Govt. and Local Bodies*	*Pvt. Aided*	*Pvt. Unaided*	*Unrecognized*	*Total*
1.	General	98,165	1,23,846	75,508	1,593	2,99,112
		–35%	–45%	–63%	–50%	(44%)
2.	SC	37,302	34,686	10,046	374	82,408
		–13%	–13%	–8%	–12%	–12%
3.	ST	27,329	16,521	3,246	156	47,252
		–10%	–5.80%	–3%	–5%	–7%
4.	OBC	73,483	69,357	21,062	792	1,64,694
		–26%	–25%	–17%	–25%	(24%)
5.	VJ	21,482	17,337	5,428	132	44,379
		–8%	–6%	–5%	–4%	–7%

Cont'd...

...Cont'd

6.	NT	10,918	8,647	1,653	62	21,280
		–4%	–3%	–1.50%	–2%	–3%
7.	SBC	6,637	3,511	1,082	33	11,263
		–2%	–1.20%	–1%	–1%	–2%
8.	NT-B	1,507	1,175	214	17	2,913
		–0.40%	–0.50%	–0.40%	–0.40%	–0.40%
9.	NT-C	2,185	354	354	10	2,903
		–1%	–0.30%	–0.80%	–0.30%	–0.40%
10.	NT-D	1,924	256	256	10	2,446
		–0.60%	–0.20%	–0.30%	–0.30%	–0.20%
	Total	2,80,932	2,75,690	1,18,849	3,179	6,78,650
		–100%		(100%)	–100%	(100%)

Source: Education Status Report of India (UDISE).

It is revealed that in 2012–13 the total number of teachers in Maharashtra was 6,78,650, in which the share of open category was 44 per cent, which was less than 50 per cent. The share of SC category was 12 per cent, which was less by 1 per cent than the norm of the Government of Maharashtra. In the same year, the proportion of OBCs to total was 24 per cent, which was greater than the government norm (19%). The STs got an opportunity in teacher employment as per the government rule. The Vinukta Jali (VJ) community got share in the total teacher employment more than the norm of the Government of Maharashtra (3%), but the Nomadic Tribes (NT) B, C, D could get a meagre share in employment than the desirable level. The Special Backward Castes (SBCs) got the desirable share in the total teacher community in the state. The analysis of institution-wise education and social stratification of teachers reveals that Open, STs and SCs have got their due shares, especially in the government institutions, but OBC and VJ have got more shares in teacher employment. The NT B, C, D have not got their desirable shares in this employment. The noteworthy feature is that in the private and government aided institutions, STs, NT B, C, D could not get their necessary shares, but Open and OBCs got more than desired shares.

Enrolment is an indicator of the involvement in education. Hence, its social stratification analysis is useful in identifying the state of educational inclusiveness in the state. The necessary data is given in Table 2.

Table 2

Gross Enrolment Ratio by Social Category-wise in School Education, 2009–10

S. No.	Category	Classes I–V (6–10 years)			Classes VI–VIII (11–13 yrs)			Classes IX–X (14–15 yrs)			Classes XI–XII (16–17 yrs)		
		Boys	Girls	Total	Boys	Girls	Total	Boys	Girls	Total	Boys	Girls	Total
1	All	104.90	102.30	103.66	91.54	86.93	89.32	75.85	69.57	72.84	59.63	50.62	55.34
2	SC	138.09	136.98	137.56	119.12	115.44	117.35	103.12	95.42	99.49	82.16	72.97	77.93
3	ST	122.09	120.65	121.40	92.54	86.82	89.81	56.43	39.85	48.46	49.78	40.71	45.37

Source: Ministry of Higher Education.

Graph 1

Gross Enrolment Ratio Across the Social Groups in Maharashtra

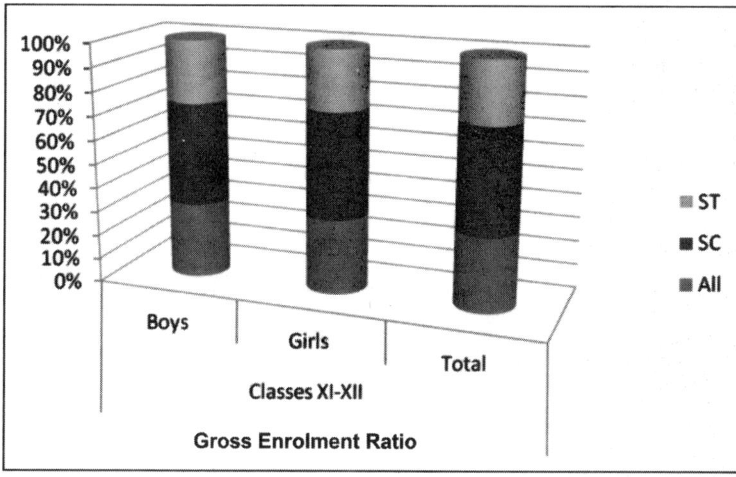

It is revealed that the enrolment of SCs and STs in primary education (I–V) is good which is more than 100 per cent, but since then it shows a falling trend. The enrolment of SCs and STs continuously decreases in higher primary (VI–VIII), high school (IX–X) and higher secondary also (XI–XII). The same trend is found in the case of Open category students also. The ST students have suffered because their enrolment is lower and also decreasing fast. Comparatively, even though in the declining enrolment situation, the position of SCs is better than all other social categories.

The higher education is considered more important than the primary, secondary and higher secondary on various grounds. Hence, the social stratification of enrolment in higher education is also essential to be analysed. The necessary statistical information about it is given in the Table 3.

The data in Table 3 highlights some very important trends about the inclusive higher education in India in general, and across the states as well as in the state of Maharashtra as well. The enrolment of Open category students in higher education is meagre at 20 per cent only at all-India level. It has wide disparities across the states. Few states like Chandigarh, Tamil Nadu, Puducherry, Manipur, Delhi, Goa, Arunachal Pradesh, Andhra Pradesh have

Table 3

—Gross Enrolment Ratio in Higher Education (Social Group-wise) (18–23 Years) 2011–12

S. No.	States/UTs	All Categories			SC			ST		
		Male	Female	Total	Male	Female	Total	Male	Female	Total
1.	Andaman and Nicobar Islands	11.6	14.9	13.1	–	–	–	14.4	25.9	20.0
2.	Andhra Pradesh	31.8	23.4	27.6	25.9	20.4	23.1	25.6	16.6	21.0
3.	Arunachal Pradesh	36.9	24.9	30.9	–	–	–	43.8	27.4	35.1
4.	Assam	14.5	14.2	14.4	11.9	11.4	11.7	14.4	12.9	13.6
5.	Bihar	14.7	11.2	13.1	10.5	6.0	8.3	12.2	9.3	10.8
6.	Chandigarh	52.4	53.8	53.0	19.4	19.0	19.2	–	–	–
7.	Chhattisgarh	12.1	9.9	11.0	10.0	7.5	8.8	5.6	4.6	5.1
8.	Dadra and Nagar Haveli	6.2	7.1	6.5	6.7	5.2	6.1	1.6	1.0	1.3
9.	Daman & Diu	3.0	7.6	4.2	10.7	22.7	16.2	18.1	9.2	13.6
10.	Delhi	35.7	33.6	34.8	19.7	15.6	17.8	–	–	–
11.	Goa	34.9	40.4	37.4	27.5	27.5	27.5	22.0	21.1	21.6
12.	Gujarat	19.3	15.7	17.6	19.6	16.2	18.0	10.1	9.4	9.7
13.	Haryana	28.4	27.3	27.9	18.8	16.9	17.9	–	–	–
14.	Himachal Pradesh	25.7	24.2	25.0	14.3	12.8	13.5	21.0	19.7	20.4
15.	Jammu & Kashmir	22.6	24.9	23.7	2.8	2.8	2.8	2.3	1.8	2.0
16.	Jharkhand	9.1	7.6	8.4	6.5	4.2	5.4	3.9	3.9	3.9
17.	Karnataka	25.2	22.8	24.0	17.1	13.7	15.4	14.4	11.0	12.7

Cont'd...

...Cont'd

18.	Kerala	19.3	26.9	23.1	12.3	22.7	17.5	11.4	13.2	12.3
19.	Lakshadweep	0.0	0.0	0.0	–	–	–	0.0	0.0	0.0
20.	Madhya Pradesh	19.8	14.6	17.4	12.0	11.1	11.6	7.6	6.2	6.9
21.	Maharashtra	29.7	24.8	27.4	27.1	22.5	24.9	15.9	9.1	12.5
22.	Manipur	32.3	34.4	33.4	76.7	72.4	74.5	24.8	20.5	22.7
23.	Meghalaya	14.3	18.3	16.4	48.6	24.0	37.0	8.6	13.4	11.1
24.	Mizoram	21.6	19.6	20.6	98.2	128.6	109.2	21.8	19.5	20.6
25.	Nagaland	22.0	13.7	17.9	–	–	–	21.3	13.1	17.2
26.	Odisha	18.4	14.3	16.3	10.2	8.1	9.1	8.4	6.6	7.5
27.	Puducherry	39.1	35.1	37.1	36.8	30.6	33.5	–	–	–
28.	Punjab	22.6	17.1	20.0	9.3	7.0	8.2	–	–	–
29.	Rajasthan	20.8	14.9	18.0	14.6	8.9	12.0	16.6	9.7	13.2
30.	Sikkim	31.2	24.4	27.9	40.0	28.2	33.9	17.4	18.2	17.8
31.	Tamil Nadu	41.1	35.2	38.2	28.7	25.6	27.1	34.2	27.9	31.0
32.	Tripura	14.2	9.1	11.6	12.3	7.7	10.0	7.7	4.1	5.8
33.	Uttar Pradesh	15.6	18.1	16.8	11.5	13.7	12.5	20.8	16.9	18.9
34.	Uttarakhand	26.5	27.9	27.2	16.3	16.7	16.5	27.4	32.6	30.0
35.	West Bengal	14.7	10.7	12.8	10.0	7.1	8.6	7.2	4.6	5.9
	All India	21.6	18.9	20.4	15.4	13.5	14.5	12.4	9.2	10.8

Source: All India Higher Education Survey, Ministry of HRD, 2011–12.

shown only considerable performance. The position of Maharashtra is not good so far as participation of Open category students is concerned. The involvement of SCs in higher education at national level is negligible, 14.5 per cent only. It has wide variations across the states and is good in few states only, such as, Meghalaya, Goa, Manipur, Mizoram, Puducherry and Sikkim. Maharashtra is not good, but it is considerable only in so far as the participation of SCs in higher education is concerned. There is a wide disparity based on the criterion of gender; only Mizoram, Manipur, Meghalaya and Puducherry have shown good performance. The situation of Maharashtra is not good but only considerable. The participation of STs in higher education is the worst. It is good only in Arunachal Pradesh and worst across the states, and Maharashtra is no exception. It has further very wide disparity across gender and states as well. Thus, even at national level the enrolment of Open category students in higher education is lower than expectations. It is worse for SCs and STs with wide disparities across the states as well as gender also. The state of Maharashtra is worse and not encouraging in so far as enrolment in higher education is concerned. Hence, higher education in India as well as in Maharashtra is not socially inclusive.

Enrolment is an indicator of educational progress in the state, but its social stratification shows the state of inclusive education. Hence it is analysed below (see Table 4).

Table 4

Social Group-wise Enrolment in Maharashtra 2012–13

S. No.	*Social Group*	*Primary (I–V)*	*Upper Primary (VI–VIII)*	*Secondary (IX–X)*	*Higher Secondary (XI–XII)*
1.	General (Open)	41,49,127 (40%)	24,15,170 (41%)	14,25,521 (42%)	9,94,448 (45%)
2.	Scheduled Castes (SC)	13,96,937 (14%)	8,47,323 (14%)	4,82,337 (14%)	2,80,170 (13%)
3.	Scheduled Tribes (ST)	12,93,321 (13%)	6,05,509 (10%)	2,81,149 (08%)	1,45,062 (06%)
4.	Other Backward Classes (OBC)	34,44,974 (33%)	20,74,182 (35%)	12,31,791 (36%)	7,84,822 (36%)
5.	Total	1,02,84,359 (100%)	59,42,184 (100%)	34,20,798 (100%)	22,04,502 (100%)

Source: Ministry of HRD.

It is revealed that the enrolment of category students in 2012–13 in different levels of education is from 40 per cent to 45 per cent. It is very much lower in the case of SCs and STs. It is good for OBCs, but not better. It is up to 14 per cent for SCs and less than 10 per cent except in primary education. This adequately proves that primary to higher secondary education in general in Maharashtra is not inclusive so far as its social stratification is taken into account.

The gender analysis of education is also an indicator of inclusive education. It is discussed below with reference to the state of Maharashtra and across the districts also. Dropout rate is a commonly used indicator of educational progress. Its social stratification indicates the situation of the inclusive education. It is therefore discussed below in the context of the state of Maharashtra (Table 5).

Table 5

Dropout Rates in Classes I–V, I–VIII and I–X

S. No.	*Year*	*Classes I–V*			*Classes I–VIII*			*Classes I–X*		
	Maharashtra	*Boy*	*Girls*	*Total*	*Boy*	*Girls*	*Total*	*Boy*	*Girls*	*Total*
	A. All Categories of Students									
1.	2006–07	–0.39	5.80	2.55	22.92	20.84	21.93	45.32	49.96	47.54
2.	2007–08	17.73	20.17	18.89	28.34	32.82	30.48	43.41	49.15	46.17
3.	2008–09	15.86	18.94	17.33	25.44	28.64	26.97	41.22	46.48	43.75
4.	2009–10	20.19	22.54	21.31	24.36	27.55	25.88	38.63	42.62	40.54
	B. SC Students									
1.	2006–07	–3.50	4.32	0.27	23.03	25.04	24.00	49.37	55.75	52.45
2.	2007–08	12.74	14.32	13.50	28.86	33.85	31.27	44.48	51.19	47.71
3.	2008–09	20.74	22.96	21.81	26.49	30.80	28.57	38.26	45.55	41.78
4.	2009–10	22.60	23.06	22.82	24.17	27.99	26.01	37.60	43.79	40.59
	C. ST Students									
1.	2006–07	10.72	20.63	15.43	45.16	47.91	46.46	71.66	79.37	75.28
2.	2007–08	27.24	31.37	29.20	40.65	45.05	42.72	67.79	76.83	72.07
3.	2008–09	32.10	34.31	33.15	46.51	51.66	48.95	65.74	75.07	70.15
4.	2009–10	24.34	23.07	23.75	46.52	51.83	49.05	65.75	74.23	69.73

Source: NSSO Report, Round No. 63, 64, 65, 66, 67, 68.

Graph 2

Dropout Rates across the Social Groups in Maharashtra

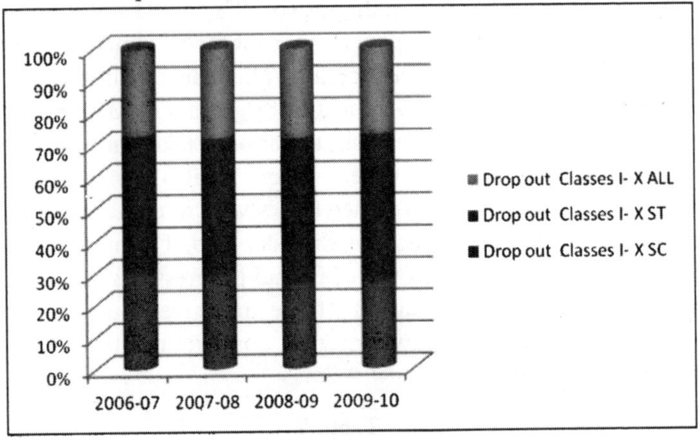

During the period 2006–07 to 2009–10, it was observed that the dropout for all categories was lower for the primary education, but significantly higher for primary to secondary education. Further, it is higher for girls than boys. The same is the case for SC and ST category students also. But it is higher in all levels namely primary, higher primary and secondary classes as compared to the Open category. It is significantly higher for STs as compared to the Open and SC category students. This is a clear indicator of the exclusive primary and higher secondary education for the SC category students and it is more exclusive for the ST category students as it is also a matter of serious concern.

Besides the dropout rates for the specific period, the annual dropout rate is also a real indicator of inclusive education.

Table 6

Annual Dropout Rate of Maharashtra, 2012–13

S. No.	*Social Groups*	*Primary*			*Upper primary*		
		Boys	*Girls*	*Total*	*Boys*	*Girls*	*Total*
1.	General	–0.13	0.55	0.18	2.89	3.86	3.34
2.	SC	1.81	2.25	2.03	3.03	4.24	3.61
3.	ST	6.33	6.47	6.40	7.51	8.60	8.02
4.	OBC	–2.01	–1.58	–1.81	–2.87	–1.85	–2.39
5.	All Social Group	0.76	1.32	1.02	2.50	2.80	2.90

Source: Education Status Report of India (UDISE).

It is observed that the annual rate of dropout in 2012–13 was lower for the general category students in both the primary as well as upper primary education in Maharashtra, but it is also a fact that it was comparatively higher for girls than boys. It is noteworthy that it was negative for OBC students. The annual dropout rate was higher for the SC category students than the General category students, and more importantly it was higher for girls than boys. This is the indicator of exclusive education and urgent need for inclusive education in a progressive state like Maharashtra.

Gender gap in education is also useful in identifying the inclusive education in the state. Hence, it is discussed in the context of Maharashtra as below (Table 7).

Table 7

Class-wise Gender Gap in Enrolment in Maharashtra (in %) 2012–13

Social Group	*Primary (I–V)*	*Upper Primary (VI–VIII)*	*Secondary (IX–X)*	*Higher Secondary (XI–XII)*
General (Open)	7.02	7.79	8.17	5.99
Schedule Castes (SC)	3.76	5.20	7.76	6.46
Schedule Tribes (ST)	4.21	7.26	10.54	13.23
Other Backward Classes (OBC)	6.05	6.99	8.58	14.51
All Social Groups	5.90	7.09	8.46	6.75

Source: Higher Education Survey, Ministry of Education, Government of India.

It is revealed that gender gap at all levels of education is higher for students of all category. But, it is higher for the Open, ST and OBC category students. It is peculiar to note that it is higher for the OBC students as compared to the other social category students, which also reveals the magnitude of exclusive education, especially from primary to higher secondary education.

While the goal of inclusive growth has become the strategic pillar in the Eleventh and Twelfth Plans, it has also raised a number of issues which require clarity, particularly the definition of inclusive growth, its measurements and indicators. The inclusive growth strategy for the Twelfth Plan also needs to be based on the experience of inclusive outcomes during the Eleventh Plan. The National Sample Survey (NSS) quiniquennial consumption expenditure data for the most recent round, 2009–10, now enables us to assess the outcome during the Eleventh Plan period, at least on poverty incidence and its implications for the Twelfth Plan strategy (Thorat and Dubey, 2012, p. 43).

Conclusion

The foregoing analysis of the data results relating to the participation of the marginalized social groups like SC, ST, NT and OBC reveals that the educational development in India is not very much satisfactory and appreciable. It apparently looks good at primary level, but when its dropout rates are taken into consideration the scenario is not very much good and satisfactory. The dropout rates are so much higher for the marginalized social groups like SC, ST, NT. The state of higher education is not very much satisfactory and appreciable in India. The gross enrolment ratio in higher education is lower; it is just 21 per cent for India as a country, which is more than 75 per cent for the developed countries like USA, UK, Japan, France, Germany, Australia, etc. More importantly, it is very much lower for the socially marginalized social groups like SC, ST and NT. Besides this, the dropout rates are very much higher for the marginalized social groups. We also found a significant gap between male and female at all the levels of education such as primary, secondary and higher secondary, and higher education. This demands an active participation of the state as well as central governments in educational development. In addition, a special treatment and education policy is a must for the marginalized social groups like SC, ST and NT.

References

Acharya, Shankar (2007), 'India's Growth: Past and Future'. Paper for presentation at the Eighth Annual Global Development Conference of the Global Development Network, Beijing, 14–16 January, pp. 1–30.

All India Management Association (AIMA) (2011), *Inclusive Growth: A Challenging Opportunity*, Deloitte, pp. 3–28. Retrieved from www.deloitte.com/in

Bairagya, Indrajit (2012), 'Employment in India's Informal Sector: Size, Patterns, Growth and Determinants', *Journal of the Asia Pacific Economy*, Vol. 17, No. 4.

Bergh, G. and C. Melamed (2012), *Inclusive Growth and a Post-2015 Framework*, London: Overseas Development Institute.

Chandra, Nirmal Kumar (2010), 'Inclusive Growth in Neoliberal India: A Facade?', *Economic and Political Weekly*, Vol. 48, No. 8, Mumbai.

Datta, Rudar (2008), *Eleventh Five Year Plan and Inclusive Growth*, Booklet by Dr Mookerjee Smruti Nyas, New Delhi.

Dev, Mahendra (2007), 'Inclusive Growth in Andhra Pradesh: Challenges in Agriculture, Poverty, Social Sector and Regional Disparities',

Working Paper No. 71, Centre for Economic and Social Studies, Hyderabad, Andhra Pradesh, March.

Hirway, Indira (2012), 'Inclusive Growth Under a Neo-liberal Policy Framework: Some Critical Questions', *Economic and Political Weekly*, Vol. 47, No. 64, p. 20.

Kanbur, R. and G. Rauniyar (2009), 'Conceptualising Inclusive Development: With Applications to Rural Infrastructure and Development Assistance', *Working Paper 2010–11*, Department of Applied Economics and Management, Cornell University, New York.

Kumar, U. and A. Subramaniam (2012), 'Growth in India's States in the First Decade of the 21st Century: Four Facts', *Economic and Political Weekly*, Vol. 47, No. 3.

Kundu and Varghese (2010), Regional Inequality and Inclusive Growth in India under Globalization: Identification of Lagging States for Strategic Intervention, Oxfam India Working Paper Series, September 2010, OIWPS VI.

Lederman, Daniel (2010), *International Trade and Inclusive Growth: A Primer for Busy Policy Analysis*, International Trade Department, World Bank, Washington, D.C.

McKinley, Terry (2010), 'Inclusive Growth Criteria and Indicators: An Inclusive Growth Index for Diagnosis of Country Progress', *ADB Sustainable Development Working Paper Series*, Asian Development Bank, June.

Mitra, A. and J. Schmid (2008), 'Growth and Poverty in India: Emerging Dimensions of the Tertiary Sector', *The Service Industries Journal*, Vol. 28, No. 8, pp. 1–22.

Nayak, P.K. et al. (2010), 'Inclusive Growth and its Regional Dimension', *Reserve Bank of India Occasional Papers*, Vol. 31, No. 3, pp. 1–66.

OIWPS-VI (2010), 'Regional Inequality and Inclusive Growth in India Under Globalization: Identification of Lagging States for Strategic Intervention', *Oxford India Working Papers Series.*

Rao, C.H. Hanumantha (2009), 'Inclusive Growth: Recent Experience and Challenges Ahead', *Economic and Political Weekly*, Vol. 44, No. 13, p. 16.

Sengupta, Arjun (2010), 'Inclusive Growth as Rights-Based Development', *Journal of Asian Public Policy*, Vol. 3, No. 3.

Subramanian, S. (2011), 'Inclusive Development and the Quintile Income Statistic', *Economic and Political Weekly*, Vol. 46, No. 4, Mumbai.

Suryanarayana, M.H. (2008), 'Inclusive Growth: What is So Exclusive About it?', *Economic and Political Weekly*, Vol. 43, No. 43, pp. 1–26.

Thorat, S.K. and Amaresh Dubey (2012), 'Has Growth Been Socially Inclusive during 1993–94 and 2009–10?', *Economic and Political Weekly*, Vol. 47, No. 10.

8

Manual Scavengers Far from Dignity and Inclusion

K.M. ZIYAUDDIN

The genesis of manual scavenging as an occupation has somewhat been understood in the origin of caste system in India. The questions of dignity and rights did never have attention in relation to certain castes in India. The discourse on identity and dignity had no meaning in the life of a manual scavenger. Perhaps, after Dalit Panther Movement in Maharashtra in 1970s, certain questions became valid to be asked and studied. For example, it was never a matter of importance to understand the life of a Dalit and a manual scavenger. They were not even accounted for as one of the fellow human beings who did the job of cleaning, the dirtiest job as their traditional and caste-based occupation. The crudest form of indignity and inhuman face emerged when certain groups of Indian society became the carrier of filth and night soil of fellow human beings. It is written in the past that killing one manual scavenger was easier than killing an animal. Thurston gave large illustrations on various castes in India largely in southern India.

The notion of scavenging which I found through the websites in my first research almost fifteen years back was entirely different from what I found while studying them in the field and among people engaged in this occupation. It was written on the website that 'the process of removing burnt exhaust gases from the combustion chamber of the engine cylinder is known as 'scavenging' but then, the process of researchers completely changed while doing ethnography on Hadis. This study on manual scavengers who are engaged in a certain occupation in Indian subcontinent since ages are least studied in sociological areas. Sachchinananda (2001) rightly observes that manual scavenging has not received proper attention, neither about its inception nor existence, desirability or epistemology. Similarly, Hadis were also missed in earlier researches.

Muslims taking the job of night soil carriers must not be very old. There is a feeling that some of the families converted to Islam in order to get rid of night soil cleaning but many of them continued with the same occupation. It is during the Muslim rule that a large number of converts took shelter under the Islamic fold. The occupation of those castes continued except for the fact that there were possibilities to find social space or a place to pray commonly together with Muslim members in the mosque. The religion would have changed but it was not an easy task to completely change from traditional occupation into a new occupation.

Hadis are one of the Scheduled Castes (SCs) in the list of 22 SCs in the census documents of 2011. Hadis have found mention in various anthropological and British records but quite often it is merely mentioned as the name of a caste, with no social history. The community's data on both Muslim and Hindu manual scavengers is discussed in the paper .

Social History of Manual Scavengers Across Religious Groups

The research on manual scavengers has taken certain pace and strength in the last five years but limited to civil society organizations and least in university academics. The Standing Committee[1] on Social Justice and Empowerment (2012–13) has accepted the reality in continuity of its earlier attempts as well. It says that the occupation of manual scavenging is inhuman and beyond acceptability. Such bold acceptance from the government has not come as far as common information is concerned. The National Advisory Committee (NAC) provided much space to civil society bodies that had been working for the eradication of most heinous and criminal occupation in human history. The report of the Standing Committee[2] (2012, p. 7) quotes a resolution dated 23 October 2010, inter alia, observed that:

(i) The National Advisory Committee (NAC) is deeply distressed to observe that the shameful practice of manual scavenging persists in India, despite being outlawed. This practice involves entrapping women, men and even children only because of the accident of their birth, into a humiliating vocation of gathering human excreta from individual or community dry toilets with bare hands, brooms or metal scrapers. It is intolerable that this endures and is the worst surviving symbol of untouchability. The persistence of dry latrines in various parts of the country violates human dignity, the law and Articles 14, 17, 21 and 23 of the Constitution.

(ii) In 1993, the Parliament passed the Employment of Manual Scavengers and Construction of Dry Latrines (Prohibition) Act, 1993, which declared the employment of scavengers or the construction of dry (non-flush) latrines to be an offence punishable with imprisonment for up to one year and a fine of two thousand rupees. But central, state and local governments have been very weak in implementing this law, and almost no one has been punished under this law in 17 years. Local bodies themselves routinely run dry toilets and employ people of specific castes to clean these manually.

(iii) One basic problem so far is that the effort has been viewed by governments more as an issue of sanitation, than an issue of human dignity as guaranteed to all citizens in the Preamble of the Constitution.

It is important to realize the significance of studying the most excluded and marginalized group of population who has been treated less than humans. The acceptance by the Government of India pushed the problem as important aspects of castes structure. It says that:

> It says, 'The obnoxious practice of manual scavenging or engaging fellow human beings into cleaning the untreated human excreta is a blot on our society. Deeply concerned about liberating the manual scavengers from the inhuman task of carrying night soil, the Parliament enacted The Employment of Manual Scavengers and Construction of Dry Latrine (Prohibition) Act, 1993. The law prohibits construction and or maintenance of dry latrines and employment of manual scavengers. However, as brought out by census 2011, there are still 26 lakh insanitary latrines in the country where nightsoil is either being deposited into open drains or removed manually. This abominable practice of manual scavenging which persists in various parts of the country violates the constitutional right of human dignity.'

The problem of manual scavenging has been seriously observed in almost all the states of India: Andhra Pradesh (erstwhile) had large number of them. Five years after the State belatedly adopted the Employment of Manual Scavengers and Construction of Dry Latrines (Prohibition) Act 1993, and announced a grandiose plan to declare the State dry toilet-free, not much has been done in this front. The Government of India has proposed to construct huge numbers of toilets by 2019 for each household across the states when there is dearth of substantial data on the accurate numbers of manual scavengers. A joint survey conducted in 2001 by the Andhra Pradesh Scheduled Caste Cooperative Finance Corporation (APSCCFC) and Safai Karamchari Andolan (SKA) estimated the number of community dry latrines (CDLs) maintained by municipalities and gram panchayats at 25,762. Kurnool headed the list with 4,782, followed by Anantapur (4,173), West Godavari (3,503), Kadapa (2,324), Visakhapatnam (2,251) and East Godavari (2,248). The number of scavengers, including dependants, was put together at 30,921. Apart from CDLs, the Andhra Pradesh Mission for Eradication of Manual Scavenging (created within the APSCCFC) estimated the existence of two to three lakh dry latrines, however, certain improvements have taken place in the last ten years. This is perhaps the largest number of such latrines in any state in South India. 'The deadline is fixed and lapsed. The initial enthusiasm that followed the survey and the formation of the mission, people has not given serious attempt to address it', says Gita Ramaswamy.[3] APSCCFC whenever asked claims that the majority of manual scavengers have been rehabilitated as part of the National Scheme for Liberation and Rehabilitation of Scavengers (NSLRS). It claims that all 28,099 scavengers and their dependants have been 'rehabilitated in dignified alternative occupations' between 2000–01 and 2003–04 at a cost of ₹ 61.43 crore. Civil society groups dismiss these programmes as a farce. 'Rehabilitation has become a charade. The beneficiaries and the middleman share the margin money provided by the State. Banks are reluctant to grant loans but ready to 'sanction and recover loans' on paper and 'close the account'. The bank is happy having 'extended the loan' to the needy. Content with his share of the margin money, the beneficiary goes back to scavenging.

However, this process has also forced the certain individuals to continue this insidious practice a reality even today (Venkateshwarlu, 2006).[4]

Historically, the practice is rooted in the caste hierarchy, just as it is elsewhere in the country, and is confined to the bottom as one of the subcaste of the Dalit community. They are called Methar (migrant Balmikis from North India largely from Haryana, Uttar Pradesh, Rajasthan and Delhi) in Hyderabad and Telengana and Paki in coastal Andhra Pradesh. Ramaswamy writes and explains how Methars were brought from Haryana by one of the Nizams, Nizam-ul Mulk, between 1855 an 1860 partly because no local was willing to take up the demeaning job. Traditionally, scavenging communities too preferred to work in areas far away from their native villages to avoid the stigma. Madigas, who were one of the populated Dalits in Rayalseema regions challenged the social history of a group who have never been examined. In bordering Anantapur district, Halalkhors (a Muslim sect) were used.[5] Muslim scavengers were found practising in Kurnool town, Karimnagar and in a few other towns. It is complex to understand their origin with the establishment of Nizams in Hyderabad. Despite this fact, their genesis is also linked with scavengers in Rajasthan who were again brought by the Nizams in Hyderabad. Gradually, lower occupational group among Muslims had to be dependent on their own occupations but with the change in the socio-political situations in Hyderabad, most of them tried to change their identifications.

It is observed that while studying the largest minority groups in India, Muslims have been historically marginalized in various spheres of their life and they stand in the same socio-economic platform of backwardness as their Dalit counterparts. Only subtle difference would be due to certain historical facts that have barely any significance to the present situation. The political metaphor to make out Muslims as the rule in past is not more than a systematic and planned attempt to divide the growing association on the basis of commonalities between the two: Dalit and Muslims. For instance in this paper, both research conducted in two different states and regions of India show similar conditions in their life. Muslims at large have never benefited from the political hegemony that lasted for centuries in India during medieval period. In fact, the loss of political dominance not only forced them to survive in socio-political marginalization, but the continuous decline in political participation excluded them from other benefits in the process of social inclusionary measures taken in independent India.

The existence of marginalized Muslims cannot be ignored. It is of greater significance to study the socio-cultural history of Muslim communities and groups among Muslims in India. Even Kaka Kalelkar's list for Hyderabad state had only six occupational communities, namely *laddaf/dudekula/pinjara/pinjari* (cotton carders), *qasa/qassab/quarishi* (butchers), *faqeer* (semi-nomad beggars), *sangtarash* (stone-carvers), *mehtar* (Muslim, Muslim scavengers) and *hajjam* (barbers). The remaining social categories were left out and large numbers of them are looking for state's affirmative support.

The educational backwardness of Muslims is due to abject poverty that forces children to drop out after attending certain level of schooling. Majority of Muslim population is concentrated and dependent in self-employment activities and in lower salaried jobs. The present condition of Muslims as minority group is quite vulnerable in their life. It is for this reasons that the classic case is witnessed into the practice of scavenging among Muslims in Andhra Pradesh and particularly in the vicinity of old city of Hyderabad. The long-term intensive studies conducted on Muslim families engaged in manual scavenging in the past have been able to shift into newer occupations but again in the repairing and mechanical subsidiary activities. The erstwhile state of Andhra Pradesh (AP) had few social groups and identified themselves as Dudekula or Pinjari or Nurbash. Two recent accounts of social groups of Muslims of Andhra Pradesh are that of Shaik Abdul Azeez Saheb contained in 'People of India', a series of Volume of Anthropological Survey of India on Andhra Pradesh. Saheb mentions that 'the Indian Muslims also have caste-like groups', but he distinguishes them from Hindu caste as the Muslim caste lacks ideological frame comparable to the traditional Hindu varna model and does not have the tendency towards rigid elaborateness. According to him, 'the Muslim castes are occupationally and culturally different'.

Mehtar as a community has been studied for people of India by S.S. Sastry. The references cited by him are Thurston, Syed Siraj Ul Hassan; the Report of Census of India in 1901; Census of India 1961 and Census of India 1981. The name Mehtar means a prince or a leader or a great man. It is a name given ironically or in compensatory consolation to the community engaged in sweeping and 'scavenging'. According to Syed Siraj Ul Hassan, those Mehtars are called Lalbegi, who are the followers of the patron-saint Lalbeg, who is considered to have been Ghazi Miyan and a saint much worshipped in Punjab among the Lalbegis wherever they are. By faith, Mehtars may be either Muslim or Hindu. This report is concerned with Muslim Mehtars. According to the Census Ethnographic Notes on Mehtar, Mahar, Mang, Mang Garodi, Dhor and Dakkal (Dakkalwar), out of the 533 sweepers and scavengers in the Hyderabad Municipal Corporation in 1966–67, 93 were Muslim by faith. This gives an idea of the proportion of Muslim Mehtar/Lalbegi in this traditional occupational community. In assessing the population of the community, it must be remembered that among Muslims, as among Hindus, all members of an 'occupational community' are not engaged in the traditional occupation, and among Hindu as well as Muslim members of communities of 'sweepers and scavengers' actually engaged in the occupation, not all, often not even a majority, are on the rolls of Municipal bodies. Their population was 4,553 in 1981 Census. It is well known that this community is treated as 'untouchable' and they are the worst victims of this practice.

But it is really difficult to find out the number of Muslim scavengers in Hyderabad because they never registered themselves in the rolls of municipal corporations and those practising or practised don't identify. The repeated trial of accessing the registered scavengers in the rolls of municipal corporations failed due to unavailability and other undefined reasons. The people were interviewed for the purpose of getting ethnographic details. This has been realized with the help of replacing their surnames with new surnames or using name without surnames. A famous Telugu writer who works with the community, who they call Dalit Muslims, suggests that they are not able to link with the mainstream Muslim society due to various socio-cultural reasons. It is believed that the deep-rooted cultural features of their community cannot be replaced with the higher elite class Muslims. Hence, it becomes essential to discuss about Dalit Muslims.

Pathak[6] (1991, pp. 37–43) in his book on *Road to Freedom* describes the existence of manual scavenging in Muslim countries too. His description focuses on manual scavenging among Hindus but not limited to any one group like Hadis. He believes that religious sanctions related to Baitul-Khula (latrine) in Muslim society suggests that latrine system existed and disposal of human excreta took place in Arabia. He rationalizes that considering Hijab as an important practice of Muslim women, they would have stopped going out for defecation. As a result, the practice of night soil disposal has prevailed even during Muslim ruled estates. But the connect between Hindu and Muslim scavengers are common on the basis of occupation for which the reasons must be many, and more needs to be clarified in future studies.

Massey[7] writes that Dalits are those who are downtrodden, broken down and an exploited section of our society. Muslims have also begun to identify themselves very close to Dalits in order to consolidate the scattered sections/groups and come together as caste-like groups. Dudekula Muslim in Andhra Pradesh has started to forego the old age traditions with Islamic rituals, traditions, customs and manners in the hope of securing a higher social status.[8] A good number of Muslims continued as manual scavengers in Hyderabad on par to Hindu Mehtar. Even Hindu Mehtar were provided land to settle down in the old city area of Hyderabad, today known as 'Mehtar-wadi' quite close to Charminar. On the contrary, Hadis in Jharkhand claimed to be not doing menial and polluted occupation in the past. The data on social history of Hadis are limited to the memory of the elder Hadis. It is worth examining the social history of Hadi caste in the state of Jharkhand, formerly Bihar. It gives a broader spectrum to analyse both the social groups engaged in same occupation. The first Muslims in Hyderabad study were found to have moved into a newer occupation but Hadis remained in the fourfold of caste structure. The next section of this paper discusses Hadis in detail.

Who are Hadis?

The Hadi community is one of the most backward caste groups among the 22 Scheduled Castes (SCs) in the state of Jharkhand (Jharkhand Population Census Data 2011. New Delhi: Registrar General India). The Census of India reports do not mention them separately as the data is available for other SCs. Bhangi and Mehtar in Chas are clubbed together in one caste category along Hadis, so they are like Hadi/Bhangi/Mehtar. It becomes somewhat clear that census does not identify them as different castes but classify them as one due to occupational history and similarity. Similarly, Halalkhor and Lalbegi are also listed in the same list of 22 SCs. The problem appear not only in the census enumeration, but in undermining the social history of a caste who could attempt changing its position and occupation in future. Hadis have been enumerated in the consecutive Census of India reports as Hair, Mehtar and Bhangi. The typographical mistake in Hadi's name refers certain aspects of indignity and exclusion. Hari, hairs are a few examples of this negligence. This paper does not study caste system in India and that which restricts the discussion on caste herein. Srinivas, in his paper 'An Obituary to Caste System', illustrates changes brought by new technological invention and introduction in the villages. Certain castes stated are getting changed in due course when technology has started taking over their works and replacing them from their traditional occupation. This argument is not to say that caste based occupation has started changing, but it shows that certain transformation is taking place. How are those products transforming the lives of villagers who are governed by caste and traditional occupation, but not into the occupation of Hadis as manual scavengers? It is exemplary to see the change in nomenclature that Hadis are not Safai Karamchari after the long struggle of Safai Karamchari Andolan (SKA). Now all manual scavengers shall be called as sweeper or karamcharis, which is near to one step of inclusion, but far from inclusion and dignity.

Hadi populations are scattered in several pockets of states across the country. Their occupational categorization of manual scavenging is confined to the lowest strata in certain pockets. The dignity is lost from the lives of each caste that stands lower in the castes hierarchy, but those in the lowest are manual scavenging castes, and Hadis are one of them. The occupational association to a filthy and unclean job is an aspect of exclusion. The doubly burdened life of those into manual scavenging is due to the deep rooted notion of caste pollution and purity. Perhaps, Muslim scavenger could manage to escape the stigma due to the absence of castes system in the Islamic way of believers and practices. However, it does not ignore the presence of caste like system, 'Biradari' among Muslims in India. Quite a lot has been written in this area of study but sociologist and anthropologists, namely Gaus Ansari, Imtiaz Ahmad, Zarina Bhat, Abul Kalam are a few. There is much more to be studied in future.

One also finds that the practice of manual scavenging has changed over a period of time and particularly during the past two decades. Manual scavengers are not carrying night soil on their heads, which was the case earlier, to dispose off in the outskirts. It took several decades to see some changes in their working conditions. Firstly, the change has arrived due to some reasons, namely conversions of septic and dry toilets into water flush toilets in the town. Secondly, the employment opportunity in the Chas Municipality, in the context of Hadis, also paved way for better working conditions. Now most Hadis in Chas town have joined the Municipal Corporation and a few in Bokaro Steel Plant, a unit of Steel Authority of India (SAIL)-public sector.

Now the following discussion brings the social history of Hadis that shows various aspects of their past. Hadis are the worst off in the ladder of socio-economic and political participation among Dalits in the state. Their engagement in menial jobs such as sweeping makes them more vulnerable. The nature of work is hazardous and filthy not only in terms of physical touch, but the pollution towards Hadis work is the highest in comparison to all other jobs carried out by any other SCs and even Muslims. Hadis residing in Bokaro were the part of my long research in the form of ethnographic fieldwork and rich data. Hadis in Bokaro district have been living in one of the Mohalla known as Hadi Cooli, commonly referred for SC localities. Bauri Caste, which is another SC group in the neighbouring Mohallas (Bauris were studied by Freeman, 1977) are not discussed in this paper. There are research studies on other manual scavenging communities in other parts of the country but not much on Hadis. Even small and scanty references are not found as it has been mentioned earlier. Before exploring the problem in question, locating it in its socio-political and historic context will help us have a better understanding of why certain things are in a certain way. Hadis are found to be four subcastes in the region but except Maghaya Hadi, rest are unknown in this study. They are Sahir Hadi, Digar Hadi, Benagli Hadi and Maghaya Hadi. It is believed that only families belonging to Maghaya Hadi are found in the entire region of Dhanbad, Hazaribagh, Ranchi, Purulia, Giridih and Ramgarh.

Aghaya means an equal caste group to Bhumihars who belong to Ghoda Gotra. As per the memory of Gandhi Hadi, a 69 years old person in the community, initially it was only three households that settled in Hadi Cooli, Chas. In fact, the available lands where Hadis are settled belong only to three members and the land belongs to only these three and incidentally they all were paternal brothers. Hadi caste is distinct as they do exist in large number of population in West Bengal and partially in Odisha including the present Jharkhand. But only a few districts have higher percentage of population such as Dhanbad, Hazaribagh, Ranchi, Giridih and Ramgarh. The field data reports that there are around 500 households in this region. Their exact figure is unknown due to the census classification of SCs in which Hadis are clubbed with Bhangis and Mehtars in the state. There is gradual but unconscious change in using the caste surnames as Hari. There are a few using Hari, while a large number continue to use Hadi. The Census of India has missed their original caste surname 'Hadi' and the document has mentioned Hadis as 'Hair' in the census report 2001, a term unrecognized by Hadis in written or other reference.

We are Small Population but Sociologically Significant

In the year 2011, the population of the three groups of people, Mehtar, Hadis and Bhangis, the urban population was 36,044 whereas in the rural context was 22,198 in Bokaro. These statistics show the existence of such occupational groups across districts that demystify the notion that they are only urban. In the same census year 2011, the district-wise scheduled caste population provides information on persons living in urban settlements as 5,286 and rural settlements as persons 5,295, which is almost equal to the urban population. Of the total population, 5,385 are males and 5,196 are females.

The largest clusters of Hadis belong to Bengali linguistic families which make them 5,81,000 Bengali speakers. Secondary languages spoken among Hadi community are as follows; Odiya, 2,12,000; Hindi, 1,26,000; Rangpuri, 44,000; Bhojpuri, 38,000; Maithili, 4,600; Santali, 4,400; Kui, 2,400; Kharia, 1,700; Kurux, 1,500; Magahi, 1,400 (Jhosua Project, 2014).

However, this population is witnessed to be scattered in the whole of Indian Territory. As per the available records about Hadis, they are populated in the following ten states of India: West Bengal (5,89,000), Odisha (2,24,000), Bihar (1,06,000), Jharkhand (84,000), Uttar Pradesh (8,300), Himachal Pradesh (2,100), Andaman and Nicobar Islands (1,600), Chhattisgarh (1,500), Tripura (1,000) and Meghalaya (1,000). Hadis are populated in small numbers, both across and outside India. Bangladesh has a population of 59,000

Hadis, whose primary language is Rangpuri and belong to Hinduism as per a report published by one non-government organization, Jhosua Project World (2014).

Mapping Hadis as Manual Scavengers and the Occupational Structure

As per the household composition census data (fieldwork data) collected over a period of three years 2009 to 2011, there are 51 in Hadi Cooli that has increased from the earlier study (Ziyauddin, 2016).[9] Hadi Cooli, the locality as known, had 38 households in 2001 data that has increased now. At present, the total population of 51 Hadi households is 306, of them 139 are male and 167 are females. It is considerably important to note that in such a small population, there are 19 widows and one divorcee woman living with her two daughters. None are found to be widowers at the time of data collection. This data also illustrates the fact that the average life of men is lower than women in Hadi Cooli. The working conditions in filthy and unhygienic environment as well as exposure to manholes expose them to ill health.

As no other caste would enter into sweeping and manual scavenging, it remained a part and parcel of generations in a few castes. Hadis in Bokaro district too remained in the same occupation despite the major industrial transformation that took place since the British took over from the regional kings, and till now it is one of the major industrial towns in the state.

Institutionalization of Manual Scavenging

Dalit, too had traditional occupations but with a distinct difference. By and large, their occupations were least desirable and defiling (Srivastava,[10] 1997; Shyamlal,[11] 1992). The regional variations in occupation among Dalits are important, but mainly two categories of occupations were popular, namely, cleaning and leather processing. Cleaning and sweeping involved sweeping of streets, drains and sewers. Removal of human and animal excreta, raising pigs, etc. are a few other ones. Since latrines in most cities were not provided with flush, the sweepers had to carry buckets of human faeces on his or her head. The most popularly known name for all those who do the so-called unclean occupation is '*Mehtar*', for which Mohammedan counterpart is '*Halalkhor*', '*Lalbeg*', and '*Khakhrob*'.

In independent India, the process of institutionalization of manual scavenging started taking place. The Indian Railways is perhaps the largest rail network in the world, employing the largest number of manual scavengers. NGOs and research groups roughly project that almost 1,20,000 persons are Dalits, of which 95 per cent are female. This trend of female dominance in scavenging is not prevalent among Hadis in Chas town which is unlike the general trend. The Government of India, as a first step to make the work of scavenging more consistent with human dignity, suggested supplying wheelbarrows or handcarts to sweepers employed by Municipalities for scavenging work, so that the practice of carrying night soil as headload could be eliminated altogether. The Government of India provided 50 per cent of the costs towards the purchase of wheelbarrow and handcarts through the state governments. The wheelbarrows provided to the scavengers were mostly improper and so heavy that they were bound to be discarded by the scavengers and this situation is reported in most towns, including Bokaro and Chas. With the beginning of urbanization, rather than practising scientific sewage system, Hindu society found it convenient to force a few castes to do menial jobs like manual scavenging across the country. For example Madigas in Andhra Pradesh (Ramaswamy, 2005) and Hadis in several region of the countryside including Bokaro. The employment of manual scavengers began systematically during British Empire, and consequently, local kings and royal families started following suit. The British rule both legitimized and systemized manual scavengers by creating official posts. In fact, the British institutions, namely the Army, Railways, Courts, Industries and major towns were equipped with dry latrines instead of waterborne sewerage. They continued to institutionalize this system of disposal as human headloads, and it remained much visible till very recently in different corners of the country in independent India.

The pan-Indian visibility of manual scavengers is due to the strong presence of British rule and their residency set-up wherever they ruled. The representatives of British rule lived permanently or for short durations in most parts of the country. Hence, this factor gave a push to the population settlement of manual scavengers in most parts of India. In view of this illustration, it is important to take note of the demographic pictures of these occupational groups in this section. However, in general, details of their population are limited and not representative due to the lack of countrywide survey by any institutions or a government body itself. Further, there is complete lack of any kind of a sociological study on the Hadi caste in comparison to other social groups. One does not get proper reference about the Hadis, not even in the edited volume of People of India series for Bihar that includes Jharkhand in Part I and Part II. The scanty references are found in the documents of Census of India. Otherwise, we do not have intensive field studies about the Hadi caste. There are good numbers of references on other castes engaged in manual scavenging but not Hadis. I did not mention those studies as they are not required at this point. Another survey by the Committee on 'Improvement of Living and Working Condition of Sweepers and Scavengers' headed by I.P.D. Salapa on the sweeper *Pourakarmiks* in Karnataka working in various municipalities in the state show that besides Scheduled Castes, there are Muslims, Christians, Lingayats, Kurubas and Mudaliars engaged in this profession. This only proves that members of different castes and communities have also taken up to this vocation mainly due to economic compulsions in the past.

As on date, there are at least 1,15,000 manual scavengers, who are also considered untouchables or Dalits, identified for benefits under a 2007 self-employment rehabilitation scheme for them being implemented by the Social Justice and Empowerment Ministry, Government of India. It is helpful to understand the problems of manual scavenging historically and discuss the practices of carrying human excreta as human headloads. Hadis were involved in doing this job for years until the introduction of flush toilets. In this background, the elaboration by Pathak (1991) in his initial writing on manual scavengers elaborates the socio-cultural history of all social groups engaged in the occupation of handling the most menial job in the human society and how they practised it as their traditional occupation. It would also be interesting to understand as to why cleaning human excreta is popularly called as *night soil*? The term 'night soil' was coined for human excreta. In American and European countries, human excreta was collected by scavengers from privy vaults at night and carried to farming areas to be used as manure. The focus of compost did not get mechanized but this practice gave rise to occupational groups in India. The practice of cleaning human excreta at night, therefore, gave it the name 'night soil'. The same got strong impetus due to already existing caste-based occupational structures in India. In fact, there have been more than a dozen types of latrines in existence, however none of them resulted in the liberation of scavengers, and they only increased the intensity of the practice (Pathak, 1991, pp. 45–52).

Why Manual Scavenger Continued?

It is worth examining to give the list of such latrines, namely sandas, closed and open sandas, septic tanks, dry toilets, portable toilets, chamber pots, urine diversion toilets, pit toilets or pit latrines, urine-diverting dry toilets (UDDTs), Dry earth closet alternative that exist. There has barely been serious attempt to replace the human involvement in manual scavenging. Doing and engaging in order to complete abolition of this occupation needed involvement of people who could research and try. Perhaps, it is also possible that even doing some research and study would attract the notion of impurity and indignity to life. But the crudest fact is the continuity of this caste in all modern society of India. India learnt everything from the western innovation and society; dress, food, language, science, etc. but never felt the need of learning a small mechanization process that was taken in the western society to handle human excreta.

The paper does not argue the best practices of western society as a whole, there are practices that continue to exclude a few populations in the West too Atluri (2011) says, 'The Zizekian toilet is never just a toilet. Rather, it reflects upon how our lives are governed by the ideologies of life, work, and well, shit'. Therefore, the problem is not only occupation but continuity of an occupation on the basis of birth in a family henceforth degraded and polluted. It is appropriate to read Zizek's[12] writings when he argues that how modern society has replaced everything, but has again used migrants as a labour to stand outside washroom in most advanced hotels and makes such people in a life of – exploitative working conditions. Those social structures in a modern hotel industry carry on inherent system of denial of dignity and inclusion similar to what Indian traditional society appreciates. Therefore Zizek argues that existence of traditional occupation in modern forms and in modern industry except that the exploited are migrants and port labourers. The important point is not narrating that Muslim and Hindu social structure.

Hadis do recall how severe forms of discrimination and practices have prevailed in the past and then gradually got reduced.

A change in toilet construction from dry to septic and later into flush based reduced the physical filth at work. Consequently, the work of Hadis, for instance, continued but only the nature of work and workplace changed. Certain changes took place due to change in the form of toilets. The crude form of doing job gradually shifted into little upgraded forms. For instance, now Hadis call themselves sweepers after the large number of Hadis getting employment in Nagarpalika as sweepers. A law passed in 1993 forced the state institution to call them as sweepers not as manual scavengers. This helped to bring changes in the mindset and perception of non-Hadis towards Hadis. The data reveals the invariable change brought about due to both change in nomenclature and invention of flush toilets. Hence, there is a noted positive change due to the above-mentioned reasons including the constitutional and legal factors. The data on untouchability does record the past experiences of Hadis. Today, manual scavenging is changed and reduced to different levels and is in various forms that is not noticeable through the lenses of law on untouchability but can be noticed in everyday lives of Hadis.

To be untouchable in Indian caste hierarchy is to be very low and partially excluded from an elaborate hierarchical social order and this order functions quite efficiently. Michael[13] (2007) gives a detailed account of untouchables in India in his new volume on *Dalit in Modern India*. He says untouchables are persons of a discrete set of low caste, excluded on account of their extreme collective impurity from particular relations with higher beings both human and divine. They make up about 16.2 per cent of the Indian population in Census 2001, and in the 2011 Census enumeration, Scheduled Castes population had increased at 16.6 per cent. The cycle of traditional and family occupation does not enforce Hadis to break the chain. The trap of caste occupation continues at large even today. Only one person among 105 workers is found to be doing non-caste and modern day work. Nirmal Hadi became an exception to the entire Hadi Cooli. He is 33 years old and works in a private firm, Tata Indicom, as an office clerk. He spends the entire day in an office, unlike all his friends who get back home in the afternoon, but he finds comfort due to nature of the work. During an interview, he questions, 'Why does the birth in a certain family and caste restricts us from the freedom of choice in all aspects of life and work?' Most are overdependent and consequently spiralled in their traditional occupation. It gives both a sense of security and over-dependency. But the result is never helpful to bring change into their life. But Nirmal overcame this barrier alone. He further asserts that 'I am the only Hadi who has completed graduation (BA) and I am not doing my caste-based occupation unlike my friends and peers in Hadi Cooli'. This context is true to the caste-based communities that are still found to be engaged in the same or similar occupation and this is much more prevalent among the low castes or SCs in the region.

Concluding Remarks

As long as the mainstream (defining this is difficult) Muslim society does not abandon the process of imposition of values of life which do not correlate with the Dalit Muslims in India or the converted, there is rare probability of marginalized and excluded occupational category of Muslims reaping the benefit of equality and equity in all spheres of man's life. Although, Dr B.R. Ambedkar did indeed give birth to a movement that encompassed all needs of human society – economic, social, cultural, political and spiritual, debating about changing occupations would have no or least meaning unless one understands the socio-cultural and political background of the community. Similarly, social exclusion helps to seek clarification about the phenomenon of exclusion which is a 'process'. Is it not a sufficient reason to argue that Muslim scavengers in Hyderabad are living in alienation and suffering from exclusion? Except a few, most of the individuals who were respondents in the study[14] (2010–2011), never disclosed their identity in terms of their names, hereditary and occupational workplace, but then provided a change that took over the period of one generation. The change is seen as an effort of families and households. They could do so because Muslims do not question the caste identity in such a way that exists in the case of Hadi caste. Hadis worked and continued for centuries and at least for the last 200 years (individual land records) to live in Bokaro region when Raja of Kashipur (presently in Purulia, West Bengal), brought them in his estate.

It would be appropriate to conclude, stating that Muslims in India may form a single religious community sharing basic Islamic percepts; they do not form a 'community' in anthropological/sociological terms. They are differentiated into various groups and subgroups along ethnic, cultural, social and occupational lines and are organized groups in a stratified order. For these reasons, the marginalized groups have begun to struggle for empowerment and self-recognition in the daily lives and interactions.[15] Muslims and Dalit Muslims are two distinguished social groups of Indian society and many Dalit Muslims share much commonality with the Hindu Dalits. The first portrays to be identified as homogenous social groups and the second is homogenous but a socially deprived group. Given the fact, that a section of 'Hindu' Dalits have received special status for decades and benefits from the state flowing from that status, it is obvious that their conditions are better than the most Muslims, or even, in a sense, more deserving of SC status in order to help them come up at least to the level of 'Hindu' Dalits. Hence, studying the dynamics and dimensions of social exclusion experienced in the community and changing occupations is an essential but difficult question. Hadis exist as an occupational group in the Hindu society and Muslim in Hyderabad have transformed their occupation into non-polluted jobs. In future, many more deep sociological studies need attention to this social category of occupation among Hindu and Muslim communities to answer the unsolved quests. The research intents to examine concerns of the social groups engaged with inhuman practice as this social reality is far from the dignity and inclusion exist among other occupational groups.

Notes

1. Standing Committee Report (2012), 'The Prohibition of Employment as Manual Scavengers and Their Rehabilitation Bill 2012', Thirty-Second Report of Social Justice and Empowerment (2012–13) (Fifteenth Lok Sabha), New Delhi: Ministry of Social Justice and Empowerment, Government of India.
2. Ibid., pp. 6–7.
3. Ramaswamy, Gita (2005), *India Stinking: Manual Scavengers in Andhra Pradesh and Their Work*, Hyderabad: Navayana Publishing.
4. Venkateshwarlu, K. (2006), 'Part of the System', *Frontline*, Vol. 23, No. 18, pp. 9–22.
5. Ramaswamy, Gita (2005), *India Stinking: Manual Scavengers in Andhra Pradesh and Their Work*, Hyderabad: Navayana Publishing.
6. Pathak, Bindeshwar (1991), *Road to Freedom*, New Delhi: Motilal Banarsidass Publishers Pvt. Ltd.

7. Massey, James (1996), *Dalits in India: Religion as a Source of Bondage or Liberation with Special Reference to Christians*, New Delhi: Manohar Publishers.
8. Saheb, S.A.A. (2003), Dudekula Muslims of Andhra Pradesh: An Ethnographic Profile, *Economic and Political Weekly*, Vol. 38, No. 46, pp. 15–21.
9. Ziyauddin, K.M. (2016), *Sociology of Health in a Dalit Community: Axes of Exclusion*, UK: Cambridge Scholars Publishing (forthcoming).
10. Srivastava, B.N. (1997), *Manual Scavenging in India: A Disgrace to the Country*, New Delhi: Concept Publishing.
11. Shyamlal (1992), *The Bhangi: A Sweeper Caste and its Socio-economic Portraits*, Bombay: Popular Prakashan.
12. Zizek, Slavoj (2004), 'Knee Deep', *London Review of Books*, Vol. 26, No. 17, September 2, pp. 12–13.
13. Michael, James (ed) (2007), *Dalits in Modern India: Vision and Values*. New Delhi: Sage
14. Ziyauddin, K.M. (2012), *Muslim Scavengers in India: Perception and Perspectives of Social Exclusion*, Germany: Lambert Academic Publishing.
15. Mondal, Seik Rahim (2003), 'Social Structure, OBCs and Muslims', *Economic and Political Weekly*, Vol. 38, No. 46, pp. 15–21.

References

Atluri, Tara (2011), You Marxist, I Clean Toilet: Racism, Labour and the Bathroom Attndent. *FRAME: A Journal of Vasual and Material Culture*. Issue One, Spring.

Freeman, James (1979), *Untouchable: An Indian Life History*, Stanford: Stanford University Press.

Jharkhand Population Census Data 2011. New Delhi: Registrar General of India.

Pathak, Bindeshwar (1991), Road to Freedom: A Sociological Study on the Abolition of Scavengining in India, New Delhi: Motilal Manarsidass Publisher.

Ramaswamy, Geeta (2005), India Stinking: Menual Scavengers in Andhra Pradesh, Delhi: Navayana Publishers.

Sachchinananda (2001), *People at the Bottom: A Portrait of the Scavengers*, New Delhi: Concept Publication.

9

Impact of Affirmative Action on Subaltern Castes

Evidence from the Recent Data

M. GOPINATH REDDY

Background

The socio-economic backwardness among various social groups and their access to services has become a matter of debate since many years. In the case of India, several mechanisms have been taken up to establish an egalitarian society through addressing the issues of inequity and unbalanced socio-economic development. In this context, the Constitution of India has also given special emphasis on the problems of backward communities such as SCs, STs, OBCs and women. Through implementing a number of constitutional and legal provisions, the Indian state has tried to address the backwardness of these communities. A main strategy of addressing backwardness and promoting economic advancement of these communities has been taken up through the policies of affirmative action. The affirmative action policies for backward communities in India is institutionalized through implementing a number of socio-economic development programmes, providing reservation and ensuring their inclusion in the political, social and economic matters.

Historically, in India, many communities such as Scheduled Castes (SCs), Scheduled Tribes (STs), Other Backward Classes (OBCs), Minorities, Women and Physically Challenged (PCPs) are being marginalized on the basis of religion, caste, creed, colour, gender and class. These communities feel excluded, alienated and often helpless to assert their rights. Current patterns of socio-economic and political inequality are often intertwined with much older systems of stratification. Many descendants of lower castes and class people continue to face socio-economic and political disadvantages. The democratic ideals of decentralization, development and increased, continuous and active popular participation in the process of nation-building can be secured only through the participation of socially excluded communities.

Rationale and Objectives

India adopted democratic form of government to address the issues of marginalized communities. Law makers have gone further to offer specific rights and privileges intended to redress past wrongs. The Constitution mandated Indian states to play the role of a transformative agency and inclusive growth. Article 38 of the Constitution of India encodes reduction of inequalities in income, status, opportunities and facilities, and Article 39 promises containing monopolization of means of production and wealth not to the detriment of common and collective goal of the society. Since India became Independent, the constitution of India has adopted Affirmative Action Policy of extending reservations to SCs and STs, to begin with, and later extended to OBCs, in the area of education, public employment, etc.

Despite the policy of affirmative action, no significant changes in the lives of marginalized communities except a segment of these sections were benefitted by the above policy. Keeping this in view, the Government of India has emphasized on 'Growth with Social Justice' in 1969 and 'Economic Reforms with Human Face' in 2004. In 2006, the World Bank advocated and described Inclusive Growth as 'growth with emphasis not only on the distribution of economic gains but also on the security, vulnerability, empowerment and a sense of full participation in social life'. The 11th and 12th Five-Year Plans recognized that the public policies and economic reforms have not succeeded in addressing the issues of social exclusion and therefore, emphasized on Social Inclusive Growth.

The Twelfth Plan, thus, defines the inclusive growth approach by observing that 'Inclusive growth should result in lower incidence of poverty, improvement in health outcomes, universal access to school education, increased access to higher education, including skill and education, better opportunities for both wage employment and livelihoods and improvement in provision of basic amenities like water, electricity, roads, sanitation and housing, etc.'

On the basis of the above raised issues, the main objective of this paper is to shed light on the impacts of policies of affirmative action on subaltern castes such as the SCs, the STs, and the OBCs in India, and how affirmative action initiatives such as programmes related to land entitlement, employment, education, health and participation in the local governments have reinforced the inclusion of these categories of people in the mainstream of development. More explicitly, this paper tries to uncover the results of various policies and programmes that have been implemented in India in recent years, and how it has promoted socio-economic advancement among the backward communities.

Data Base and Sources

The paper demonstrates the result of the secondary data gathered from various sources at national level. The paper has particularly tried to examine the result of affirmative action policies and their implications on the subaltern castes such as SCs, STs, OBCs and women. The key parameters looked at to understand the relative position of the marginalized vis-à-vis others are: (i) Land (owned as well as operation holdings), (ii) Amenities, (iii) Employment, (iv) Poverty, (v) Participation in Panchayati Raj Institutions (PRIs), and (vi) Participation in MGNREGS.

Result and Discussion

Land Ownership

In land distribution pattern, there are two types, mainly Household Ownership Holdings (HOH) and Operational Holdings (OH).[1] In this part, we will deal with HOH, whose data is available decennially but the data related to social groups is available in 59th round only in full scale for 2003. Thus, we analyse the data for 2003 among ST, SC, OBC and Others among all social groups. Table 1 presents the status of land ownership among the various social groups in India.

In 2003, among the estimated number of households in India, both for rural and urban areas together, the share of STs forms 8.5 per cent, but their ownership of land is 10.7 per cent of the total agricultural land. The share of ownership is higher than their share of households by 2 percentage points. But, the share of ownership of area (8.8%) among SCs is not even half of their share of households (19.8%). Among OBCs, the share of land ownership (43.1%) is higher (by 3 percentage points) than the share of households. But among others, the former share is higher by more than 5 percentage points. The position of others in land ownership (36.3%) is higher by 10 percentage points than their share of households.

Table 1

Distribution of Land Ownership among Social Groups, 2003

S. No.	Item	ST	SC	OBC	Others	All
				Rural Households		
1.	Estimated No. of HOH (in 000)	15,592	31,908	61,513	38,816	1,47,838
2.	Percentage of HOH	10.55	21.58	41.61	26.26	100.00
3.	Total Area of Land (in 000 ha)	11,952	9,692	46,652	38,938	1,07,228
4.	Percentage Area of Land Owned	11.15	9.04	43.51	36.30	100.00
5	Average Area (ha) Owned per Household	0.767	0.304	0.758	1.003	0.725
				Urban Households		
1.	Estimated No. of HOH (in 000)	1,616	8,350	19,133	26,407	55,508
2.	Percentage of HOH	2.91	15.04	34.47	47.57	100.00
3.	Total Area of Land (in 000 ha)	235	344	2,652	3,982	7,212
4.	Percentage Area of Land Owned	3.25	4.76	36.77	55.21	100
5.	Average Area (ha) Owned per Household	0.145	0.041	0.139	0.151	0.130
				All Households (Rural + Urban)		
1.	Estimated No. of HOH (in 000)	17,208	40,258	80,646	65,223	2,03,346
2.	Percentage of HOH	8.46	19.80	39.66	32.07	100.00
3.	Total Area of Land (in 000 ha)	12,187	10,036	49,304	42,920	1,14,440
4.	Percentage Area of Land Owned	10.65	8.77	43.08	37.50	100.00
5.	Average Area (ha) Owned per Household	0.708	0.249	0.611	0.658	0.563

* includes cases of social group not recorded.

Source: NSSO (2006), *Household Ownership Holdings in India, 2003,* Report No. 491(59/18.1/4), November, p. 23.

In urban areas also, the relative position is similar to rural areas. But the land ownership among SCs (4.8%) is less than 1/3rd of their share of households. The average size of area owned among STs is higher than that of all groups in rural, urban and rural and urban areas together. Among SCs, the position seems bad at rural and urban level collectively, where the average area for SCs is less than half of the average of all groups. Whereas in urban areas, their position turns from bad to worst, as their average size is only 0.04 ha as compared to 0.13 ha for all groups.

Amenities

The Census of India has provided data in 2001 and 2011 on the amenities possessed by the households among STs, SCs and all Social Groups. The data covered in 2011 are: (i) Mode of Transportation: bicycle, scooter/motor cycle/moped, and car/jeep/van, (ii) Mode of Communication: radio/transistor, television, computer/laptop with internet, computer/laptop without internet, telephone (landline only), telephone (mobile only), both types of telephones, (iii) TV, computer/laptop, telephone/mobile and scooter/car, and (iv) None of the specified items.

As regards amenities at all-India level, in 2001, radio/transistor possessed among STs was 21.8 per cent, whereas by 2011, the share decreased to 14.0 per cent. On the contrary the possession of TVs rose from 12.1 per cent to 21.5 per cent. While among all social groups, the share of TVs rose from 31.6 per cent to 45.3 per cent, among SCs this share rose from 28.1 per cent to 30.5 per cent. In regard to the possession of landline telephone, among STs it decreased from 2.5 per cent in 2001 to 2.0 per cent in 2011, but the mobile possession by 2011 assumed the share of 30.8 per cent. Among SCs, the landline decreased from 3.5 per cent to 2.8 per cent, but the possession of mobiles became 46.3 per cent. Among all social groups, the possession of telephone came down drastically from 9.1 per cent to 3.9 per cent, whereas the possession of mobiles got the share of 52.5 per cent. In 2011, if we consider the possession of TV, computer/laptop, telephone/mobile phone and scooter/car as a combination, calling it amenities hybrid group, it is found only 1.2 per cent of STs, as against 1.6 per cent among SCs, while the same is 4.1 per cent among all social groups (see Table 2).

Table 2

Amenities Possessed by the Households among STs, SCs and all Social Groups in 2011 and 2001 Censes

Social Groups	Radio/ Transistor	TV	Computer/Laptop		Telephone/Mobile			Bicycle	Scooter/ Motor-cycle/ Moped	Car/ Jeep/ Van	HHs with TV, Computer /Laptop, Telephone/mobile phone and Scooter/Car	None of the Assets**
			With Internet	Without Internet	Landline only*	Mobile only	Both					
							Census–2011					
ST	13.96	21.51	0.82	4.35	1.95	30.81	3.76	82.17	8.93	1.46	1.21	37.42
SC	16.01	36.48	1.19	5.23	2.84	46.34	2.41	43.87	10.93	1.72	1.60	23.85
All	19.79	45.31	2.80	6.21	3.93	52.45	5.59	44.51	19.84	4.08	4.12	18.55
							Census–2001					
ST	21.77	12.06	–	–	2.51	–	–	32.03	4.13	0.89	–	54.03
SC	28.09	21.28	–	–	3.47	–	–	40.94	5.38	1.04	–	42.64
All	35.12	31.59	–	–	9.14	–	–	43.67	11.71	2.50	–	34.48

* Telephone of 2001 is taken as identical with Landline of 2011

** HHs with None of the Items from Radio/Transistor to Car/Jeep/Van

Employment

For all-India level, the WPRs (Work Participation Rates) according to usual status *(ps* and *ss)* for different social groups over the period 1983 to 2009–10 have been presented in Table 3. The survey periods for which the WPRs have been presented in this statement refer to those of NSS 38th (1983), 43rd (1987–88), 50th (1993–94), 55th (1999–2000), NSS 61st (2004–05) and NSS 66th (2009–10) rounds. It may be noted that the estimates for *Others* category included OBCs in the 38th, 43rd and 50th rounds, since in those surveys, OBC was not a separate social group.

Table 3

No. Employed per 1,000 Persons (WPR) during 1983 to 2009–10

NSS Round	*Year of Reference*	*Worker Population Ratio (WPR)*				
		ST	*SC*	*OBC*	*Others*	*All*
			Rural Male			
66th	(2009–10)	559	548	540	552	547
61st	(2004–05)	562	545	537	557	546
55th	(1999–00)	558	531	532	520	531
50th	(1993–94)	591	554	–	547	553
43rd	(1987–88)	567	538	–	535	539
38th	1983	588	551	–	540	547
			Rural Female			
66th	(2009–10)	359	269	267	199	261
61st	(2004–05)	464	333	330	262	327
55th	(1999–00)	438	325	302	223	299
50th	(1993–94)	482	355	–	297	328
43rd	(1987–88)	454	358	–	294	323
38th	1983	478	381	–	310	340
			Urban Male			
66th	(2009–10)	510	550	543	542	543
61st	(2004–05)	523	537	554	550	549
55th	(1999–00)	480	503	530	518	518

Cont'd...

...Cont'd

50th	(1993–94)	520	505	–	523	521
43rd	(1987–88)	504	492	–	509	506
38th	1983	531	490	–	514	512
			Urban Female			
66th	(2009–10)	203	178	145	113	138
61st	(2004–05)	245	200	185	134	166
55th	(1999–00)	204	185	169	108	139
50th	(1993–94)	234	199	–	145	155
43rd	(1987–88)	225	213	–	140	152
38th	1983	255	205	–	139	151

Source: NSSO (2012), NSS Report No 543(66/10/3), September, p. 35.
WPR = (No. of Employed Persons/Total Population) 1,000

In rural areas, for male category among STs between 1983 and 1993–94, it was lying between 56.7 and 59.1 per cent while between 1999–00 and 2009–10, its levels decreased to between 55.8 and 56.2 per cent. What is significant is to find that rural male STs exhibit higher levels of WPR in each of the rounds than those of all groups. Not only this, the SCs who have more or less the same levels of WPR as those of all groups, automatically lag behind the STs. Thus, WPRs of both rural males and females among STs, being located in forest areas mostly, are higher than those of their counterparts among SCs, OBCs and others, as the earning of livelihoods are precarious and time consuming, along with manual work.

Poverty

Panagariya and More (2013), computed the estimates of the poverty rates as percentages of population below the Tendulkar poverty line in rural and urban regions and in the combined areas (Rural and Urban), for Scheduled Castes, Scheduled Tribes and Others (OT) for years 1993–94, 2009–10 based on NSS reports for the respective years. As regards the comparability, the surveys allow us to identify only SC, ST and, All Others (AO) in the first of these years, whereas in the last three years All Others (AO) were further classified into OBCs and Others (OT) and thus, there are four social groups in the latter case instead of three in the former case.

Table 4

State-wise Rural Poverty Ratio among Social Groups (1993–94 and 2009–10)

States	*1993–94*			*2009–10*		
	ST	*SC*	*Others*	*ST*	*SC*	*Others*
Andhra Pradesh	58.4	64.5	42.4	40.2	25.7	20.4
Assam	55.3	58.4	54.5	32.0	36.9	42.1
Bihar	73.3	76.3	57.6	64.4	68.1	50.8
Chhattisgarh	65.9	53.4	48.2	66.8	67.6	45.4
Gujarat	53.1	56.3	37.2	48.6	17.9	19.2
Haryana	69.7	63.1	30.4	49.6	33.6	11.8
Himachal Pradesh	62.4	43.6	33.0	22.0	14.4	5.7
Jammu & Kashmir	74.5	34.4	30.3	3.1	8.5	8.3
Jharkhand	72.6	73.7	59.9	51.2	44.1	33.6
Karnataka	70.3	72.4	50.2	21.3	35.6	23.7
Kerala	40.9	53.3	31.6	24.4	27.7	10.0
Madhya Pradesh	69.9	59.4	36.0	61.9	42.4	32.4
Maharashtra	74.1	73.9	53.1	51.7	37.6	23.4
Odisha	82.1	62.8	54.6	66.0	47.1	25.2
Punjab	35.9	35.0	10.7	16.1	27.2	4.3
Rajasthan	63.9	55.3	30.8	35.9	38.6	19.5
Tamil Nadu	57.0	66.4	45.4	11.5	31.2	18.1
Uttar Pradesh	48.5	68.6	45.2	49.8	53.6	33.7
Uttarakhand	54.9	43.5	33.4	20.0	20.0	11.5
West Bengal	66.5	48.2	36.1	32.9	31.5	27.1
NE States (excluding Assam)	42.9	40.6	38.4	24.3	22.3	25.2
Other States and UTs	39.8	23.3	17.7	22.8	5.6	5.0
All India	65.7	62.2	43.9	47.3	42.2	28.0

Source: NSS unit level data of Household Consumption Expenditure, 43rd and 66th rounds.

Poverty is markedly high among STs and SCs in rural areas: even in 2009–10, nearly half the STs and about 42 per cent of SCs were poor (see Table 4). Between 1993–94 and 2004–05, the rate of decline in the incidence of poverty among these social groups was sluggish at less than 1 per cent annually. Also, during this period, the social group 'others' registered a faster rate of decline in poverty. Decline in poverty of all social groups accelerated considerably between 2004 and 2010. In fact, trends suggest that poverty of SCs and STs declined faster than the average between 2004–05 and 2009–10. Yet, SCs and STs constitute 44 per cent of the rural poor.

Participation in Panchayati Raj Institutions (PRIs)

The proportion of elected representatives from SCs is 19.4 per cent and it varies from state to state, depending on their population and in comparison to STs that is 11.7 per cent. Whereas, the proportion women elected representatives stands at 46.7 per cent. This is due to recent decision by few state governments to enhance women reservation to 50.0 per cent (see Table 5).

Table 5

State-wise Proportion of Elected SC, ST and Women Representatives in Panchayats (per cent) as on 1 March 2013)

States	*SC*	*ST*	*Women*
Andhra Pradesh	18.4	8.3	33.5
Arunachal Pradesh	NA	100.0	41.6
Assam	5.0	3.3	36.9
Bihar	16.3	0.8	50.0
Chhattisgarh	12.4	40.2	54.5
Goa	NA	5.9	32.3
Gujarat	7.0	20.0	33.0
Haryana	21.5	NA	36.5
Himachal Pradesh	26.8	4.4	50.1
Jammu & Kashmir	NA	NA	NA
Jharkhand	11.0	34.1	58.6
Karnataka	18.6	10.8	43.6
Kerala	4.5	0.6	51.9
Madhya Pradesh	15.1	273	50.5
Maharashtra	10.9	14.9	49.9
Manipur	1.2	2.2	48.5
Odisha	16.2	22.0	50.0
Punjab	32.0	NA	34.9
Rajasthan	17.2	12.6	50.0
Sikkim	7.0	38.0	50.0
Tamil Nadu	24.0	1.0	35.0
Tripura	26.6	5.4	36.0
Uttar Pradesh	23.9	NA	40.0
Uttarakhand	19.9	3.4	56.1
West Bengal	34.2	8.1	38.4
All India	19.4	11.7	46.7

Source: Ministry of Tribal Affairs, Govt of India, 2014.

Participation in MGNREGS

India's National Rural Employment Guarantee Scheme NREGS is renamed as Mahatma Gandhi National Rural Employment Guarantee Scheme. From 2010 onwards, it is considered as one of the most creative initiatives of our times in the field of social policy. The most novel and remarkable features of the MGNREGS's are: (i) a legally binding response by the state to ensure right to work to the poor and unemployed persons, (ii) a development initiative, chipping with crucial public investments for creation of durable assets, (iii) emphasis on water conservation, drought and flood proofing underscoring water security for rural transformation, (iv) payment of statutory minimum wages, (v) provision for unemployment allowance to be paid to the workers in case the state is unable to provide the guaranteed days of work, i.e. 100 days employment for every household in a year, and (vi) undertake the programmes benefiting more to the SCs, STs and women.

Given the above objectives, it is pertinent to see that to what extent these laudable objectives are being met. The analysis of 2009–10 MGNREGS data state wise/social category wise (see Table 6), reveals that at All India level, nearly 40.0 per cent of STs, 33.0 per cent of SCs, 21.0 per cent of OBCs and 15.0 per cent of 'others' have got employment under MGNREGS. It is understandable that both STs and SCs have got work more than their proportion of population as the focus of the programme is more on creation of work for the benefit of STs and SCs. In addition, large chunk of labour force is drawn from STs and SCs and hence, their participation in MGNREGS is more than their share in the total population. In the tribal dominated states like Madhya Pradesh (49.6%), Odisha (32.3%), Chhattisgarh (51.9%), Rajasthan (77.6%), Gujarat (31.4%) and Andhra Pradesh (56.7%), participation of STs in MGNREGS is high, while in some other ST dominated States like Jharkhand (18.9%) and Maharashtra (only 6.3%), their participation was very low. Of course, in the North East States where STs are predominant, their participation in MGNREGS is satisfactory.

Nearly 40.0 per cent of STs, 33.0 per cent SCs, 21.0 per cent OBCs and 15.0 per cent other got work under MGNREGS. This figure shows that not all who are seeking employment, particularly from the marginalized groups, are getting employment.

Table 6

State-wise Proportion of Households that Received MGNREGS Work by Social Category (per cent) (2009–10)

States	*ST*	*SC*	*OBC*	*Others*	*All*
Andhra Pradesh	56.7	43.4	38.2	15.0	35.4
Arunachal Pradesh	21.8	11.6	7.5	8.1	17.9
Assam	19.0	17.2	15.9	18.5	17.6
Bihar	8.7	17.3	8.5	1.5	9.5
Chhattisgarh	51.9	43.5	50.4	21.4	47.9
Goa	0.0	0.0	7.9	2.3	2.2
Gujarat	31.4	26.5	14.7	5.4	18.1
Haryana	0.0	10.5	4.4	1.8	5.1
Himachal Pradesh	39.2	41.3	29.4	29.8	33.4
Jammu & Kashmir	3.6	12.3	9.3	7.5	8.1
Jharkhand	18.9	22.2	12.4	12.0	16.3
Karnataka	18.6	16.0	4.2	5.4	8.0
Kerala	16.8	23.8	9.8	8.8	11.2
Madhya Pradesh	49.6	40.5	30.6	18.0	36.4
Maharashtra	6.3	1.7	7.4	1.5	4.4
Manipur	86.0	98.1	62.1	61.2	73.6
Meghalaya	42.4	70.9	5.7	37.2	42.2
Mizoram	88.6	89.2	0.0	0.0	88.5
Nagaland	61.9	0.0	0.0	6.5	59.4
Odisha	32.3	22.0	22.4	10.0	21.9
Punjab	0.0	10.4	1.6	0.9	5.2
Rajasthan	77.6	62.8	56.4	39.6	59.0
Sikkim	52.2	30.9	46.9	2.3	44.1
Tamil Nadu	28.6	52.3	27.9	6.9	33.5
Tripura	87.6	78.4	76.3	63.5	77.4
Uttar Pradesh	14.0	32.4	11.8	4.4	16.2
Uttarakhand	37.3	46.7	7.6	25.8	27.1
West Bengal	65.3	50.7	44.8	36.0	43.0
All-India	39.8	32.9	20.9	15.1	24.2

Source Ministry of Tribal Affairs, Govt of India, 2014.

Nearly 20 STs, 22.2 of SCs, 18.3 per cent OBCs and 18 per cent Others did not employment even though they sought the work under MGNREGS (see Table 7). There is no evidence of any compensation given in lieu of those who were not given employment on demand.

Table 7

State-wise Proportion of Households that Sought but did not get MGNREGS Work by Social Category (per cent) (2009–10)

States	*ST*	*SC*	*OBC*	*Others*	*All*
Andhra Pradesh	18.1	14.8	10.7	9.1	11.7
Arunachal Pradesh	28.5	13.7	26.1	13.2	24.6
Assam	28.2	22.7	22.8	20.1	22.4
Bihar	52.2	36.1	34.0	30.0	34.4
Chhattisgarh	23.3	24.1	15.0	35.7	21.1
Goa	0.6	0.0	5.3	8.5	5.5
Gujarat	9.6	29.0	11.9	15.8	14.1
Haryana	6.0	20.4	12.1	12.1	14.4
Himachal Pradesh	14.3	12.7	7.0	6.1	8.5
Jammu & Kashmir	3.2	19.2	34.9	18.0	19.7
Jharkhand	24.5	33.6	27.5	27.1	27.5
Karnataka	9.8	12.8	17.4	13.0	14.8
Kerala	6.2	15.7	11.3	12.4	12.0
Madhya Pradesh	23.6	20.7	21.5	17.9	21.5
Maharashtra	21.8	27.4	21.8	23.5	23.2
Manipur	0.9	0.0	6.2	8.3	3.8
Meghalaya	14.1	10.7	0.0	18.8	14.2
Mizoram	3.5	0.0	0.0	0.0	3.5
Nagaland	15.4	0.0	4.0	31.6	15.6
Odisha	25.5	31.6	31.8	24.4	28.7
Punjab	32.2	28.5	24.3	23.8	26.0
Rajasthan	8.2	12.5	10.0	14.2	10.8
Sikkim	0.8	2.0	2.9	0.0	1.9
Tamil Nadu	1.1	8.0	7.8	10.9	7.8
Tripura	3.9	7.3	6.2	14.5	7.7
Uttar Pradesh	30.4	21.6	19.0	13.7	18.7
Uttarakhand	25.9	16.3	8.7	8.6	10.5
West Bengal	19.3	25.2	19.5	21.8	22.5
All-India	19.7	22.2	18.3	18.1	19.3

Source: Ministry of Tribal Affairs, Govt of India, 2014.

Conclusion

The above trend shows that affirmative action policies that have been formulated and implemented in India for promoting inclusion among subaltern castes has brought many changes, despite backwardness prevailing among these sections of people. The policies related to providing land title, employment, basic amenities and various poverty eradication measures demonstrated changes in their position. However, there is still a wide range of disparity existing among these sections of people which calls for further policy reforms.

References

Ministry of Tribal Affairs, Government of India (2014), Report of the High Level Committee on Socio-Economic, Health and Educational Status of Tribal Communities of India, New Delhi.

National Sample Survey Organization (1998a), Morbidity and Treatment of Ailments (52nd Round NSS Report No. 441), Ministry of Statistics and Programme Implementation, Government of India, New Delhi.

—— (1998b), Small Trading Units in India and Their Basic Characteristics 1997 (Volume I), (53rd Round NSS Report No. 443), Ministry of Statistics and Programme Implementation, Government of India, New Delhi.

—— (2003), Unorganised Service Sector in India 2001–02: Characteristics of Enterprises (57th Round NSS Report No. 483), Ministry of Statistics and Programme Implementation, Government of India, New Delhi.

—— (2006a), Employment and Unemployment Situation among Social Groups in India 2004–05 (61st Round NSS Report No. 516), Ministry of Statistics and Programme Implementation, Government of India, New Delhi.

—— (2006b), Household Assets Holding, Indebtedness, Current Borrowings and Repayments of Social Groups in India (as on 30.06.2002): All-India Debt and Investment Survey (59th Round NSS Report No. 503), Ministry of Statistics and Programme Implementation, Government of India, New Delhi.

—— (2006c), Household Ownership Holdings in India 2003 (59th Round NSS Report No. 491), Ministry of Statistics and Programme Implementation, Government of India, New Delhi.

—— (2006d), Morbidity, Health Care and the Condition of the Aged (60th Round NSS Report No. 507), Ministry of Statistics and Programme Implementation, Government of India, New Delhi.

—— (2007), Household Consumer Expenditure among Socio-Economic Groups 2004–05 (61st Round NSS Report No. 514), Ministry of Statistics and Programme Implementation, Government of India, New Delhi.

—— (2010a), Education in India 2007–08: Participation and Expenditure (64th Round NSS Report No. 532), Ministry of Statistics and Programme Implementation, Government of India, New Delhi.

—— (2010b), Migration in India 2007–08 (64th Round NSS Report No. 533), Ministry of Statistics and Programme Implementation, Government of India, New Delhi.

Panagariya, Arvind and Vishal More (2013), Poverty by Social, Religious and Economic Groups in India and Its Largest States, 1993–94 to 2011–12, Working Paper No. 2013–02, School of International and Public Affairs, Institute for Social and Economic Research and Policy, Columbia University.

10

Dalits and Human Development Indices

SHIDDALINGASWAMI V. HANAGODIMATH

Human Development Index has been accepted as the measurement of development of the people world over. The basic objective of human development is to enhance the choices of people. This indicates that all people in the society should be well educated, healthy and with good standard of living, irrespective of their race, caste, religion, creed, ethnicity or colour. This index has been prepared for the first time in 1990 by UNDP (United States Development Programme), considering 159 countries of the world. In the development of the concept of Human Development Index, the contribution of Amartya Kumar Sen is remarkable. To fulfil the objective of attaining a higher level of human development, the government of every country has formulated policies and programmes towards it. India is also not lagging behind in this regard. Till now, India has two National Level Human Development Reports, taking into consideration states, i.e. for the year 2002 and 2012. To know the status of human development of districts, many Indian states have developed State Human Development Reports. Karnataka is in the pioneer states, not only in the publication of state human development reports (taking into consideration of districts) but also in publishing the District Human Development Reports (DHDRs), taking into consideration taluks as the unit of analysis in the year 2015. All these national, state and district level reports have suggested various policy interventions for human development.

India has a rigid caste based hierarchical system in the society along with diversity in various aspects like language, culture, costume, ritual, custom, practice, and so on. The development of a particular region (state, district, taluk) cannot be considered as the entire development because, due to hierarchical caste system, some of the social groups enjoy more fruits of the development and some are deprived from the same. Developmental measures should capture all social groups of all regions. For this purpose, developmental indicators are analysed by categorizing them into region-wise, genderwise, castewise, incomewise groups, and so on. Similarly, attempts are made to construct and analyse the Human Development Index for different social groups. Countries like, Nepal, Gabon, Malaysia, USA, Canada, Gautemala, and so on have already tried this. Among these efforts, studies by Thorat (2007) and Corrie (1995) are very important in India. Thorat has constructed Human Development Index for SC, ST, Non-SC and Non-ST and all social groups of 16 major states of India for the years 1980 and 2000.

In recent years, the concept of Dalit Development Index has been developed by the researchers but it is based on field survey, which has not been very successful. However, after Thorat's social group-wise HDI, no attempts have been made significantly to construct social groups wise HDI. Given this background, using the available data, an attempt has been made in this study to find out the gap of HDI in Dalits (SC) and non-Dalits non-SC-ST. The objectives of this study are to:

- find out the status and gap of HDI of Dalits, and non-Dalits in Indian states
- examine the gap in HDI of Dalits and non-Dalits of different taluks of Karnataka State

Data and Methodology

The study is based on secondary-data collected from various published sources. They are State wise and Social Group-wise HDI values for years 1980 and 2000, which have been used from the study by Thorat (2007). District-wise HDI values have been taken from Economic Survey of Karnataka 2015–16. Further, Taluk-wise HDI values have been computed from data available from District Human Development Reports of all districts of Karnataka.

The gap in HDI values of Dalits and non-Dalits can be studied in two ways. First is the direct way, where HDI values of Dalits and non-Dalits are used for which, the exercise data on HDI for Dalits and non-Dalits should be available. In the second way which is called the indirect way, the data on HDI of only overall is available. In this method, the percentage of Dalit population is used and correlated with the overall HDI values for different region. In the present study, both methods have been used.

Inter-State Comparison of HDI of Dalits and Non-Dalits

For the year 1980 and 2000, comparison of human development indices of Dalits and non-Dalits has been made in the direct way. In Table 1, information related to this (i.e. state-wise HDI for Dalits and non-Dalits and Overall) has been presented. The table reveals that HDI value of overall was 0.241 in the year 1980, which increased to 0.366 in 2000 (1.5 times of increase). HDI value of Dalits was 0.162 in 1980, which increased significantly to 0.303 in 2000 (the increase is 1.9 times). On the other hand, HDI value of non-Dalits was 0.285 in 1980, which increased to 0.393 in 2000 (1.4 times increase). It should be noted here that the gap in HDI of Dalits and non-Dalits (non-Dalits HDI minus (-) Dalits HDI) was 0.123 in 1980, which decreased significantly to 0.09 in the year 2000. It clearly shows the decrease in the developmental disparities among social groups in India.

However, these statuses and gaps are not similar in all states. The performance of some states is good and in some states it is very low. Kerala is found in the first position in HDI of all social groups, i.e. SC, non-SC/ST and all groups. On the other hand, Bihar is at the last position in all social groups. Along with Kerala, states like Himachal Pradesh, Maharashtra and Tamil Nadu are found in top position in HDI of Dalits, non-Dalits and all social groups. Contrary to this, along with Bihar, states like Uttar Pradesh and Odisha are found in lower position. In the year 1980, out of 16 states, none of the states have registered higher HDI value of Dalits than non-Dalits, but an interesting observation is that in the year 2000 Assam has recorded higher HDI value for Dalits than that of non-Dalits. In the year 1980, Assam, Gujarat, Uttar Pradesh and Rajasthan have shown lower gap in HDI values between Dalits and non-Dalits. The gap between HDI value of Dalits and non-Dalits is lower in Gujarat, Maharashtra and Tamil Nadu in the year 2000.

Overall, it is found that HDI values of Dalits are lower in all states (except Assam in 2000) than non-Dalits in India. Further, over the period of time, the gap between HDI of Dalits and non-Dalit has decreased significantly.

Table 1

Human Development Index of SC, non-SC and ST and All for the years 1980 and 2000

States	*1980*			*2000*		
	Dalits	*Non-Dalits*	*All*	*Dalits*	*Non-Dalits*	*All*
Andhra Pradesh	0.163	0.262	0.237	0.283	0.382	0.348
Assam	0.283	0.296	0.274	0.407	0.358	0.360
Bihar	0.119	0.212	0.198	0.195	0.301	0.279
Gujarat	0.252	0.303	0.275	0.371	0.433	0.406
Haryana	0.182	0.296	0.270	0.340	0.419	0.428
Himachal Pradesh	0.228	0.346	0.287	0.450	0.524	0.505
Karnataka	0.184	0.309	0.263	0.308	0.417	0.389
Kerala	0.448	0.565	0.539	0.661	0.755	0.715
Madhya Pradesh	0.153	0.247	0.206	0.294	0.368	0.326
Maharashtra	0.227	0.343	0.295	0.416	0.480	0.453
Odisha	0.145	0.241	0.201	0.289	0.364	0.316
Punjab	0.233	0.376	0.331	0.343	0.446	0.444
Rajasthan	0.144	0.230	0.196	0.291	0.365	0.338
Tamil Nadu	0.183	0.324	0.317	0.411	0.461	0.447
Uttar Pradesh	0.121	0.202	0.183	0.250	0.323	0.307
West Bengal	0.183	0.308	0.265	0.359	0.452	0.412
India	0.162	0.285	0.241	0.303	0.393	0.366
CV (%)	39.7	28.3	31.2	30.0	24.6	25.7

Source: Thorat (2007).

Dalits and HDI in Karnataka

At present, no separate HDI for Dalits has been constructed for Karnataka taking into consideration taluks or districts. However, the district Human Development Reports 2014, which have been prepared for all districts of the state, have constructed an index called Dalit Development Index. This index has been constructed using the case study method considering villages. These indices give partial status of the district, as it has considered 2–3 villages in each district.

In this circumstance, where HDI values for Dalits is not separately available, the second method which has been mentioned in the methodology is the indirect method of finding out the gap between Dalits and others in HDI.

Table 2

District-wise HDI, GII, CDI, FSI and Share of Dalit Population

District	*HDI*	*GII*	*CDI*	*FSI*	*SC (%)*
Udupi	0.675	0.038	0.746	0.664	6.41
Dakshina Kannada	0.691	0.050	0.840	0.694	7.09
Uttara Kannada	0.565	0.070	0.734	0.547	8.10
Dharwad	0.610	0.111	0.624	0.695	9.63
Belgaum	0.449	0.112	0.547	0.544	12.08
Bengaluru Urban	0.928	0.056	0.690	0.589	12.46
Kodagu	0.658	0.069	0.664	0.568	13.27
Haveri	0.406	0.089	0.525	0.422	13.77
Mandya	0.491	0.092	0.603	0.364	14.69
Gadag	0.350	0.123	0.628	3.452	16.36
Bagalkot	0.384	0.130	0.474	0.519	16.89
Shivamogga	0.596	0.088	0.743	0.358	17.58
Mysuru	0.533	0.093	0.537	0.493	17.88
Koppal	0.280	0.169	0.303	0.269	18.61
Ramanagara	0.533	0.092	0.725	0.343	18.83
Tumkur	0.471	0.080	0.466	0.393	18.92
Hassan	0.576	0.069	0.730	0.362	19.42
Davanagere	0.528	0.124	0.575	0.405	20.18
Vijayapura	0.330	0.105	0.617	0.508	20.34
Raichur	0.165	0.150	0.231	0.266	20.79
Ballari	0.354	0.167	0.569	0.350	21.10
Bengaluru Rural	0.603	0.084	0.733	0.280	21.57
Chikkamagaluru	0.627	0.057	0.783	0.380	22.29
Yadgir	0.196	0.110	0.416	0.348	23.28
Chitradurga	0.386	0.115	0.469	0.301	23.45
Bidar	0.430	0.115	0.530	0.569	23.47
Chikkaballapura	0.486	0.105	0.685	0.216	24.90
Kalaburugi	0.407	0.130	0.334	0.466	25.28
Chamarajnagar	0.401	0.105	0.555	0.398	25.42
Kolar	0.543	0.114	0.479	0.346	30.32
Belagaum Division	0.442	0.106	0.593	0.955	13.71
Bengaluru Division	0.564	0.095	0.618	0.359	17.72
Kalaburugi Division	0.305	0.140	0.397	0.378	22.28
Mysuru Division	0.582	0.072	0.682	0.490	15.58

Source: Economics Survey of Karnataka, 2015–16 and Census, 2011.

Udupi, Dakshina Kannada and Dharwad districts have lower proportion of Dalit population, whereas the HDI values of these districts are higher. On the other hand, Kalaburagi, Chamarajnagar, Chikkaballapur, Bidar, Yadgir district have higher Dalit population but their HDI value is very lower comparatively (see Table 2).

Taluk Level HDI and Dalits

HDI of Karnataka has been constructed using the nine indicators from three dimensions of health, education and standard of living. In the following diagrams (Figures 1–4), these dimensional indices and the share of Dalits in each taluk has been presented to see the association. It is found that there is a significant negative association between HDI (and its dimensional indices) and the share of SC population (i.e. Dalits). The correlation coefficient have also been calculated and presented in Appendix-Table 1. It also shows the significant negative association between Dalits and dimensional indices of HDI. It means that higher the SC population, lower is the HDI value of a particular taluk and vice versa. It is clear from this analysis that Dalits have comparatively lower HDI status than that of others. Further, another interesting observation is that among the divisions, the taluks of Kalaburagi division has higher share of SC population and lower status of HDI and its dimensional indices, which can be seen through the diagrams. Among the three dimensional indices of HDI, negative association is very high in educational index followed by health index and standard of living index.

DHDRs 2004 have also constructed GII (Gender Inequality Index) for all the taluks of the state. Gender inequality is found in all the taluks (see Appendix-Table 2 for more details). Further, in Figure 5, GII and share of Dalit population of the 176 taluks have been scattered to see the association between them. It is found that positive association between these two are observed. It means that Dalit women face higher gender discrimination than non-Dalit women.

In this index also, the taluks of Kalaburagi division are in the lower position. Totally, it can be observed that gender inequality is higher in backward taluks in general and SC population of backward taluks in particular.

Figure 1

Scatter Diagram of per cent of SC Population and Standard of Living Index

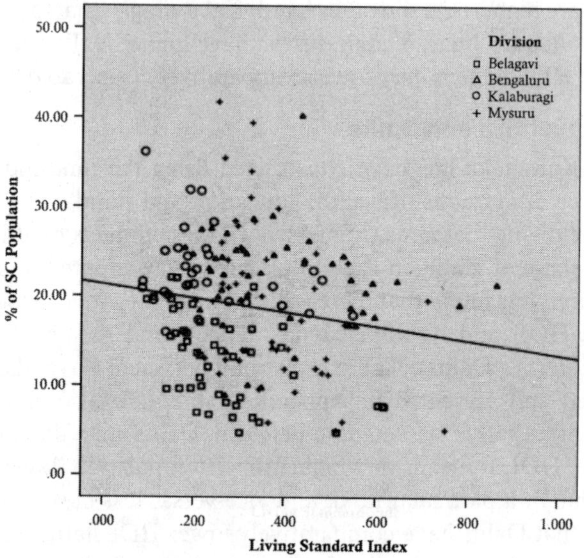

Figure 2

Scatter Diagram of per cent of SC Population and Health Index

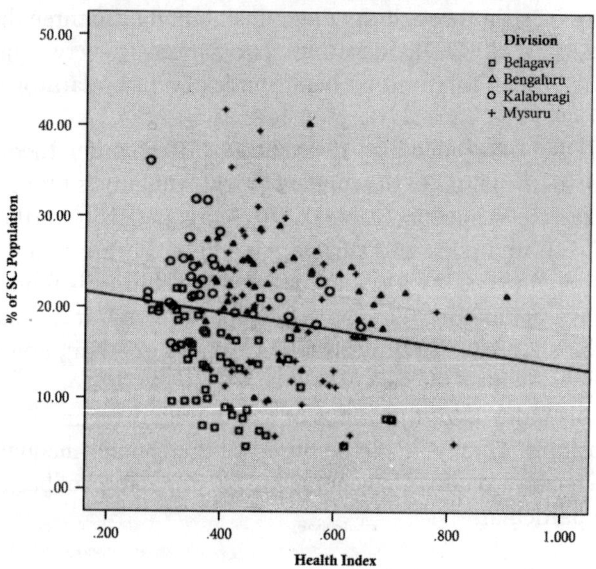

Figure 3

Scatter Diagram of per cent of SC Population and Education Index

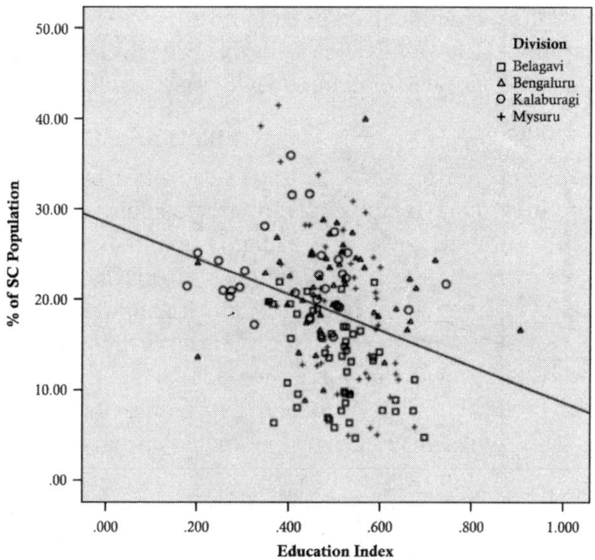

Figure 4

Scatter Diagram of per cent of SC Population and HDI

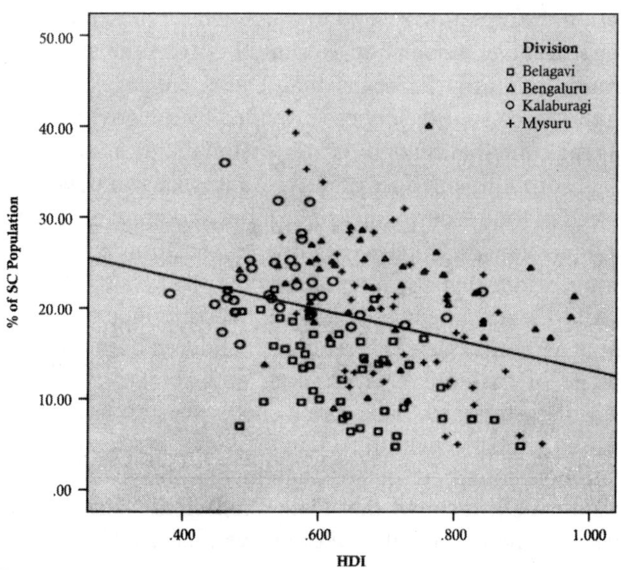

Figure 5

Scatter Diagram of per cent of SC Population and GII

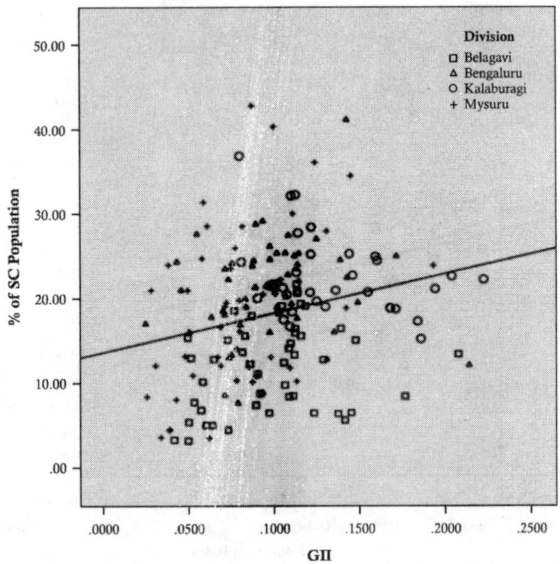

Another very important index namely Food Security Index (FSI) has also been used to see the association with Dalit population. Information related to this has been presented in Figure 6. Strong negative association is found between the share of Dalit population and FSI. It means that Dalits are lagging behind in getting the food security services provided by the government. This index is the combination of three dimensional indices namely, availability, absorption, and accessibility. As it is known that Dalits are in the need of food security measures more as compared to others, in such circumstances, higher negative association between Dalit population and FSI is not acceptable.

Child Development Index is a composite index of indicators like Child Mortality Rate, percentage of children born underweight, percentage of malnourished children and percentage of dropout children mainstreamed. This index shows the proxy indication of the status of next generation Dalits. In this index also, negative association is found. It means that higher the Dalit population, lower is the CDI. It shows that Dalit children are lagging behind in development than non-Dalit children (see Figure 6A).

Figure 6

Scatter Diagram of per cent of SC Population and FSI

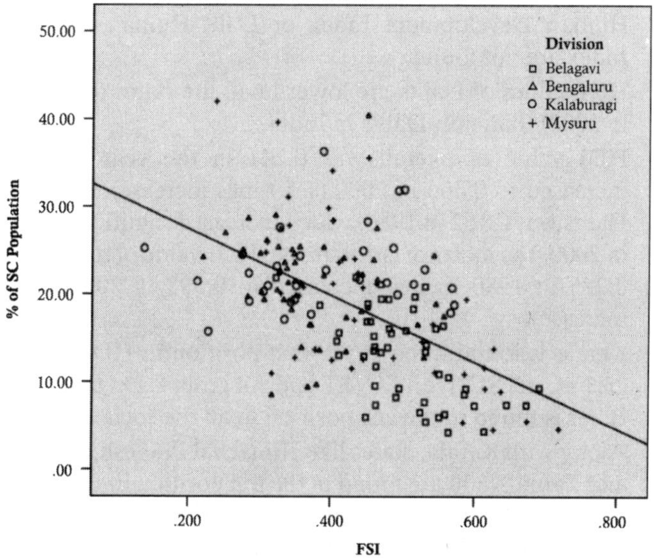

Figure 6A

Scatter Diagram of per cent of SC Population and CDI

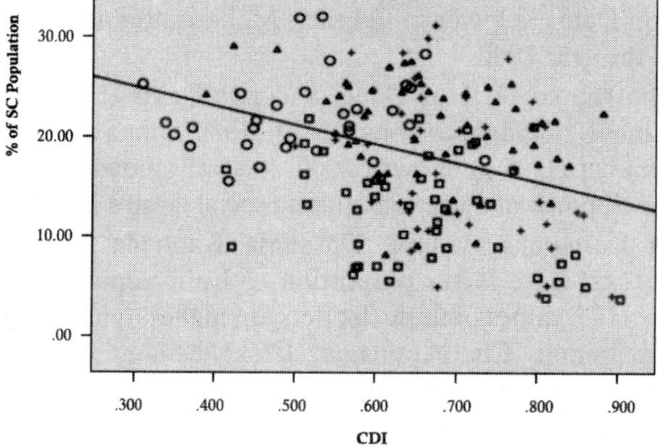

Findings

- Except Thorat (2007), attempts to construct Social Group-wise Human Development Index or Dalit Human Development Index are not found.
- HDI values of Dalits are lower in all the states (except Assam in 2000) than non-Dalits in India.
- HDI value of overall was 0.241 in the year 1980, which increased to 0.366 in 2000 (1.5 times increase). HDI value of Dalits was 0.162 in 1980, which increased significantly to 0.303 in 2000 (the increase is 1.9 times). HDI value of non-Dalits was 0.285 in 1980, which increased to 0.393 in 2000 (1.4 times increase).
- Kerala is found to be in the first position in HDI of all social groups, i.e. SC, Non-SC/ST and All groups. On the other hand Bihar is found in the last position in all the social groups.
- Along with Kerala, states like Himachal Pradesh, Maharashtra and Tamil Nadu are found in the top position in HDI of Dalits, non-Dalits and all social groups. Contrary to this, along with Bihar, states like Uttar Pradesh and Odisha are found in the lower position.
- In the year 1980, out of 16 states, none of the states have registered higher HDI value of Dalits than non-Dalits. But an interesting observation is that in the year 2000 Assam has recorded higher HDI value for Dalits than that of non-Dalits.
- In the year 1980, Assam, Gujarat, Uttar Pradesh and Rajasthan have shown lower gap in HDI values between Dalits and non-Dalits. The gap between HDI value of Dalits and non-Dalits is lower in Gujarat, Maharashtra and Tamil Nadu in the year 2000.
- The gap in HDI of Dalits and non-Dalits (Non-Dalits HDI minus (-) Dalits HDI) was 0.123 in 1980, which decreased significantly to 0.09 in the year 2000. It clearly shows the decrease in developmental disparities among social groups in India.
- In Karnataka, Udupi, Dakshina Kannada and Dharwad, districts have lower proportion of Dalit population, whereas the HDI values of these districts are higher. On the other hand, Kalaburagi, Chamarajnagar, Chikkaballapur, Bidar, Yadgir district have higher Dalit population but their HDI value is comparatively lower.

- With respect to taluk level analysis of Karnataka State, among the three dimensional indices of HDI, negative association is very high in educational index followed by health index and standard of living index.
- Dalit women face higher gender discrimination than non-Dalit women. Gender inequality is higher in backward taluks in general and SC population of backward taluks in particular.
- Dalits are lagging behind in getting the food security services provided by the government as there is a negative association between FSI and share of Dalit population.
- Dalit children are lagging behind in development than that of non-Dalits. It shows that the next generation of Dalits are also underdeveloped than non-Dalits.

Conclusion

Systematic methodology should be developed to construct Social Group-wise Human Development Index starting from village level, so that it will be a great help for researchers and policy makers to take proper measures to decide what and where is the gap in HDI. It also helps a lot for proper coping mechanism.

Increasing public expenditure on social sector, especially for rural area, is very important. Further, it should be made with more inclusive approach. Serious steps should be taken against the bureaucrats who deny or make delay in providing the public social services.

In case of Karnataka, Gulbarga division has found more share of SC population and lower status of HDI. Therefore, the Government of India has made 371 Constitutional Amendment which should be implemented more meaningfully.

References

Corrie, Bruce P. (1995), 'A Human Development Index for the Dalit Child in India', *Social Indicators Research*, Vol. 34, No. 3, pp. 395–409.

GoK (2015), *District Human Development Reports 2014 of All Districts*, Planning Department.

Thorat, Sukhadeo (2007), 'Human Poverty and Socially Disadvantaged Groups in India', *UNDP Discussion Paper 18*, New Delhi.

Appendix

Table 1

Correlation Coefficients of Different Indices with per cent of SC Population of Karnataka

Indices	*Coefficients*
Living Standard Index	–.155*
Health Index	–.284**
Education Index	–.292**
HDI	–.121
GII	.230**
CDI	–.304**
FSI	–.550**

** Correlation is significant at the 0.01 level (2-tailed).

* Correlation is significant at the 0.05 level (2-tailed).

Table 2

Taluk-wise Different Indices and Share of SC Population

District	*Taluks*	*LSI*	*HI*	*EDI*	*HDI*	*GII*	*CDI*	*FSI*	*CTDI*	*SC*
Bagalkot	Badami	0.173	0.584	0.476	0.363	0.1108	0.720	0.473	0.441	14.11
	Bagalkot	0.397	0.778	0.553	0.555	0.1112	0.518	0.549	0.514	16.55
	Bilagi	0.165	0.549	0.450	0.344	0.1019	0.540	0.378	0.432	18.83
	Hungund	0.212	0.548	0.522	0.393	0.1113	0.426	0.444	0.439	17.02
	Jamkhandi	0.245	0.626	0.516	0.430	0.1379	0.763	0.449	0.455	17.04
	Mudhol	0.195	0.647	0.459	0.387	0.0761	0.698	0.445	0.436	19.00
Bellary	Bellary	0.454	0.727	0.443	0.527	0.1046	0.729	0.559	0.544	18.03
	Hadagali	0.175	0.614	0.495	0.376	0.1130	0.547	0.322	0.467	27.61
	H.B. Halli	0.229	0.427	0.504	0.366	0.1592	0.518	0.270	0.471	24.55
	Hospet	0.463	0.280	0.462	0.391	0.2022	0.621	0.386	0.550	22.81
	Kudligi	0.193	0.495	0.521	0.368	0.2206	0.563	0.279	0.474	22.46
	Sandur	0.551	0.369	0.443	0.448	0.1825	0.599	0.366	0.463	17.84
	Siraguppa	0.226	0.537	0.291	0.328	0.1926	0.641	0.471	0.437	21.42
Belgaum	Athani	0.176	0.888	0.467	0.418	0.0490	0.603	0.498	0.415	16.01
	Bailhongal	0.206	0.234	0.483	0.286	0.1402	0.576	0.518	0.460	6.86
	Belgaum	0.621	0.731	0.631	0.659	0.1362	0.579	0.593	0.668	7.58
	Chikodi	0.328	0.826	0.490	0.510	0.0823	0.608	0.539	0.517	16.24
	Gokak	0.212	0.723	0.395	0.393	0.1054	0.635	0.557	0.448	10.77

Cont'd...

...Cont'd

	Hukkeri	0.244	0.799	0.523	0.467	0.0807	0.601	0.526	0.472	14.41
	Khanapur	0.294	0.552	0.512	0.436	0.0963	0.629	0.457	0.500	7.67
	Raibag	0.152	0.755	0.415	0.363	0.0861	0.663	0.508	0.409	18.44
	Ramdurg	0.158	0.596	0.402	0.335	0.1465	0.676	0.478	0.454	15.72
	Saundatti	0.167	0.476	0.418	0.321	0.1752	0.433	0.489	0.433	9.54
Bangalore Rural	Devanahalli	0.504	0.810	0.485	0.583	0.0706	0.741	0.329	0.616	23.62
	Doddaballapur	0.579	0.770	0.463	0.591	0.0823	0.731	0.297	0.613	20.29
	Hoskote	0.594	0.763	0.450	0.589	0.0994	0.708	0.334	0.600	21.37
	Nelamangala	0.648	0.782	0.494	0.630	0.0883	0.796	0.343	0.642	21.59
Bangalore Urban	Anekal	0.870	0.794	0.674	0.775	0.0452	0.785	0.352	0.615	21.27
	Bangalore East	0.529	0.948	0.715	0.711	0.0428	0.706	0.536	0.693	24.43
	Bangalore North	0.787	0.920	0.631	0.770	0.0694	0.762	0.539	0.638	18.96
	Bangalore South	0.599	0.935	0.662	0.718	0.0246	0.792	0.550	0.662	17.58
Bidar	Aurad	0.188	0.765	0.441	0.341	0.1115	0.538	0.495	0.421	31.85
	B. Kalyana	0.197	0.710	0.476	0.405	0.1348	0.570	0.508	0.435	21.26
	Bhalki	0.162	0.546	0.524	0.359	0.1429	0.327	0.480	0.443	25.30
	Bidar	0.394	0.784	0.658	0.588	0.1095	0.532	0.564	0.512	18.89
	H. Bad	0.203	0.716	0.513	0.421	0.1448	0.579	0.523	0.453	22.92
Chamarajnagar	Chamarajanagar	0.273	0.786	0.380	0.434	0.1915	0.654	0.409	0.495	23.99
	Gundlupet	0.240	0.556	0.371	0.368	0.1410	0.507	0.338	0.506	19.30
	Kollegal	0.289	0.705	0.432	0.445	0.0604	0.572	0.396	0.450	28.37

Cont'd...

...Cont'd

	Yelandur	0.265	0.555	0.378	0.382	0.1229	0.790	0.445	0.484	35.40
Chikkaballapura	Bagepalli	0.270	0.590	0.371	0.390	0.1237	0.617	0.246	0.455	26.93
	Chikkaballpura	0.452	0.808	0.514	0.573	0.0968	0.651	0.304	0.551	26.12
	Chintamani	0.376	0.692	0.552	0.524	0.0874	0.632	0.268	0.513	24.52
	Gowribidanur	0.308	0.424	0.444	0.387	0.1702	0.732	0.271	0.501	25.05
	Gudibanda	0.260	0.656	0.377	0.401	0.0748	0.402	0.215	0.503	24.24
	Sidlaghatta	0.347	0.885	0.464	0.522	0.0725	0.868	0.321	0.529	22.47
Chikkamagalore	Chikkamagalur	0.539	0.822	0.596	0.642	0.0741	0.785	0.404	0.642	23.68
	Kadur	0.261	0.945	0.542	0.512	0.0280	0.800	0.396	0.528	21.27
	Koppa	0.465	0.746	0.586	0.588	0.0928	0.699	0.438	0.604	20.82
	Mudigere	0.468	0.560	0.581	0.534	0.0574	0.598	0.303	0.582	24.77
	Narasimharajapura	0.437	0.844	0.592	0.602	0.0680	0.765	0.426	0.627	17.19
	Sringeri	0.401	0.486	0.631	0.497	0.0892	0.711	0.423	0.617	11.75
	Tarikere	0.359	0.905	0.531	0.557	0.0379	0.706	0.426	0.568	24.08
Chitradurga	Challakere	0.235	0.466	0.399	0.352	0.1414	0.592	0.323	0.465	22.66
	Chitradurga	0.443	0.762	0.506	0.555	0.0865	0.680	0.453	0.562	23.95
	Hiriyur	0.291	0.569	0.449	0.420	0.1109	0.569	0.339	0.480	25.07
	Holalkere	0.214	0.638	0.484	0.404	0.1074	0.635	0.323	0.492	27.37
	Hosadurga	0.259	0.499	0.450	0.388	0.1059	0.554	0.319	0.499	20.53
	Molakalmuru	0.251	0.649	0.351	0.385	0.1092	0.578	0.278	0.431	19.78
Dakshina Kannada	Bantwal	0.514	0.820	0.527	0.605	0.0613	0.879	0.620	0.642	4.87

Cont'd...

...*Cont'd*

	Beltangady	0.345	0.870	0.503	0.532	0.0255	0.808	0.608	0.565	9.50
	Mangalore	0.756	0.867	0.591	0.729	0.0336	0.794	0.710	0.736	4.95
	Puttur	0.469	0.799	0.565	0.596	0.0520	0.802	0.607	0.614	11.83
	Sulya	0.409	0.891	0.520	0.574	0.0474	0.794	0.620	0.590	13.97
Davanagere	Channagiri	0.302	0.661	0.510	0.467	0.1134	0.760	0.383	0.551	25.34
	Davanagere	0.543	0.747	0.655	0.643	0.1340	0.616	0.514	0.606	16.64
	Harappanahalli	0.195	0.426	0.478	0.341	0.1376	0.663	0.342	0.449	24.60
	Harihara	0.423	0.550	0.606	0.521	0.2121	0.686	0.523	0.544	12.96
	Honnalli	0.318	0.675	0.517	0.480	0.1021	0.588	0.383	0.530	22.16
	Jaglur	0.177	0.688	0.514	0.397	0.1008	0.654	0.320	0.467	25.36
Dharwad	Dharwad	6.078	0.540	0.602	0.583	0.1440	0.604	0.638	0.623	7.70
	Hubli	0.618	0.593	0.669	0.626	0.1221	0.582	0.665	0.675	7.66
	Kalghatgi	0.206	0.587	0.485	0.388	0.1276	0.641	0.464	0.514	13.56
	Kundgol	0.139	0.720	0.531	0.376	0.1078	0.685	0.581	0.437	9.50
	Navalgund	0.192	0.810	0.520	0.433	0.1102	0.745	0.683	0.481	9.58
Gadag	Gadag	0.394	0.521	0.595	0.496	0.2060	0.671	0.455	0.565	14.19
	Mundargi	0.160	0.206	0.583	0.268	0.1121	0.523	0.317	0.467	21.96
	Nargunad	2.169	0.584	0.518	0.402	0.0911	0.582	0.456	0.480	9.83
	Ron	0.147	0.569	0.521	0.352	0.1086	0.613	0.454	0.503	15.39
	Shirhatti	0.186	0.625	0.511	0.390	0.1124	0.787	0.463	0.462	21.21
Hassan	Alur	0.295	0.274	0.514	0.347	0.1296	0.756	0.335	0.455	27.81

Cont'd...

...Cont'd

	Arasikere	0.319	0.707	0.588	0.510	0.0788	0.646	0.324	0.428	20.15
	Arakagud	0.291	0.864	0.466	0.489	0.0491	0.729	0.457	0.457	21.26
	Belur	0.324	0.839	0.535	0.526	0.0583	0.671	0.333	0.449	31.00
	Channarayapatna	0.255	0.629	0.551	0.446	0.1122	0.772	0.312	0.487	11.19
	Hassan	0.492	0.989	0.630	0.675	0.0305	0.838	0.481	0.542	12.93
Haveri	Byadagi	0.230	0.683	0.524	0.435	0.0895	0.674	0.457	0.530	11.99
	Hanagal	0.183	0.582	0.518	3.814	0.1076	0.567	0.402	0.524	14.82
	Haveri	0.286	0.657	0.533	0.465	0.0852	0.580	0.440	0.536	13.13
	Hirekerur	0.212	0.436	0.581	0.378	0.1048	0.683	0.405	0.536	13.26
	Ranebennur	0.327	0.803	0.582	0.534	0.0641	0.521	0.525	0.553	13.63
	Savanur	0.182	0.612	0.470	0.374	0.0721	0.592	0.405	0.461	15.76
	Shiggaon	0.260	0.874	0.513	0.489	0.0509	0.736	0.454	0.490	13.76
Kalaburugi	Afzalpur	0.140	0.637	0.458	0.344	0.1238	0.501	0.486	0.336	20.05
	Aland	0.133	0.608	0.467	0.336	0.1581	0.642	0.438	0.364	24.99
	Chincholi	0.088	0.516	0.400	0.263	0.0792	0.573	0.382	0.353	36.11
	Chitapur	0.213	0.674	0.403	0.387	0.1090	0.511	0.487	0.405	31.73
	Jewargi	0.482	0.737	0.739	0.641	0.0967	0.461	0.433	0.539	21.78
	Kalaburugi	0.083	0.623	0.411	0.277	0.1065	0.570	0.561	0.361	20.80
	Sedam	0.241	0.633	0.344	0.375	0.1207	0.659	0.444	0.399	28.25
Kodagu	Madikeri	0.497	0.780	0.637	0.627	0.0866	0.664	0.579	0.621	11.12
	Somwarpet	0.533	0.742	0.587	0.614	0.0792	0.672	0.535	0.661	16.72

Cont'd...

...Cont'd

	Virajpet	0.483	0.746	0.572	0.590	0.0773	0.651	0.538	0.602	11.30
Kolar	Bangarpet	0.436	0.719	0.562	0.561	0.1414	0.541	0.444	0.573	40.18
	Kolar	0.442	0.850	0.561	0.584	0.1118	0.543	0.343	0.568	23.61
	Malur	0.404	0.684	0.446	0.498	0.1057	0.566	0.350	0.535	25.40
	Mulbagal	0.373	0.510	0.471	0.447	0.0927	0.434	0.316	0.543	28.93
	Srinivasapur	0.330	0.608	0.500	0.464	0.0886	0.485	2.478	0.510	28.59
Koppal	Gangawati	0.275	0.428	0.503	0.390	0.1667	0.383	0.280	0.435	19.30
	Koppal	0.314	0.616	0.507	0.461	0.1698	0.496	0.338	0.493	19.20
	Kushtagi	0.136	0.349	0.494	0.286	0.1843	0.429	0.223	0.404	15.89
	Yelbarga	0.108	0.402	0.500	0.279	0.1289	0.450	0.343	0.411	19.46
Mandya	Krishnarajpet	0.223	0.809	0.468	0.439	0.0682	0.641	0.344	0.549	12.95
	Maddur	0.307	0.808	0.481	0.492	0.0664	0.631	0.372	0.574	13.88
	Malavalli	0.275	0.806	0.406	0.448	0.0997	0.654	0.355	0.542	20.87
	Mandya	0.383	0.779	0.573	0.555	0.0973	0.597	0.372	0.642	13.87
	Nagamangala	0.269	0.812	0.427	0.453	0.0844	0.697	0.439	0.545	12.77
	Pandavapura	0.300	0.806	0.459	0.481	0.1083	0.845	0.395	0.504	12.68
	Shrirangapattana	0.373	0.810	0.481	0.526	0.0777	0.645	0.520	0.541	14.78
Mysore	Heggadadevanakote	0.251	0.481	0.373	0.356	0.0864	0.588	0.233	0.497	41.73
	Hunsur	0.333	0.756	0.441	0.481	0.0807	0.633	0.395	0.534	28.36
	Krishnarajanagar	0.305	0.566	0.539	0.453	0.1030	0.632	0.431	0.527	22.48
	Mysore	0.716	0.814	0.502	0.664	0.0707	0.592	0.581	0.707	19.51

Cont'd...

...*Cont'd*

	Nanjangud	0.325	0.448	0.460	0.406	0.1438	0.620	0.394	0.515	33.94
	Periapatna	0.259	0.630	0.476	0.427	0.0767	0.647	0.305	0.543	25.93
	T Narasipur	0.327	0.447	0.335	0.366	0.0990	0.610	0.318	0.522	39.41
Raichur	Devadurga	0.084	0.412	0.177	0.183	0.1042	0.354	0.207	0.351	21.55
	Lingasugur	0.178	0.443	0.302	0.288	0.1120	0.485	3.318	0.417	23.25
	Manvi	0.181	0.415	0.255	0.267	0.1538	0.386	0.306	0.381	21.06
	Raichur	0.374	0.359	0.273	0.332	0.1200	0.458	0.345	0.510	21.03
	Sindhanur	0.208	0.261	0.323	0.260	0.1082	0.465	0.329	0.415	17.26
Ramanagara	Channapatna	0.412	0.752	0.435	0.513	0.0793	0.828	0.415	0.550	17.46
	Kanakapura	0.302	0.737	0.394	0.444	0.1009	0.787	0.328	0.543	19.42
	Magadi	0.317	0.805	0.427	0.478	0.1478	0.647	0.345	0.571	19.90
	Ramanagara	0.546	0.831	0.583	0.642	0.0705	0.683	0.445	0.618	18.57
Shimoga	Bhadravati	0.546	0.898	0.519	0.634	0.0946	0.811	0.458	0.662	21.74
	Hosanagara	0.268	0.650	0.433	0.423	0.0780	0.614	0.312	0.494	8.79
	Sagara	0.350	0.808	0.533	0.532	0.0704	0.651	0.362	0.542	9.65
	Shikaripura	0.315	0.445	0.542	0.424	0.0968	0.597	0.295	0.604	24.67
	Shimoga	0.573	0.780	0.592	0.642	0.1124	0.814	0.436	0.682	18.15
	Soraba	0.201	0.599	0.492	0.390	0.0827	0.569	0.301	0.543	19.44
	Thirthahalli	0.319	0.699	0.473	0.473	0.0925	0.719	0.374	0.570	9.92
Tumkur	CN Halli	0.211	0.622	0.466	0.394	0.0627	0.584	0.339	0.492	18.29
	Gubbi	0.262	0.592	0.465	0.416	0.0966	0.650	0.364	0.513	16.61

Cont'd...

...Cont'd

	Koratagere	0.231	0.626	0.346	0.368	0.1072	0.765	0.332	0.542	22.97
	Kunigal	0.315	0.889	0.456	0.503	0.0728	0.807	0.378	0.562	13.78
	Madhugir	0.245	0.473	0.200	0.285	0.1127	0.558	0.411	0.518	24.12
	Pavagada	0.236	0.778	0.534	0.461	0.0544	0.643	0.457	0.474	27.50
	Sira	0.263	0.604	0.660	0.471	0.1133	0.677	0.437	0.520	22.29
	Tiptur	0.374	0.652	0.419	0.468	0.0742	0.692	0.353	0.576	14.08
	Tumkur	0.557	0.807	0.901	0.740	0.0499	0.605	0.366	0.601	16.63
	Turuvekere	0.270	0.611	0.201	0.322	0.1297	0.724	0.415	0.570	13.62
Udupi	Karkala	0.424	0.949	0.619	0.629	0.0424	0.644	0.630	0.554	9.18
	Kundapur	0.366	0.960	0.576	0.587	0.0385	0.675	0.577	0.556	5.71
	Udupi	0.529	0.950	0.672	0.696	0.0386	0.803	6.966	0.610	5.84
Uttara Kannada	Ankola	0.271	0.771	0.416	0.443	0.0567	0.820	0.524	0.525	8.01
	Bhatkal	0.255	0.905	0.631	0.526	0.0527	0.836	0.579	0.499	8.88
	Haliyal	0.303	0.783	0.521	0.498	0.0886	0.668	0.485	0.578	8.55
	Honavar	0.301	0.831	0.543	0.514	0.0493	0.889	0.557	0.520	4.58
	Karwar	0.516	0.948	0.693	0.697	0.0412	0.802	0.607	0.621	4.66
	Kumta	0.286	0.774	0.530	0.489	0.0596	0.817	0.544	0.459	6.29
	Mundgod	0.278	0.661	0.537	0.462	0.1147	0.655	0.475	0.561	16.21
	Siddapur	0.233	0.868	0.486	0.462	0.0496	0.792	0.552	0.450	6.63
	Sirasi	0.421	0.691	0.672	0.580	0.0577	0.673	0.544	0.522	11.13
	Supa	0.331	0.744	0.366	0.448	0.0632	0.619	0.443	0.608	6.29

Cont'd...

...Cont'd

	Yellapur	0.346	0.798	0.497	0.516	0.0723	0.848	0.526	0.575	5.77
Vijayapura	BasavanBagewadi	0.148	0.677	0.377	2.336	0.0992	0.652	0.428	0.375	22.01
	Indi	0.109	0.817	0.354	0.316	0.1146	0.718	0.510	0.353	19.80
	Muddebhihal	0.148	0.405	0.400	0.289	0.1036	0.518	0.464	0.362	19.56
	Sindagi	0.093	0.643	0.363	0.279	0.1172	0.714	0.474	0.286	19.54
	Vijayapura	0.331	0.775	0.437	0.482	0.1127	0.708	0.524	0.442	20.96
Yadgir	Shahapur	0.183	0.618	0.245	0.303	0.0801	0.442	0.350	0.338	24.40
	Shorapur	0.132	0.433	0.270	0.249	0.0895	0.364	0.300	0.323	20.37
	Yadgir	0.224	0.599	0.200	0.300	0.1204	0.637	0.133	0.423	25.26

Source: District Human Development Reports of all Districts of Karnataka, 2014 and Census, 2011

11

Dalit Discourse and Democracy

SUBHANKAR BASU AND SRIKAKOLLI ELIAH

The basic theme of the National Seminar was Dalit situation in India after economic reforms. It was held at the backdrop of the 125th birth anniversary of Dr B.R. Ambedkar. The theme draws the sterling dichotomy when efforts have been made to put facts into perspectives. The towering figure of Dr Ambedkar as the architect of the Constitution stands opposite to his conversion to an egalitarian religion – Buddhism – owing to the discrimination prevalent in Hinduism. His two other identities as an eminent economist and the first Law Minster of India get lost in the whole issue of Dalit discourse.

Way back in 1990s, the economic reforms were inevitably initiated with liberalization, privatization and globalization (LPG) at the backdrop of economic crisis that emerged out of the workings of the planned economy, nationalization of key economic sectors, protection of indigenous market, etc. The basic postulate was to reduce the public (Govt.) control over private sector. Mixed economy, as the structure of Indian economy, remains the same but the control comes down as it was not fruitful in the long run. The competition grew considerably. Herbert Spencer became relevant for his justification of the survival of the fittest. In this competition, the appropriation of wealth took place in the name of the creation of wealth. The rich became richer and the poor became poorer. The economic reforms post-90s have made Dalits more vulnerable in terms of displacement of (land) holdings and habitats. POSCO and Vedanta may be a few examples (*The Hindu*, 11 January 2014; *The Frontline*, 20 November to 3 December 2010).

There is little political reform to deal with this LPG model of economic reforms. The already marginalized Dalits remain vulnerable in the market economy, but got a little more incentive from the state sponsored welfare schemes. In the subsequent generations of economic reforms, Dalits became more vulnerable and remained excluded from what is known as the main stream; the promoters of Indian politics, shaping and sharing of power. Anybody who does not have access to this main stream is vulnerable. Today, the Indian National Congress is vulnerable in national politics. Therefore, Dalit issues are to be understood in the context of politics. The constitutional schemes relied on a sagacious axiom: fair treatment is better than equal treatment. In spite of the Right to Equality guaranteed in Article 14 of the Constitution, SCs and STs got special reference in the Fifth Schedule (Art. 244) of the Constitution. In the name of reservation, equal treatment is denied to Dalits.

The word Dalit comes with a picture of plight. Let us understand who constitute Dalits? The word 'Dalit' reflects more on the downtrodden status of down to earth people in the public space. The economic backwardness over generations will invariably lead to social backwardness in India as there is no social security in place. With the fast track economic reforms, the social exclusion pushes a large number to the downtrodden segment. This segment constitutes a mixed lot. Even among Christians and Muslims, there are Dalits. In the framework of Hindu social hierarchy, those who do not belong to any of the four *Varnas* may also be called Dalits or untouchables. A few lines of the Indian Institute of Dalit Studies (IIDS) Report 2008–09, can make things little more clear. 'Established in 2003, Indian Institute of Dalit Studies (IIDS) is amongst the first research organizations in India to focus exclusively on development concerns of the marginalized groups and socially excluded communities. Over the last six years, IIDS has carried out several studies on different aspects of social exclusion and discrimination of the historically marginalized social groups, such as, Scheduled Castes, Scheduled Tribes and Religious minorities in India and other parts of the Subcontinent.' However, there are two separate commissions – one for SC and another for ST. The erstwhile National Commission for Scheduled Castes and Scheduled Tribes has been replaced by National Commission for Scheduled Castes and, National Commission for Scheduled Tribes by the 89th Constitution Amendment Act, 2003 (w.e.f. 19 February 2004). The technical issue that SCs do not belong to STs may be true, but both are historically backward and downtrodden. Again, the operational definition of being downtrodden or backward will not work as there are laws as to who constitute the SC, ST, OBC, and general category. The issue of reservation is specifically defined in law. The poor Brahmins, equally downtrodden, do not come under the scheme of reservation. All Dalits are not downtrodden; all downtrodden people are not Dalits. The rule of law being paramount, it is the government that defines Dalit since the issue is linked to reservation. A person who does not come under the scheme of reservation is otherwise not a Dalit in law. The reservation for SC, ST, and OBC has gone up to 50 per cent and it cannot go beyond 50 per cent as per the Supreme Court Judgment. This can be interpreted from two aspects. The social exclusion is growing, and therefore, the Supreme Court has increased reservation up to 50 per cent. As per the 2011 Census, SCs, STs form 25 per cent of the population (*The Indian Express*, 1 May 2013). States such as Rajasthan, Haryana and Gujarat have faced the Gurjjar, Jat, and Patidar movements in the recent past. There is a growing demand for reservations and an equally growing demand for being Dalits.

Reservation holds something more than an opportunity of being equitable. Therefore, there is a growing demand for reservation, and no political party is in a position to put an end to this system made available in the Constitution for the first 10 years from the commencement of the Constitution. Though reservation does not necessarily signify only Dalit, but it has not yet been extended to the poor backward Brahmins who are equally downtrodden. In Article 16(4), the term 'backward classes' is used as a generic term and comprises various categories of backward classes, viz., Scheduled Castes, Scheduled Tribes, Other Backward Classes, De-notified Communities (Vimukta Jatiyan) and Nomadic/ Semi-nomadic communities. The OBC stands for other backward class and not castes. The concept of class is of economic and not social nature like castes. This duality is the reality – socio-economic exclusion on one side and inclusion to (Dalit) vote banks on the other. The Supreme Court was critical of the Jat quota in its judgment stating that competitive backwardness cannot be the ground for Jat quota. The Supreme Court observed that historical perception, i.e. caste, is not good enough for reservation (http://scroll.in/article/714288). The question is whether reservation system is the solution for what the Dalits are known for. Reservation, no doubt, has created a creamy layer among Dalits, and that, in turn, demands for competitive backwardness. There has been a structural transformation of the public sphere (Habermas, 1989) since Mandal Commission (1979–80) report came to the public domain. Are the creamy layers among Daits discriminated? Does Ram Vilas Paswan, the Union Minster of Food and Public Distribution, meet social discrimination in his home state Bihar where the caste discrimination is well known? The answer may be negative, but Brahmins would not dare to boycott him. Jeetan Ram Manjhi, the Ex-CM of Bihar, once alleged that a temple in Madhubani was washed after his visit. He also added that people behind the incident, however, do not hesitate to touch his feet to seek 'personal favours' (*The Indian Express*, 29 September 2014). One thing appears to be clear that among Dalits, the majority are downtrodden and discriminated. There is sufficient literature on it. Quoting the National Crime Records Bureau, the Home Ministry informed the Rajya Sabha that over 47,000 cases of atrocities against the Scheduled Castes were registered in 2014, up from 39,000 cases the previous year (http://www.ndtv.com).

It provides us with a question as to how variables (downtrodden and discrimination) relate and respond to. Can we ignore discrimination among Dalits? Is the downtrodden upper caste community not discriminated? The basic question is whether discrimination serves the purpose of the society being functional. How can the social structure be in favour of discrimination when it does not serve the purpose? What is about the modernization of Indian tradition? Does the caste system as well as corresponding discrimination suggest the failure of the modernization of tradition? A statement of Leninmay sums up the issue clearly: 'The supporters of reforms and improvements will always be fooled by the defenders of the old, as long as they will not realize that every old institution, however absurd and rotten it may appear, is kept in being by the forces of one or other of the ruling classes' (http://revcom.us/avakian/science/01ba-science...revolution-foolish-victims-of-deceipt-en.html.).

Historically speaking, India has never ever gone through the process of enlightenment like the way the West passed through. Even authority remains devoid of rationality, and this makes the social institutions – be it caste, religion, or patriarchy – confronting with the demands of modernity. Even the West confronted with the dialectics of enlightenment failed to fulfil the promises made. Thesis develops anti-thesis in the due process of rationalization. At the end, Hegel's dialectics came to an end in the Prussian state of Marx's dialectics in communism. Democracy demands some sort of rationality. We have opted not democracy but electoral politics. One can represent a constituency even with minimum percentage of votes polled. In a multiparty electoral politics, Dalits are the vote banks. The BJP has to honour Ambedkar with ₹ 99 crore memorial (*The Hindu*, 30 May 2015). The Party President takes lunch in a Dalit family in UP (http://scroll.in/article/print/809217). Moreover, Dalits have their own political party (BSP). Therefore, there is a constant demand for Dalit identity and consolidation of vote banks. Amidst Dalit discrimination, the matter of disproportionate assets by some of the BSP leaders draws more sociological imagination.

The Dalit issue needs critical appreciation from the postmodern and post-structural perspectives. The whole issue needs deconstruction. What modernity stratified in terms of functional pre-requisite, the postmodernity justifies that in terms of cultural identity/diversity. The legacy may come from UNESCO's Universal Declaration on Cultural Diversity. The basic question is whether Dalits are proud of their culture? The answer may be affirmative. Let this question be asked differently? Are Dalits proud of being Dalits? The answer, in all likelihood, is negative. Does it suggest that the Dalit discourse is based on structuralism? Can structuralism deny the basic structure of society? There is no single answer to these questions. The basic contention lies in the text and texture of social discourse. Social Science is not an experimental science in search of laws, but an interpretative science in search of meaning (Geertz, 1973). Moreover, Social Science has a cognitive purpose for an equitable social order.

Construction of Self

The construction of self is made either on three probable structures: 'I am what I am' or 'I am what I think you think I am' or 'I am not what you think I am'. There are two classes – one is the defining class and another is the defined class. Going by the literature available, it would not be wrong to say that Dalit in India is the defined class. However, there are exceptions. Being denied access to water, a Dalit man digs a well in Maharashtra village (*The Hindu*, 9 May 2016). One is poor not necessarily because of being a Dalit while the other is rich, not necessarily because of being a Brahmin. However, one is Dalit by birth and so is the Brahmin. This is not just the domain of society, it is the domain of law too. A Dalit is Dalit by birth and by law in spite of 'We, the People of India, …' made in the Preamble to the Constitution of India. The reservation, over decades has offered Dalits some jobs, but at the same time, it has robbed them of their being equal. They are less equal than others. The duty of the state (reservation to Dalits) for the first ten years has, over time, become the rights of Dalits to be 'differently' treated with state amnesty. The so-called Dalit movement by umbrella organizations in the name of Dr Ambedkar has got Dalits consolidated, but got trapped in the vote bank politics. Mayawati has become the Dalit cult. Such is the power of discourse. Can she be the redeemer? Discourse, however, is not free from hegemony. It is 'From Harijan to Bahujan: Dalit Politics in Search for an Identity' (Mondal, 2014; Bandyopadhyay, 2000). In every society, there are some charismatic figures [for more details, read Barnes (1978)].

Every election is an acid test for democracy. The last Bihar election is not an exception. What is to be critical is the deliberate efforts of political parties to debilitate democracy. The victory of Lalu Prasad Jadav, his language, his body language, the caste equation, the backwardness – all that he stands for, have been voted to power. In such a situation, how can it help democracy to make India modern? How can democracy eradicate caste inequality and discrimination and the backwardness of Bihar? Reservation on ascribed status is not the long-term solution for caste discrimination and inequality. Bihar must not be dragged to backwardness because of its leaders being backward. This is the dark side of democracy.

Let us take the matter simply. Equal treatment is guaranteed in the Article 14. In addition, there are ample Constitutional and statutory provisions for the protection of Dalits. If so, how can there be discrimination and atrocity against Dalits? The state today is powerful enough to enter into someone's bedroom with its instrument called Domestic Violence Act, 2005. Can Dalit discrimination and atrocity be understood as the failure of the state and the victory of Brahminical society? If so, are Brahmins above laws? The answer lies in how we address the issue. Let us try to understand a dilemma of discourse on the population of India. The word 'population' invariably comes with another word 'explosion'. Who are we going to call being extra or unwanted? Population is human resource with knowledge, skill and character. Population can be an asset or liability with or without education. This is, however, not the right structure of discourse. The governments still rely more on totalitarian sterilization and Dalits are the prime targets (*The Indian Express*, 25 November 2014; *The Hindu*, 11 November 2014). Dalits do not define discourse either on national televisions or on social media. An African proverb goes like this: So long lions will not have their own historians, the story of hunting will always appreciate the hunter. The Dalits have to have their own historian to set the text and texture of discourse.

The Working of Discourse

While refusing to say *'Bharat Mata Ki Jay'*, the antagonists uttered it more than once in public to register protest. In the same way, the BJP leaders kept uttering *'Bharat Tere Tukde Honge. Insha Allah Insha Allah'*, while condemning it. Interestingly, we utter in protest and speak in praise. What is not supposed to be said is vociferously uttered to register protest. The discourse itself creates space to justify the unjust. This is the power of discourse. Dalits may not be so much downtrodden or untouchable except in literature. The social life consists of activities promoted by discourses. Foucault's argument is that even identity is constituted by discourse. People are who they are, they think what they think, know what they know, say what they say and do what they do because of discourses. So, for Foucault, discursive practices are at the root of social life. The exercise of power through discourse is everywhere (Jones, 2005: pp. 145–48). Let us take the Sapir-Whorf hypothesis into account. The common sense idea that words are merely labels that people attach to things is wrong. Language has embedded within it the ways of looking at the world. Thus, thinking and perception are not only expressed through language but are also shaped by language. When we learn a language, we learn not only words but also particular ways of thinking and perceiving (Henslin, 1997: pp. 44–45). Kuhn (1962) argues that even the production of scientific knowledge is influenced by fashion and trend, by politics and the exercise of power and by choices about what should be known about and what not. Scientific knowledge is produced within a dominant paradigm that decides what is to be done and how it is to be done. Scientists belong to one of the traditions/paradigms. Scientific knowledge for relativists is not powerful because it is true; it is true because it is powerful (Jones, 2005: p. 148).

'Rights can never be higher than the economic structures of society and its cultural development conditioned thereby.' Drawing similar analogy from Marx (1875/1970), it can be said that discourse can never be higher than the hegemony of the ruling ideology. In the Indian Constitution, rights are protected from public authorities but not guaranteed to the people. The right to life does not guarantee food, shelter and medicine. Indian politics is growing in-between the sacred and secular – a potent dichotomy in Indian politics. The caste system needs to be understood from this perspective. What (caste reservation) was a blessing in 1950s has become a burden over the years. A vast lot remains to be the victims of caste politics simply because it is imposed on them in spite of the right to equality being guaranteed.

There are, no doubt, protests against Dalit atrocities by media and by the so-called elites and intellectuals. However, the main focus is on the discrimination by upper castes. Yet, people are not critical of caste system. Those who honestly deliver lectures on Ambedkarin public forum do not forget to recollect on what Ambedkar had to say on the annihilation of caste, but at the same time, they prefer to be in the same system. A glance of the same is available in the matrimonial advertisements of middle class in newspapers. It is the middle class dilemma to be both modern in public life and traditional in private life. The discourse is meticulously silent on the ruling hegemony and the role of state apparatus. The middle class does not want to offend the state. The discourse is not about the empowerment of Dalits, but their plights that evokes empathy and amnesty to downtrodden at the receiving end. It is not always true that Brahmins are killers of Dalits as Dalits themselves are busy in fighting. Moreover, hierarchy among Dalits is undeniable. It is the space, the political space and the accessibility to it that defines vulnerability.

It is the irony of Dalit history that Dalits have picked up the ascribed status of Dr Ambedkar, giving up his achieved status which could have, otherwise, acted as a social force for their social uplift more equal to the so-called upper caste. The upper caste today is not silent on the achieved status of Ambedkar, but they do not necessarily link it to his ascribed status in order to keep Dalits at bay. Will the proliferation of studies on Ambedkar in several universities, including foreign universities, help dismantle the caste system and/or make Dalit voice heard louder which could again help consolidate Dalit vote bank? Does the solution of this complex issue lie in dismantling the caste system or in dignifying Dalit which, in turn will provide opportunities to remain Dalits? It is interesting to point out that the last public lecture of Srinivas was 'Obituary on Caste as a System', delivered on 7th October 1999 at the National Institute of Advanced Studies, Bangalore (Menon, 1999). Is there any sociologist today to come forward to deliver a lecture on the obituary of the Dalit system? His study on 'Sanskritization' categorically suggests the upward mobility of lower strata. They are in need of a different discourse, not of amnesty or charity of the state, but of dignity and self-determination to the very cause of justice – social, economic and political as envisaged in the Preamble to the Constitution, wherein everybody is the co-author of the Constitution. Why should Dalits be treated with charitable discourse? More importantly, what would happen to the caste identity when the digital (biometric) identity becomes the reality?

There are social movements (Shah, 1990) including the Dalit movements, but there is no social reform movement under the aegis of the elite upper castes in spite of the world-view of humanity, human dignity, human rights, etc. The (registered) crimes committed against Dalits can give a pen picture of the cleavage existing in the society in spite of laws like Untouchability Offence Act, 1955, Prevention of Atrocity Act, 1989, etc. If the SC/ST candidates cannot get elected even in their own tribal majority constituencies without reservation of seats, what does this really suggest? Even in reserved seats in Puducherry, the non-Dalit castes use their dominance to determine the candidates (*The Hindu*, 13 May 2016). In Bengal, there are about 50,000 odd schools being run by the RSS in Bengal, which is at the heart of a raging debate in Keshiyari seat, reserved for Scheduled Tribes (*The Indian Express*, 8 April 2016).

The tribes will remain tribes not because their remote ancestors lived on forest resources, but because they are born to a caste under the constitutional scheme made to protect their backwardness. It cannot be understood in terms of welfare as it is promoting social inequality and discrimination. Ours is a stratified society. The dispensation of justice in all likelihood will remain stratified. The equality before law is equality within the stratification. There is no reference to the right to justice as a fundamental right. It is left to the mercy of the state under the Directive Principles of State Policy (39A). The difference between playing with democracy and playing democratically seems to have created anomie in the duality of structure, both constraining and enabling social actors to structuration in the dichotomous pattern variables. The fact is that the gap between pattern variables and functional imperatives is inherent in any given society with structural and cultural plurality.

The basic structure of the Left ideological discourse remains to be 'no caste, no capitalism' but dictatorship of the proletariat. The dialectics of polarity between the bourgeois and proletariat that Marx argued as the epicentre of revolution, is no more existent. The Indian communists find 'To a large extent, the most exploited classes in our society constitute the most socially oppressed castes. And, to that extent, the struggle against class exploitation and the struggle against social oppression complement each other' (Yechury, 1977). Bengal's ruling elite have always been drawn from the state's upper castes. Brahmins in Bengal form just two per cent of the state's population, but they have held most of the important portfolios in successive regimes' (*The Times of India*, 9 February 2013). The Left heavily suffered from the dilution of dialectics. Gail Omvedt has shown in her book, *Dalits and the Democratic Revolution*, that the Brahman-bourgeois Congress had been appropriating Dalit politics during the last phase of colonial rule, and this was weakening Ambedkar's political base (Omvedt, 1994: p. 304). The situation is not different today. Brahmin vote helps the BSP party of low caste to win in India (*The New York Times*, 12 May 2007). This time, Mayawati has chosen a Brahmin and a Dalit for the Rajya Sabha elections held recently. The Newton-Oweiss Law in Social Sciences is that every action has a reaction, not necessarily opposite in direction and not necessarily equal in force, and herein lies the power of discourse.

Some Recommendations

These recommendations may help the discourse to be different. One such recommendation is the liquidation of the ascribed status and accordingly reservations. The introduction of the Uniform Civil Code may streamline the fragmented groups. The Social Security

System is a must for vulnerable who can't afford to help themselves survive in the market economy. They will surrender to the state, if need be, for immediate rehabilitation and then will get back to normal social life. India is unique in terms of unity in diversity, but the government is to make sure that such diversity must not be the source of disparity and discrimination. There should be a discourse on democratic social reforms for a just and equable society.

References

Bandyopadhyay, Sekhar (2000), 'Transfer of Power and the Crisis of Dalit Politics in India, 1945–47', *Modern Asian Studies*, Vol. 34, No. 4, pp. 893–942.

Barnes, Douglas F. (1978), 'Charisma and Religious Leadership: An Historical Analysis', *Journal for the Scientific Study of Religion*, Vol. 17, No. 1, pp. 1–18.

Bidwai, Praful (2010), 'The Posco Question', *Frontline*, Vol. 27, No. 24, November 20–December 3.

Geertz, Clifford (1973), *The Interpretation of Cultures*, New York: Basic Books.

Habermas, J. (1989), *The Structural Transformation of the Public Sphere*, Cambridge: Polity Press.

Henslin, James M. (1997), *Essentials of Sociology*, Boston: Allyn and Bacon.

Jones, Pip (2005), *Introducing Social Theory*, Cambridge: Polity.

Kuhn, Thomas (1962), *The Structure of Scientific Revolutions*, Chicago: University of Chicago Press.

Marx, Karl (1875/1970), 'Critique of the Gotha Programme', in Marx/Engels, *Selected Works*, Vol. 3, Moscow: Progress Publishers, pp. 13–30.

Menon, Parvathi (1999), 'A Scholar Remembered', *Frontline*, Vol. 16, No. 26, pp. 11–24.

Mondal, Anindita (2014), 'From Harijan to Bahujan: Dalit Politics in Search for an Identity', *European Academic Research*, Vol. 2, No. 7.

Omvedt, Gail (1994), *Dalits and the Democratic Revolution: Dr Ambedkar and the Dalit Movement in Colonial India*, New Delhi: Sage Publications.

Shah, Ghanshyam (1990), *Social Movements in India: A Review of Literature*, New Delhi: Sage.

The Frontline, 20 November to 3 December 2010.

The Hindu, 11 January 2014.

The Hindu, 11 November 2014.

The Hindu, 30 May 2015.

The Hindu, 31 March 2016.

The Hindu, 9 May 2016.

The Hindu, 13 May 2016.

The Indian Express, 1 May 2013.

The Indian Express, 29 September 2014.

The Indian Express, 25 November 2014.

The Indian Express, 8 April 2016.

The New York Times, 12 May 2007.

The Times of India, 9 February 2013.

Yechury, Sitaram (1977), 'Caste and Class in Indian Politics Today', P. Sundarayya Memorial Lecture.

Web References

http://revcom.us/avakian/science/01ba-science...revolution-foolish-victims-of-deceipt-en.html.

http://scroll.in/article/714288

http://scroll.in/article/print/809217

http://ww.ndtv.com

12

Bonded Labour and its Implications

Sociological Reflections of a Mahadalit Community in Bihar

VINOD KUMAR YADAV

A Brief View on Dalits

The traditional society in India, particularly the Hindu society, was constituted of numerous castes and subcastes functioning within the wider frame of *varnas*. The caste system was, in principle, rigid and no person belonging to certain caste was allowed to accept membership of the other castes. Ritual and social distances were observed strictly, through taboos on pollutary interactions, and restrictions on inter-dining and intermarrying.[1] However, there were some channels built on the system, especially in the forms of the *jajmani* (patron-client) relations and the pursuits of occupations other than the caste specific ones, through which members of all castes were, in a way, related to one another. Thus, the system maintained an independence of castes through ritual obligations and through performance of roles assigned and sometime unassigned to them.[2]

A person's caste status vis-à-vis his/her rank was determined by his/her birth in the caste and by its place in ritual hierarchy, though the other factors also, like economic and political power, added substantiality to his/her esteem. But, according to Dumont, both status and power were separated in their functions in the caste system even in early periods, and power was subordinate to status.[3] Thus, a person having more power had inferior ritual and social status in the caste hierarchy if he belonged to a lower caste.

Contrary to the view mentioned above, there are some historians, sociologists and social anthropologists[4] who have argued that one or the other type of flexibility existed in the caste system even during the early periods. Theoretically, there were only obvious means of improving status. One was by opting out of the society and become an ascetic. The other was by ensuring rebirth in a higher status (caste) in one's next life.[5] The caste system was found to have inbuilt mechanism for social mobility, whereby a caste which improved its secular position sought to consolidate this gain by restoring to the process of Sanskritization or cultural change in the direction of high, and in particular, 'twice born' caste.[6]

Untouchability is one of the unique features of the Indian society, particularly attached to Dalits. Those castes within the orbit of the Hindu religion which were treated as untouchables were listed in a schedule in 1936 by the British Government[7] for the purpose of giving these castes some concessions because of their disadvantageous position in the social hierarchy. They came to be known as Scheduled Castes, and were called 'Harijan' by Gandhiji.[8] These groups in the course of time, during the nineteen seventies called themselves Dalits. 'Dalit Panthers', a militant organization founded by two writers, Namdeo Dhasal and Raja Dhale in April 1972,[9] already famous for its celebration of 'Black Independence Day' like the American movements. Dalit Panther and Dalit School of literature represent a new level of pride, militancy and sophisticated creativity. The Marathi word Dalit, like the word Black, was chosen by the group itself and is used proudly. Dalit implies those who have been broken, ground down by those above them in a deliberate and active way. There is in the word itself an inherent denial of pollution, karma and justified caste hierarchy.[10] The clearest definition of Dalits was seen in a letter written to Eleanor Zelliot by a Marathi Professor Gangadhar Pantawane. He writes, 'to me, Dalit is not a caste. He is a man exploited by the social and economic traditions of this country ... he does not believe in God, rebirths, soul, holy books, teaching separatism, fate and heaven because they have made him a slave. He does not believe in humanism. Dalit is a symbol of change and revolution'. Recently, Bhopal Declaration (2002), refers that the term 'Dalit in general encompasses the communities known as untouchables, Scheduled Castes and the tribes who are officially treated Scheduled Tribes'.[11]

In the question of who is a Dalit, The Dalit Panther manifesto says that members of Scheduled Castes and Tribes, neo-Buddhists, the working people, the landless and poor peasants, women and all those who are being exploited politically, economically and in the name of religion are Dalits.[12] The key here is a radical rejection of the religious legitimization of poverty and untouchability of those who have suffered from either.[13] The Indian untouchable, though increasingly alienated from the caste Hindu, continues to share the civilizational structure that marginalizes a section of Indian population for many centuries. As contemporary untouchables stake claim for social improvement, their dissatisfaction mounts alongside those of the caste Hindus. This is because the democratic promise of 'free and fair play' clashes with the traditional concept of Karma-Dharma, of 'cosmic fair play'. Hence, whatever the untouchables gain threatens the established notions of caste privilege and justice.[14]

Caste system in India has legitimized the dehumanization of a large section of society known differently as Chandal, Pariah, Harijan, etc. in various parts of the country. Max Weber identified Pariah groups more or less with guest residents and defined them 'as underprivileged social groups who, though their occupations were economically indispensable for their host societies were nevertheless treated as "impure" and consequently ritually avoided. For this reason, they were obliged to live as unsteady wanderers, or as people forcibly restricted to settling only on the fringe of the cities, towns and villages. Often they were aliens who were refused admittance into a closely knitted society'.[15] These Pariah groups are treated as inferior and devoid of human rights as they are outsiders, aliens of different race and culture, often they are regarded as less than human. They live on the fringes of society, often excluded from social contact with its members though their services are highly valuable and often necessary for the survival of the host society.[16]

Despite minor similarities among these heterogeneous communities, the fundamental uniting feature is their segregation as 'untouchables' and religious legitimacy accorded to their servile status. They are now recognized under a generic term 'Dalit' – an embodiment of a new consciousness along with an inherent desire to rebel against the exploitative structure as a whole. It should be made clear at the outset that the term 'Scheduled Caste' is primarily an administrative category with all-India applicability. At the local level, there exist numerous castes, each with a strong sense of its own identity and separateness from others. Consequently, its endeavour to establish a new social system which would restore dignity and human rights to Dalits necessitated the growth of consciousness by constructing a collective identity.[17]

The Perspective on Dalit Movements

However, studies of successful or even partially successful Dalit movements may broadly be divided into three categories. In the first category those studies have made passing reference to few Dalit movements in their analysis of social structures and on going process of change either in a village or in the caste system or, for that matter, the backward class movements in certain regions, which have exclusively focussed on individual Dalit movements.[18] While some studies have provided an overview of Dalit movements organized over a period of time, others have tried to analyse their forms and styles.[19]

Since the last few decades of previous century, Dalit movements have addressed prime issues like untouchability and related social disabilities of Dalit emanated from Hindu religion and its caste system, their concern for sharing political power and privileges, gaining self-respect and dignified social identity, their liberation from socio-economic exploitation and bondage. Against untouchabilty and related social disabilities within the Hindu religion, they organized a number of religious movements leading to a withdrawal from Brahmin dominated Hinduism and self-organizing themselves. Some of their religious movements studied by different scholars are the Izhava movement in Kerala,[20] the Satnami movement in Madhya Pradesh,[21] the Adi-Dharm movement in Punjab,[22] the Adi-Hindu movement in Uttar Pradesh[23] and so on.

Dalits in Maharashtra, since the early nineteen seventies and later in other states, have realized that the established literature written by Hindu literature is primarily anti-Dalits in its glorifying the Hindu culture and social system alongwith portraying their negative image in it. In response they started writing their own literature – popularly known as Dalit literature, which is accepted as the Dalit literature movement,[24] attacking the caste system and socio-economic exploitation of Dalits and also asserting their self-respect and dignified social identity. Besides, they also organized separate movements for gaining self-respect and dignified social identity, both within and outside the Hindu religion in north India, especially in the Agra region of Uttar Pradesh.[25] Since Dalits have suffered more from socio-economic exploitation and bondage, especially in rural areas, they had organized a couple of successful movements even in the past for their social and economic liberation.

At least two of them, which have drawn attention of social scientists, need to addressed here – one is the Bairwa movement organized in the adjoining areas of Rajasthan and Madhya Pradesh during 1943–56[26] and the other is the land grab movement of 1970 – grabbing the benami or government's barren land – organized in the Basti district of eastern Uttar Pradesh.[27]

Government Measures for Scheduled Castes

In the above-mentioned situation of numerous religious and social disabilities of untouchable castes and occurrences of both the recurrent and patterned changes in the past in the country, it is difficult to ascertain the number of mobile persons from amongst these castes and the degree to which they had adopted changes, especially before independence. Yet one can agree with Moore's statement, 'One may even hesitate to claim that their relation to their employers changed fundamentally during British period'.[28] Ambedkar also blamed the British government for adopting a policy of non-interference in the indigenous traditions and beliefs of Indian people. This indirectly supported the dominance of upper castes and thereby, the retention of the caste system. Thus, British rule in India could not remove social and religious disabilities of untouchables as they, by and large, could not rise from their position of the earlier times.

Several state governments were committed measures of 'protection', to end inhumane practices against lower castes. Besides that powers were delegated for dealing with offenders to the local government. They passed a series of laws throwing open public spaces and prohibiting all restrictions on worship for scheduled castes in state-controlled temples. The Caste Disability Removal Act was passed at the national level as early as 1850.

In spite of all such legislative measures no significant change occurred among scheduled castes because, there was lack of uniformity in laws at the national level and implementation of these laws was slack and faulty. Similar was the case with efforts made by various voluntary associations though the dynamic leadership of Mahatma Gandhi provided an ease to what he called Harijans.

After independence, more systematic attempts have been made by the government to deal with the problems of scheduled castes. They have been provided with special rights. India has one of the best Constitutions in the world with provisions and laws for the protection and development of Dalits. Some of them are:

- Bonded Labour Abolition Act, 1976.
- The Child Labour (Prohibition and Regulation) Act 1986.
- Scheduled Castes and Scheduled Tribes (Prevention of Atrocity) Act, 1989, and Rules, 1995.
- The Employment of Manual Scavengers and Construction of Day Latrines (Prohibition) Act, 1993.
- Reservation of 22.5 per cent in Education and Jobs for SCs/STs, and
- Reserved seats in the Local, State and Federal Parliament, and so on.

Background of the Community

The Musahars are a group of people living in India, mainly in the states of Bihar, Jharkhand, West Bengal, Assam and Uttar Pradesh. They are also found in adjoining Nepal. They form the lowest strata of the Scheduled Castes category. Dalits in Bihar constitute 14.51 per cent of the total population of the State comprising 23 caste groups.[29] The different socio-economic and development indices available on Dalits in India show that even in an independent India, their situation has not improved, and they continue to suffer from manifold forms of oppression and discriminations. The plights of Dalits in Bihar is much worse than that of their brothers and sisters elsewhere in the country.

Coming to Musahars in particular, they are among the five major groups in Bihar today – Chamars (31.24), Dusadhs (30.86), Musahars (16.19), Dhobis (4.96) and Pasis (5.45%). These five groups together form 79.78 per cent of the total Dalit population of Bihar.[30] Except Musahars, all the four groups have made considerable development economically, educationally and politically since India attained independence. But Musahars have remained underdeveloped and is going backward as per development indices. Since Musahars have been categorized into so-called low caste Hindus for about two centuries,[31] unlike tribal communities, they have lost most of their indigenous traditions of subsistence and culture. They are considered a group of dispersed people who remain on the periphery in spite of selling their human labour for the maintenance and development of mainstream society.

The Rajwars and Musahars of eastern Uttar Pradesh and Bihar belong to the same category.[32] Their features clearly betray their aboriginal descent. The Rajwars (1,96, 307 in 1961) who have now taken to field cultivation are slightly higher social rank than Musahars, and even employ degraded Brahmins for their religious functions. They have largely retained their original social organization. At present they are mainly field labourers and are of low caste, though some have acquired small holdings as tenants and since the abolition of landlordism, as owners. According to their own traditions they are related to Musahars.

It is still under dispute whether Musahars (11,98,517 in 1961) are descendent from the Mundas through the Bhuiyas or from Dravida-speaking tribes through Cheros. But they are undoubtedly of aboriginal stock. This is proved not only by their physical appearance, but also by their social organization and their religion.[33]

Musahars, like many other similar castes, are divided into a settled and Hinduised and a nomadic section. They derive their name from a curious association with the field rat.[34] They are supposed to possess a hereditary instinct for locating underground burrows and grain catches of these animals. After each harvest they drive rats from their homes and take a portion of their grain. But they do not kill rats and take care to leave them sufficient grain to survive until the next harvest. The relationship is thus symbiotic.

Though Musahars do not observe ordinary Hindu restrictions about food and behaviour and have retained much of their original social structure as also much of their old form of worship, they occasionally invite Brahmins to serve at their religious feasts. But most of their celebrations do not require any Brahmins as official priests. The settled Musahars live in villages, do menial jobs and work in the field as daily labourers, while the nomadic Musahars prefer hunting in the jungles and collecting forest produce and fuel which they sell in the villages.[35] They refuse employment as field labourers.

The cultivating castes of Bihar have given an interesting reason for their habit of employing Musahars to watch their crops in the fields, namely that they are alone able to exorcise the older gods who have been driven away by plough and resent the intrusion of alien peasantry. They obviously connect Musahars with the older gods, and thus acknowledge that they are the earlier settlers in the region.[36]

Musahars are so low in their status that they are placed below the Chamars from whom they accept food. Their impure food habits and in particular, their association with field rats may be the reason for their low social status.

More towards the west in Bihar and in the northern districts of Uttar Pradesh, south of Jamuna, are found Bhars who in their physical appearance must also be descendent from a dark aboriginal race. About hundred years ago, they were still of rather unsettled habits. Their favourite occupation was breaking up fresh land when a village area had been brought fully under cultivation.

Between the fertile stretch of the Ganga and southern highland of Chotanagpur plateau, Musahars are spread over middle Ganga plains. Although criss-crossed by numerous streams and rivers, this region is characterized by high agricultural period as the water retaining capacity of the soil here is low, there being a strong downward slope from north-south. Availability of moisture through the year and fertile alluvial soil in northern part of the flood plain of Bihar allows agricultural activities through the year, while in southern parts, the agricultural season is restricted to paddy cultivation during winter season with the help of irrigated water.

It is believed that historically, descendants of the tribes of the Chotanagpur area, Musahars had migrated from the hills to the valley.[37] Today, they live in the districts of Gaya, Nawada, Munger, Bhagalpur, Purnea, Muzzafarpur, Darbhanga, Saran and Champaran.[38] In this region, high agricultural seasonality has created a high demand for permanent agricultural labour. Paddy cultivation being a dominant mode of economic practice for centuries in the middle Ganga plains, this persistent demand for agricultural labour has been primarily to maintain the irrigation system of the south[39] during peak agricultural season. It also produced a land-labour system by which labourers were compelled to function through long-term ties to the *maliks* or landlords. *Kamiauti*, a permanent land-labour arrangement, emerged out of the historical-geographical characteristics of this area, whereby the whole Musahar community was transformed through time into bonded labourers. Under the *Kamiauti* system, a *Kamia* worked all his life for the same landlord, earning wages for the days that he worked and in principle, expecting assistance when needed. For his son's marriage, he received some grains, money and traditionally a small plot of land from the landlord. After the conclusion of this transaction called *Kamiauti*, the son too becomes the same malik's *Kamia*. Women also became attached to the same master in a labour arrangement in perpetuity through their marital relationship with the *Kamia* husbands.

The obligation to live in the land of the malik bound them to continue with a long labour work tie with maliks. At the same time, having come down from hills to plains, Musahars came into contact with the agricultural caste-based society, characterized by Brahminical concepts of purity and pollution. Musahars have been incorporated in the hierarchy than the lowest level. They have become untouchable because they were kept outside the four Hindu varnas.[40] From mountains and hills to the plains of paddy fields, the fate of Musahars appears to have had a clear downward slope. The closer they came to the rice bowl, deeper they got into indigence and misery. Those settled in Bhagalpur and Munger regions worked as ghatwals and tikaits, collecting transit fees at the mouth of valley or pass under the local lords and enjoying privileges. Into the plains, they were settled as untouchables and coerced into labour bondage. Contemporary social and economic positioning of Musahar community within the larger societal structure bears the twin impact of being a *Kamia* and an untouchable, marked by almost total denial of entitlements, especially land which forms an integral part of their everyday struggle for existence.[41] Of course, as agricultural labourers,[42] they carry out the toughest agricultural work of soil-cutting, earth-removing and heavy spadework particularly on barren and uncultivable hard soils and form the backbone of the present agricultural economy of Bihar.

The Musahars or rat-eaters are one of the lowest divisions of Dalits, and are, therefore, placed at the bottom of the social and economic scale. Most of them were bonded labourers and were given tracts of barren lands ranging from 0.5–3 acres Bhoodan and Gramdan Schemes. Placed at the lower rungs of social and ritual ladder, they have largely remained socially, politically and economically backward despite their own government's and NGO's efforts at raising their standard of life. Unlike some SC communities elsewhere in India, which have made substantial economic development, the relatively large Musahar community in Bihar has remained an economically poor and illiterate community. In recent years, they seem to have attempted to rise in society through education, government welfare programmes, and so forth. By and large, their life appears to be one of struggle for survival as has been evident from their involvement in the Naxalite movement in some areas of Bihar.

The interest in Dalits is not related to the fact that they (the Scheduled Castes [SCs] and Scheduled Tribes [STs]) constitute a substantial proportion of the total population of the country (24%). Rather, it is related to two facts. First, in the system of social stratification in India, Dalits are placed the lowest in the social rungs among the caste Hindus. Musahars, who are real *antyaja* (untouchables), are placed at the bottommost rung – even among Dalits. Due to cumulative poverty and discrimination, modern development programmes have only made a minor impact on them. Though they have tried to avail of the educational facilities for their children, medical care, mid-day meal scheme, food for work, immunization schemes and facilities of the public distribution system, such schemes have little impact on them. In fact, they have been exploited for such a long time that they have become used to starvation and other deprivations. Their living conditions are subhuman. The task of upliftment of Musahars is not merely a humanitarian one; it is a matter of complete overhaul of the national polity. It will, therefore, be necessary in our study to see the issues in that perspective.

Several studies have been made on the problems of Dalits in India.[43] There are also some community-specific studies highlighting the socio-economic and cultural changes of the Chamars, Bhangis, Dusadhs, Dhobis and Musahars.[44] However, a study on Musahar community in the vortex of change has not been made as yet.

Background of Welfare Schemes

Since the first Five-Year Plan, commencing to respond to what was identified as 'the special needs of Scheduled Castes/Tribes/Other Backward Classes' to be supported only by bureaucratic and political machinations waivers of the welfare state. Five successive plans emphasized that 'the general development programmes must be designed to support the needs of Backward classes'. The concept of Tribal sub-plan was presented during the Fifth Plan and Special Plan for Scheduled Castes during the Sixth Plan to facilitate the monitoring of development programmes for the benefit of Scheduled Castes and Tribes.[45] Important poverty reduction approaches for planning the development of the Community Development in India in the sixties and seventies to Integrated Rural Development Programme (IRDP) of the nineties have paid special attention to the Scheduled Castes and Tribes families.

However, though a number of special programmes aimed at ameliorating the conditions of weaker sections have been sponsored by the government, not a single agency has been created specifically for the economic development of the SCs. Some of the special programmes implemented for Dalits are: Special Component Plan (SCP) for the development of SCs and STs, Tribal Sub-Plan, the 'Pre-Matric scholarship' for the children of those engaged in unclean occupations; the Indira Awas Yojana, Food for Work scheme, Mid-day Meal scheme, and so on.

Policy interventions in the early seventies saw the essence of socialist policies of the government and the public sector was in its commanding heights; all banks were nationalized, the license permit raj was at its peak and *Garibi Hatao* rhetoric was powerful. Foreign trade represents about 5 per cent of national income to the share in world trade less than one per cent. The overall growth rate during 1950–1980, however, was 3.5 per cent per year (called the Hindu rate of growth). The low growth rate is explained by policy makers as a result of ideology to continue socialist orientations. Ironically, the score card of socialist goals was less brilliant. Poverty levels remained very high at nearly 50 per cent in the 1970s. This is despite the fact that numerous special programmes to reduce poverty and increased employment were formulated and implemented with a high rhetoric Garibi Hatao in the seventies. The focus of the campaign was to the launch some of the most ambitious programmes for employment generation and poverty reduction, such as the Integrated Rural Development Programme (IRDP), small farmers and Agricultural Labourers Programme (MFAL), Small and Program Marginal Farmers development, (SFDA), Development of Women and Children in Rural Areas (DWCRA) for rural women, youth Training for Self-Employment (TRYSEM) for unemployed youth, National Rural Employment Programme (NREP) and Program rural Employment Guarantee (RLEGP), and Jawahar Rojgar Yojana (JRY) for generating employment in rural areas.

One of the important features of the SCP was the launching of special mechanism for Dalits to ensure that these groups received their due share of funds/benefits from the other development sectors. But the 'hunger deaths' in various states have exposed the gross failure of the food-related schemes – the Public Distribution System (PDS), Antyodaya Anna Yojana, National Mid-day Meal

Programme, and so on. Deaton and Dreze say that the PDS has completely broken down in most of the states.[46] They further say that about 80 per cent of the food meant for Dalits and their children, released by the Food Corporation of India for the PDS, were sold in black markets.[47] This is a clear-cut violation of the Supreme Court's order, which ruled that cooked mid-day meals should be provided in all the primary schools.[48] Moreover, it was observed that non-release of SCP funds on time to the beneficiaries concerned has been adversely affecting the smooth running of various income-generation programmes for Dalits living below the poverty line.[49]

The fact that disparities have become more pronounced during the 1990s, or have not been reduced despite government programmes, for example in education, suggest that the processes have been influenced by liberalization of the economy, accompanied by structural adjustment. This relationship is complex and often simplified in popular discourse. Liberalization and adjustment are neither responsible for sustained deprivation in the area and disparities across the state, nor are they likely to do much to address these issues. One key issue is related to ensuring that the new paths of development of the economy inserting in a new, faster, global economy should benefit poor people in remote rural regions. The inequalities described above are neither just, nor efficient. Moreover, they are cumulative, and human development disparities reinforce those related to income, poverty and vice versa. They leave out a large section of the population, unable to be economically productive, leading to needs for schemes of social protection, and potentially to political unrest.[50]

Creation of Mahadalit

From a sociological standpoint, Dalits in no way constitute a homogeneous community. They are divided into 22 Scheduled Caste groups in Bihar as per government classification. Dalits constitute nearly15 per cent of Bihar's population of 100 million.[51] Although grouped together as Dalits, they occupy varying locations on the bottom rungs of the caste hierarchy, some being poorer and more discriminated against than others. The poorest of Dalit groups were declared 'Maha Dalits' by the Bihar government in 2007. Nitish Kumar, the Chief Minister of the state, constituted Mahadalit Commission to identify the most vulnerable groups among the Dalit caste for their development and propose measures. The Commission classified 21 out of 22 castes as Mahadalits and details are provided in Table 1.[52]

Table 1

Population of Scheduled Castes in Bihar

S.No.	*Dalit Castes in Bihar*	*Population in Bihar*	*Share in Bihar's SC Population (%)*
1.	Chamar	40,90,070	31.34%
2.	Dusadh	40,29,411	30.88%
3.	Musahar	21,12,136	16.19%
4.	Pasi	7,11,389	5.45%
5.	Dhobi	6,47,491	4.96%
6.	Bhuiya	5,68,403	4.36%
7.	Rajwar	2,13,795	1.64%
8.	Hari/Mehtar	1,81,748	1.39%
9.	Dom	1,55,383	1.19%
10.	Bantar	1,01,223	0.78%
11.	Chaupal	1,00,111	0.77%
12.	Nat	38,615	0.30%
13.	Turi	33,638	0.26%
14.	Bhogta	12,659	0.10%
15.	Kurariyar	6,567	0.05%
16.	Pan	3,653	0.03%
17.	Halalkhor	3,960	0.03%
18.	Dabgar	3,590	0.03%
29.	Bhumij*	2,333	0.02%
20.	Bauri	2,096	0.02%
21.	Lalbegi	809	0.01%
22.	Kanjar	1,620	0.01%
23.	Ghasi	674	0.01%
	Total	1,30,48,608	

* Bhumij was later dropped from the list of SCs in Bihar, leaving only 22 castes in the list.

The creation of Mahadalits by Nitish Kumar government has been criticized by the opposition as an election stunt and to electorally marginalize Ramvilas Paswan and Dusadhs vote-banks among whom he is a very influential leader, who was left out of this category only for Dalit caste. But whatever the differences between

Dalits and Mahadalit politics, and an internal hierarchy of castes in Bihar, Dusadh, is the second largest, with its traditional occupation of watchman, and is ranked higher than the other Dalit groups. Musahar (rat catcher), one of the nation's largest Mahadalit, is considered the lowest in the caste hierarchy. Here Musahars are the main focus of this study. On the one hand this Musahar community clearly demonstrates extreme form of caste oppression, but on the other hand several members of this caste have actively taken part in various resistance movements, including the Maoist struggle.

Everyday Life of Musahar

Musahars mostly live in different states of Bihar, Jharkhand, Uttar Pradesh and West Bengal. Large number of Musahar population has also settled in Nepal.[53] In Bihar, with a population of more than over two million, this community constitutes the third largest Dalit group in the state. They are the poorest and most discriminated Dalit castes in Bihar. Any reflection on the lasting effects of poverty and untouchability in the community must take into account every day actions and social arrangements that while seemingly 'normal' or 'harmless', still result in irreparable damage to self-image and agency community. They include untouchability practices, illiteracy, lack of land, infant mortality, the low status of women and Dalits dominant discourses representing Dalits in a negative way, all being submerged under deep forms of violence. Consequently, social inequalities, structural, political and economic relations built on land and caste hierarchies are perceived as 'natural' and even as part of a 'divinely ordained scheme.' The 'naturalness' and perceived 'inevitability' in the creation of social order accordingly, while creating a sense of resignation among Musahars and other Dalit groups.

Within this conceptual framework of structural violence, I analyse how the dominant discourses, both Brahmanical and colonial, have constructed Musahar identities and their way of life. Religion, proverbs, myths and folktales give legitimacy and sanctity to these dominant renderings. Further, I examine the economic and social implications of Musahars' total landlessness and large-scale illiteracy in relation to their transformation into 'complying subjects'.

Landlessness and its Socio-Economic Implications

Compliance among Musahars and other Dalits is linked to their poverty and dependence on the landowning castes. In Bihar, as everywhere in rural India, power and dominance are linked to the ownership of land, which in turn is related to caste status. Of the four upper castes in Bihar (Brahmans, Bhumihars, Rajputs and Kayasths), who constitute 12.7 per cent of the population, the Rajputs and the Bhumihars own the most land and are dominant in rural areas. The upper stratum of the Other Backward Classes (OBC), comprising mainly Yadav, Kurmi and Koeri, and constituting 19 per cent of the population are also among the landowning dominant castes in the state.[54] While 26.2 per cent of the population owns 88.8 per cent of the land, the bulk of the population, 73.8 per cent, owns just 21.2 per cent.[55] Dalits, who constituted over 15 per cent of the state population, are mostly landless agricultural labourers. Among them, Musahars suffer the worst because of their absolute landlessness. According to the Census of India for 2001, over 97 per cent of Musahars are considered labourers, of whom around 92 per cent are landless agricultural labourers.

As shown in Table 2, Musahars have the highest percentage of labourers compared to other major Dalit castes in Bihar.

Table 2

Percentage Distribution of Workers in Four Economic Categories

Economic Category	*All SCs*	*Chamar*	*Dusadh*	*Musahar*	*Pasi*	*Dhobi*	*Bhuiya*
Cultivators	7.9	7.9	10.3	2.7	12.3	14.8	6.6
Agricultural Labourers	77.6	80.2	75.9	92.5	46.5	48.1	86.8
Household Industry Workers	3.3	2.1	1.6	0.8	12.2	9.6	1.0
Other Workers	11.2	9.8	12.2	4.0	29.0	27.5	5.6

Source: Census of India, 2001.

Every year in December-January they start migrating towards different regions of Punjab, Haryana and Uttar Pradesh. They do wheat harvesting and rice-sowing there. By June end they come back and go again in September and do rice harvesting. Thus, they work primarily as agricultural labourers for six-seven months a year.

Large-scale migration of Musahars is a recent history, starting largely from the early nineties. Villages are now found totally deserted of young and middle age male members during most of the agricultural seasons. It enables Musahars to survive and helps in meeting their basic needs

Musahars do not own even their homestead land but build their huts on *gairmazaruazamin* (public land). The irony is that Musahars, who are an offshoot of the Bhuiya tribe – etymologically meaning of the land (*bhumi*) – have no land, not even to erect their own huts. In an agrarian society like Bihar, landlessness means much more than material poverty. Land represents many things, including economic, social and political power and with it, respect. Musahar and other Dalit groups' total lack of land has effectively prevented their participation in the decision-making process in rural India. This powerlessness has also led to their lack of influence, especially over local manifestations of the state, including the police and welfare officials.[56]

Poverty and dependence are maintained and reinforced by the chronic deficit that characterizes the untouchables budget. In other words, contrary once again to what Srinivas claims 'an untouchable's income is never sufficient to meet even his most basic needs'. Traditionally, untouchables were paid in kind with a set quantity of grain at harvest time. This was much less than the amount received by other social categories. As Gyan Prakash[57] mentioned in one of the case study as follows:

> I, Somar Rajwar, son of Geyan Rajwar, of Andherbari, pargana Jarra, district Gaya, am by profession a labourer and a kamia. As I have to pay off the debt of Babu Bhikhari Singh of aforesaid village, to make some clothes and also to incur expenditure on food, and which cannot be done without recourse to borrowing, and because nobody gives a loan without my executing a Kamiauti document, I requested Babu Dhanpat Singh, son of Babu Gajadhar Singh, deceased, of village Andherbari, by profession agriculturist and service-holder, to advance a loan of ₹ 13–4–0 on Kamiauti terms and to get a document executed by me on stamped paper. To this the aforesaid Babu agreed. I, therefore, of my own free will, have taken a loan of ₹ 13–4–0 (half of which comes to ₹ 6–10–0) from the aforesaid Babu Dhanpat Singh of the above-named village and have put the money to my personal use. I, therefore, bind myself and execute this document agreeing to assist the agriculturist with my wife in all the work of a kamia and in the agricultural operations, e.g. sowing, etc. I shall receive antia, dinora, and wages as per custom of the village and shall raise no objection. I shall also have to repay the money at a lump in Jeth of the year 1916, when I shall take back the stamped document. And so long I do not repay the money, I shall always discharge my duties, and if I happen to go away elsewhere I shall pay to the said Babu Dhanpat Singh interest at one anna per rupee per month until the aforesaid loan is

> paid off. On my failing in this the said Babu Dhanpat Singh shall be entitled to realize the money from any of my properties that he may find, and to this neither I nor my descendants or successors-in-interest shall have any objection. I have therefore executed this document concerning interest to be made use of later on if required. Be it noted that if I have to go elsewhere for a day or two I shall put my son in charge of the said agriculturist as my substitute and the said agriculturist will have authority to take work from my son. (dated 2 August 1914)

The chronic deficit has come down to modern times, where agricultural labourers are more than ever in need of cash. As they are insolvent, the only thing untouchables can do is sell their labour as the same reflects with Musahar community; and that is why, in exchange for an advance, they are willing to themselves serve for an indefinite period of the time to their creditors. The widespread system of bonded labour, *Kamia-malik* (labourer-landlord) is another consequence of this chronic deficit across Musahars.[58]

The outcome of Musahar powerlessness was their transformation into agricultural slaves totally dependent on upper-and middle-caste landlords. Musahars' dependence was based on and reproduced by a mechanism of credit and indebtedness centred on *Kamia-malik* relations. By extending small loans to labourers in times of distress, marriage, etc. the landlords ensured their control over the *Kamia*'s labour until the debt had been repaid. At the same time, the repayment conditions were formulated in such a way that the labourer would never be able to pay back the debt. For instance, repayment day was fixed for a certain day in *jyeth* (July–August), a time of recession.[59] Due to the *Kamia*'s inability to pay back the debt, the landlord ensured that the labourers' wives and children also worked for him. This bondage subjected them all to a 'system of restrictions: restrictions on their movements, their labour, and their persons'.[60] Although bonded labour was abolished by law in 1976, one report indicated that during the 1980s and 1990s, more than 4,00,000 Musahars continued to live in bondage to upper-caste landowners in Bihar.[61] The People's Union for Civil Liberties (PUCL) Bulletin of June 2002 reports the release of 46 bonded labourers, aged 7 to 60, all local Musahars from a brick kiln owned by a powerful person in Phulpur sub-division of Varanasi district in Eastern Uttar Pradesh.[62]

The practice of bonded labour, at least in theory, seems to have undergone some changes in recent years. Presently, Musahars and other Mahadalit castes work as either *laguamazdur* (attached labourers) or *chuttamazdur* (free labourers). The *lagua* labourers or *harvaha* (ploughmen), as they are also called (involving only men; women mostly work for the same landlords to whom their men are bound by these contracts), are bound to a landlord on a one-year contract. This contract is different from the type of bonded labour described above, in which the labourers were bonded from one generation to another. As a result, most of the Dalit households have to take loans from moneylenders or landlords; Dalits remain in 'chronic deficit',[63] and the cycle of bondage never ends. Musahars are considered the toughest labourers for basic agricultural work of land-levelling and soil cutting, but they are not considered as part of agrarian labour. They are still considered only as additional class of village labour.

Musahar Illiteracy Rate in Bihar

The wretched situation of Musahars is further reflected in their dismally low rate of literacy. In the Census reports of 1991, the Musahar literacy rate in Bihar was recorded as 2.25 per cent whereas, the Musahar female literacy rate was 1 per cent. Ten years later, the Census of 2001 recorded 9 per cent of the community as literate, with the literacy rates among Musahar women being 3.9 per cent. Even this record of marginal increase, as the statistics given in the report of the SC and ST Welfare Department of the Government of Bihar (2012) indicate, is rather optimistic. According to this report the literacy rate among Musahars is 4.6 per cent (male: 7.7 and female: 3.3). As Table 3 demonstrates, the literacy rate among Musahars is the worst of all Mahadalit castes in the state.

The high rate of illiteracy among Musahars is closely linked with their position at the bottom of the caste and class hierarchy. In some villages, Musahar parents even have to ask permission from landlords to send their children to school. Mendelsohn and Vicziany[64] refer to the story of: 'Jitan Ram Manjhi, the Musahar politician from Bihar. Seeing his son's interest in learning, Jitan Ram's father approached the Bhumihar landlord to whom he was bonded, asking for permission for his son to go to school. The response was a sound thrashing for the presumptuousness of even asking'.

'The everyday practice of the school often fulfils the social purpose of maintaining established power relations',[65] 'thus reproducing domination and subordination by favouring some children and disfavouring others'.[66] Musahar children dare not go to schools attended by children from other castes for fear of ridicule and discrimination. 'Those children who do persist initially leave very soon, not only without the education they deserve, but also with a sense of failure and internalizing the violence meted out to them at the hands of an educational system that is designed to perpetuate the dominant culture'.[67]

Table 3

Literacy Rates of Dalit Castes in Bihar

S. No.	*Dalit Castes in Bihar*	*Literacy Rates (%)*		
		Female	*Male*	*Total*
1.	Turi	6.5	28.6	17.9
2.	Rajwar	5.2	29.6	18
3.	Pasi	12.9	44.5	29.6
4.	Pan	19.1	47.7	33.9
5.	Nat	6.2	20.6	13.8
6.	Musahar	1.3	7.7	4.6
7.	Lalbegi	12.2	30.6	21.7
8.	Kurariyar	8.8	30.2	19.5
9.	Kanjar	4.5	15.1	10.7
10.	Hari/Mehtar	13.4	38.7	26.9
11.	Halalkhor	12.4	39.2	26.2
12.	Ghasi	13.9	36.6	25.4
13.	Dusadh	8.4	35.7	22.9
14.	Dom	7.4	26.3	17.4
15.	Dhobi	14.2	48.2	32.3
16.	Dabgar	13.2	42.8	29.2
17.	Chaupal	6.4	29	18.8
18.	Chamar	7.1	35.3	21.8
19.	Bhuiya	2.8	14.5	8.9
20.	Bhogta	4.5	21.9	13.6
21.	Bauri	7.8	35.2	22.1
22.	Bantar	3.7	20.4	12.4
	Total	7.1	30.6	19.5

Source: SC and ST Welfare Department, Government of Bihar 2012: 62.

Conclusion

Many think that Musahars since they lead a life of impoverishment, with most of them being landless labourers, they have nothing of their own, materially and culturally. Yet, the fact that they have showed remarkable tenacity to survive in spite of sickness and starvation, oppression and marginalization and manifesting a resilience amidst the forces of globalization, is a remarkable proof that they owe something of their own; their knowledge, their skills, their worldview and their culture. It is a case of sheer neglect on the part of academia and government machinery that the traditions of a large chunk of people remain unknown and hidden. Should we take this on the part of the educated and conscientious people of the nation as an attempt to silence and marginalize a group of people? It is a matter of challenge for scholars and activists to bring the everyday practices of Musahars community to the gaze of the nation, which is claiming to be a nation leaping forth into one of the most economically competitive nations in the world.

The sad plight of one of India's lowest castes is directly linked to sheer government apathy to improving their lot. Musahars are mainly landless agricultural labourers. They have only their physical labour to sell. They do not have any fixed economy and their annual income is less than a primary school fee. The state of the community in North Bihar is much worse than any of the indigenous tribals of the country. 'Today the Musahars of north Bihar are fighting for their survival and nobody takes any notice of it. So it's not surprising that they are selling off their children to the brokers. They are not left with any alternatives.'

Yet, even after four decades of land-labour reforms involving Musahars, nothing much appears to have changed; the incremental system of bonded labour continues to subsist.

Notes

1. Ram, Nandu (1989), *The Mobile Scheduled Castes: Rise of a New Middle Class*, Delhi: Hindustan Publishing Corporation.
2. Ibid.
3. Dumont, Louis (1972), *Homo Hierarchicus*, London: Paladin.
4. Srinivas, M.N. (1966), *Social Change in Modern India*, Bombay: Allied Publishers and Rowe, W.L. (1968), 'The New Chauhans: A Caste Mobility in North India', in J. Silverberg (ed.), *Social Mobility in the Caste System in India*, The Hague: Mouton, pp. 66–78.
5. Thapar, Romila (1975), *The Past and Prejudice*, New Delhi: National Book Trust.
6. Srinivas, M.N. (1966), *Social Change in Modern India*, Bombay: Allied Publishers.

7. Deliege, Robert (1999), *The Untouchables of India*, New York: Berg.
8. Ibid.
9. Joshi, B. (1986), *Untouchable! Voices of the Dalit Liberation Movement*, London: Zed Books.
10. Zelliot, Eleanor (1992), *From Untouchable to Dalit: Essays on the Ambedkar Movements*, New Delhi: Manohar Publications.
11. *The Bhopal Document* (2002), Government of Madhya Pradesh, Bhopal.
12. Dalit Panthers Manifesto, Mumbai (1973).
13. Ibid., p. 107.
14. Khare, R.S. (1984), *The Untouchable as Himself*, Cambridge: Cambridge University Press, p. 120.
15. Weber, Max (1958), *The Religion of India: The Sociology of Hinduism and Buddhism*, New York: The Free Press.
16. Fuchs, Stephen (1981), *At the Bottom of Indian Society*, Delhi: Munshiram Manoharlal.
17. Yagati, Chinna Rao (2003), *Dalit Struggle for Identity*, New Delhi: Kanishka Publishers and Distributors.
18. See Hardgrave, R.L. (1969), *The Nadars of Tamil Nadu: The Political Culture of a Community in Change*, Bombay: Oxford University Press, p. 115; Gokhale, J. (1979), 'The Dalit Panthers and the Radicalisation of the Untouchables', *Journal of Commonwealth and Comparative Politics*, Vol. 17, No. 1, pp. 77–93; Gooptu, N. (1993), 'Caste, Deprivation and Politics: The Untouchables in UP Towns in the Early Twentieth Century', in Peter Robb (ed.), *Dalit Movements and the Meaning of Labour in India*, New Delhi: Oxford University Press, pp. 277–298; Gore, M.S. (1993), *The Non-Brahman Movement in Maharashtra*, New Delhi: Segment Book Distributors; Aiyappan, A. (1965), *Social Revolution in a Kerala Village*, London: Asia Publishing House; Babb, L.A. (1972), 'The Satnamis: Political Involvement of a Religious Movement', in J.M. Mahar (ed.), *The Untouchables in Contemporary India*, Arizona: University of Arizona Press, pp. 143–151 and Sharma, S.K. (1985), *Social Movements and Social Change: A Study of Arya Samaj and Untouchables in Punjab*, Delhi: B.R. Publishing House.
19. Oommen, T.K. (1990), 'Sources of Deprivation and Styles of Protest: The Case of the Dalits', in T.K. Oommen (ed.), *Protest and Change: Studies in Social Movement*, New Delhi: Sage Publications and Ram, Nandu (1995), *Beyond Ambedkar: Essays on Dalits in India*, New Delhi: Har-Anand Publications.
20. Rao, M.S.A. (1979), *Social Movements and Social Transformation: A Study of Two Backward Classes Movements in India*, Delhi: Macmillan.

21. Babb, L.A. (1972), 'The Satnamis: Political Involvement of a Religious Movement', in J.M. Mahar (ed.), *The Untouchables in Contemporary India*, Arizona: University of Arizona Press, pp. 143–151 and Dube, S. (1992), 'Myths, Symbols and Community: Satnampanth of Chhattisgarh', in P. Chatterjee and G. Pandey (eds), *Subaltern Studies: Writings on South Asian History and Society*, Vol. 7, New Delhi: Oxford University Press, pp. 121–158.
22. Juergensmeyer, M. (1982), *Religion as Social Vision: The Movement against Untouchability in 20th Century Punjab*, Berkeley: University of California Press.
23. Gooptu, N. (1993), 'Caste, Deprivation and Politics: The Untouchables in UP Towns in the Early Twentieth Century', in Peter Robb (ed.), *Dalit Movements and the Meaning of Labour in India*, Delhi: Oxford University Press, pp. 277–298.
24. Bhoite, U. and A. Bhoite (1977), 'Dalit Sahitya Movement in Maharashtra: A Sociological Study', *Sociological Bulletin*, Vol. 26, No. 1, pp. 60–75.
25. Lynch, O.M. (1974), *Politics of Untouchability*, New Delhi: National Publishing House and Ram, Nandu (1995), *Beyond Ambedkar: Essays on Dalits in India*, New Delhi: Har-Anand Publications.
26. Vashishtha, V.K. (1985), 'Struggle of the Chamar Peasants for the Removal of Social Disabilities in Feudal Estate (Uniara Thikana) in Rajasthan, 1946–47', *Proceedings of the Indian History Congress (45th Session)*, Annamalai Nagar, Tamil Nadu, pp. 717–728.
27. Singh, R. (1974), 'Agrarian Social Structure and Peasant Unrest: A Study of Land-Grab Movement in District Basti, East UP', *Sociological Bulletin*, Vol. 23, No. 1, pp. 44–70.
28. Moore, W.E. (1964), *Social Change*, New Jersey: Prentice Hall.
29. See Census of India (2011), New Delhi: Registrar General of India.
30. Ibid.
31. In *A Statistical Account of Bengal: Districts of Patna and Saran, 1877, Vol. XI*, W.W. Hunter reports that the Musahars were classified as Semi-Hinduised Aborigine, pp. 50–52.
32. Fuchs, S. (1991), *At the Bottom of Indian Society*, Delhi: Munshiram Manoharlal Publications.
33. Ibid.
34. Ibid.
35. Notes from fieldwork.
36. Fuchs, S. (1991), *At the Bottom of Indian Society*, Delhi: Munshiram Manoharlal.

37. The origin of the Musahars, who are known by different names in Bihar and its adjoining states, has still remained debatable. In colonial ethnographic works, they have been related to different tribes both within and outside the region based on etymological explanation and anthropometrical indices. Nesfield, J.C. (1888), 'The Musahars of Central and Upper India', *Calcutta Review*, Vol. 171, pp. 1–52.
38. Presently it is in the Magadh region of Bihar where they have the greatest concentration, and are known as 'Bhuinyas'.
39. Traditionally tank irrigation was the most popular mode of irrigation in south Bihar. Locally known as Ãhars (tanks) consisting of a maze of Pains (irrigation channels) to store water from rainfall and rivers.
40. In the 1935 census, Musahars (together with Bhuinya population) were considered as tribes but for the first time in the 1961 census they were put in the Scheduled Caste category. In Bihar, according to the 1981 census, the entire population of the Musahars amounted to 13,91,000 and that of the Bhuinya as to 8,50,469. According to this count, the population of the Musahars and the Bhuinyas taken together made up nearly 20 per cent of the entire Dalit population. In short, out of the three 'millionaire castes' in the state of Bihar, Musahars is one of them. The other two being the Chamars (3 million) and the Dusadhs (2.7 million).
41. A recent household survey carried out by the Planning Commission of India, 2004, Scheduled Communities: A Social Development Profile of SC/STs (Bihar, Jharkhand and West Bengal), New Delhi: Government of India, revealed that out of 392 Scheduled Caste households, only 18.4 per cent own cultivable land, and 11.2 per cent possess assets. The study found that the Musahars and the Chaupals have neither land nor agricultural assets.
42. According to the 1981 census, out of the total population in Bihar, 46.7 per cent are workers and among them 95.34 per cent are agricultural labourers. Only 2.52 per cent are involved in cultivation and the remaining 2.14 per cent are in other services.
43. Louis, P. (2003), *Political Sociology of Dalit Assertion*, New Delhi: Gyan Publishing House; Yogeshwar, P. (1995), *Economic Development of Scheduled Castes in Bihar during the Plan Period* (Volume 1), Patna: Janki Publications; Oommen, T.K. (1990), 'Sources of Deprivation and Styles of Protest: The Case of the Dalits', in T.K. Oommen (ed.), *Protest and Change: Studies in Social Movement*, New Delhi: Sage Publications; Sachidananda (1997), *Harijan Elite*, Faridabad: Thomson Press and Wankhede, G.G. (1999), *Social Mobility and Scheduled Castes*, Jaipur: Rawat Publications.

44. Gokhale, J. (1979), 'The Dalit Panthers and the Radicalisation of Untouchables', *Journal of Commonwealth and Comparative Politics*, Vol. 17, No. 1, pp. 77–93; Joshi, B.R. (1986), *Untouchable: Voices of the Dalit Liberation Movement*, London: Zed Books Ltd.; Mukherjee, A.B. (1980), *The Chamars of Uttar Pradesh: A Study in Social Geography*, New Delhi: Inter-India Publications; Lal, S. (1984), *The Bhangis in Transition*, New Delhi: Inter-India Publications and Prasad, A. (1986), *Samanwaya Ashram in the Service of Harijans*, Patna: Janki Prakashan.
45. See discussion in Section 2.1 Poverty Alleviation in Rural India: Programmes and Strategy, 9th Five Year Plan (Volume 2), GoI, http://planningcommission.nic.in/plans/planrel/fiveyr/welcome.html
46. Deaton, A. and J. Dreze (2002), 'Poverty and Inequality in India: A Re-examination', *Economic and Political Weekly*, September 7, pp. 3729–3749.
47. Ibid.
48. *The Hindustan Times* (2002), 'Hunger Deaths Expose State Government's Food-related Schemes', New Delhi, August 3.
49. Planning Commission of India, *Tenth Five Year Plan: 2002–07* (Volume 2).
50. Haan, Arjan de and Amaresh Dubey (2005), 'Poverty, Disparities, or the Development of Underdevelopment in Orissa', *Economic and Political Weekly*, Vol. 40, No. 22/23, pp. 2321–2329.
51. Census of India (2011), New Delhi: Registrar General of India.
52. Population of Scheduled Castes in Bihar (Source: SC and ST Welfare Department, Government of Bihar, 2012), p. 57.
53. In the Tarai region of Nepal, the Musahars, with a population of 1,72,434 are listed as the second largest Dalit group after the Chamars (Giri, 2013).
54. Blair, Harry (1980), 'Rising Kulaks and Backward Classes in Bihar: Social Change in the Late 1970s', *Economic and Political Weekly*, Vol. 15, No. 2, pp. 64–74.
55. Prasad, Pradhan (1979), 'Caste and Class in Bihar', *Economic and Political Weekly*, Vol. 14, No. 7/8, pp. 481–484.
56. Mendelsohn, O. and M. Vicziany (1998), *The Untouchables: Subordination, Poverty and State in Modern India*, Cambridge: Cambridge University Press, pp. 58–59.
57. Prakash, Gyan (1990), *Bonded Histories: Genealogies of Labour Servitude in Colonial India*, Cambridge: Cambridge University Press, pp. 226–227.
58. From field notes.

59. Mukherjee, R. (1961), *Land Problems of India*, London: Oxford University Press.
60. Prakash, Gyan (1990), *Bonded Histories: Genealogies of Labour Servitude in Colonial India*, Cambridge: Cambridge University Press, p. 1.
61. Bhushan, Shashi (2002), 'Reflections on the Material Conditions of the Musahars', in Hemant Joshi and Sanjay Kumar (eds), *Asserting Voices: Changing Cultural Identity and Livelihood of the Musahars in Gangetic Plains*, Delhi: Deshkal Publications.
62. People's Vigilance Committee on Human Rights (2002a), 'Bonded Labour from Musahar Community in Danger', *PUCL Bulletin*, June.
63. Prasad (1979) uses this term to describe the condition of agricultural labourers in Bihar, who are perpetually in debt.
64. Mendelsohn, O. and M. Vicziany (1998), *The Untouchables: Subordination, Poverty and State in Modern India*, Cambridge: Cambridge University Press, pp. 218–234.
65. Herr, K. (1999), 'Institutional Violence in the Everyday Practices of School: The Narrative of a Young Lesbian', *Journal for a Just and Caring Education*, Vol. 5, No. 3, pp. 242–255.
66. Bourdieu, P. (1977), *Outline of a Theory of Practice*, London: Oxford University Press.
67. Herr, K. (1999), 'Institutional Violence in the Everyday Practices of School: The Narrative of a Young Lesbian', *Journal for a Just and Caring Education*, Vol. 5, No. 3, pp. 242–255.

13

Different Constitutional Provisions and its Impact on Occupational Diversification among Social Groups in India

M. THANGARAJ

> You have no land because others have usurped them;
> you have no posts because others have monopolized them.[1] (Keer, 2005)
>
> – Dr Ambedkar

Several factors contribute to the economic development and occupational diversification is one among them. Occupation determines income of the individual and occupational diversification is expected to change in the traditional order of occupation based on birth. Indian society is a stratified society where there is a close linkage between the caste system and occupational pattern. 'Upper castes were landowners, middle ranked castes were farmers and artisans and the lowest ranked castes, the Scheduled Castes were the labourers and performers of menial tasks' (Béteille, 1996). After independence, government of India enacted several legislative provisions for the all-round development of socially neglected and ostracized sections of the people, viz. Scheduled Castes and Scheduled Tribes in India.

Objectives of the Study

The objectives of the study are to analyse:

1. Different constitutional provisions/safeguards for the development of SCs and STs.

2. (i) Distribution of landholdings by social groups; (ii) Central government and public sector employment and (iii) Representation of SCs/STs in government services.
3. Diversification of Occupation: (i) self-employment in rural areas in agriculture and non-agriculture, (ii) self-employment in urban areas, (iii) regular wage/salaried in urban areas and (iv) casual workers in urban areas.
4. Reservation in private sector.

Data Base

Data on landholdings were collected from All-India Report on Agricultural Census; data on central government employees were collected from the Census of Central Government Employees; data on representation of SCs/STs were collected from Report on National Commission for Scheduled Castes; data on occupational pattern/labour force participation were collected from the NSS Reports on 'Employment and Unemployment Situation Among Social Groups in India'.

Tools of Analysis

The change in occupational diversification was studied with the help of F-Ratio.

Constitutional Provisions/Safeguards

Constitutional Safeguards for Social Justice/Fundamental Rights

Indian Constitution guarantees the fundamental rights to citizens. The following provisions deal with the Fundamental Rights:

1. Article 14: Right to equality before the law.
2. Article 15: Prohibition of discrimination on grounds of religion, race, caste, sex or place of birth.
3. Article 16: Equality of opportunity in matters of public employment.
4. Article 17: Abolition of untouchability.
5. Abolition of titles, Article 18 prevents the state from confirming any title except for military and academic distinction. Article 18 prohibits the Indian citizens from receiving titles from any foreign state. The foreign nationals holding the office of profit under the state may accept titles from the foreign government with the consent of President. In a

true democracy, there is no space for artificial distinctions among the same society. Titles such as Rai Bahadur, Sawai, Rai Sahab, Zamindar, Taluqdar, etc. were prevalent in medieval and British India.

Article 19: Protection of certain rights regarding freedom of speech, etc.

Article 20: Protection in respect of conviction for offences.

Other Articles from 21 to 35 also deal with the issues relating to the social justice.

Social Safeguards

Article 17: 'untouchability' is abolished and its practice in any form is forbidden. The enforcement of any disability arising out of untouchability shall be an offence punishable in accordance with law.

The Protection of Civil Rights Act, 1955

The Scheduled Castes and Scheduled Tribes (Prevention of Atrocities) Act, 1989

Article 23 prohibits traffic in human beings and beggars (compulsory work) and other similar forms of forced labour. It also provides that any contravention of this provision shall be an offence punishable in accordance with law. Although it does not deal with SCs and STs, but a majority of the bonded labour belongs to SCs/STs.

Bonded Labour System (Abolition) Act, 1976, was enacted in pursuance of the Article 23. There is a centrally sponsored scheme for the identification, liberation and rehabilitation.

Article 24 provides that no child below the age of 14 years shall be employed to work in any factory or mine or engaged in any other hazardous employment. Although it does not deal with SCs and STs, but a majority of the child labour belongs to SCs/STs.

Article 25 (2) (b) Provides that Hindu religious institutions of public nature shall be thrown open to all classes and sections of Hindus. But the problem of entering into temple still persists for SCs.

Economic Safeguards

1. Fifth Schedule of the Constitution: The schedule contains administration and control of Scheduled Areas and Scheduled Tribes. There are eight states having scheduled areas, viz.,

Andhra Pradesh, Bihar, Gujarat, Himachal Pradesh, Madhya Pradesh, Maharashtra, Odisha and Rajasthan. These states have Tribal Advisory Councils (TACs). The TACs have powers to:

(i) Prohibit/restrict transfer of lands.
(ii) Regulate the allotment of land.
(iii) Regulate the carrying on of business as moneylenders.

Part XVI Special Provisions Relating to Certain Classes (Articles 330–342)

330. Reservation of seats for Scheduled Castes and Scheduled Tribes in the House of the People.
331. Representation of Anglo-Indian community in the House of the People.
332. Reservation of seats for Scheduled Castes and Scheduled Tribes in the Legislative Assemblies of the States.
333. Representation of the Anglo-Indian community in the Legislative Assemblies of the States.
334. Reservation of seats and special representation to cease after seventy years.
335. Claims of Scheduled Castes and Scheduled Tribes to services and posts.
336. Special provision for Anglo-Indian community in certain services.
337. Special provision with respect to educational grants for the benefit of Anglo-Indian Community.
338. National Commission for Scheduled Castes.
338A. National Commission for Scheduled Tribes.
339. Control of the Union over the Administration of Scheduled Areas and the welfare of Scheduled Tribes.
340. Appointment of a Commission to investigate the conditions of backward classes.
341. Definition of the term Scheduled Castes.
342. Definition of the term Scheduled Tribes.

Article 244(2) is dealing with provisions as to the administration of tribal areas in the states of Assam, Meghalaya, Tripura and Mizoram. The Sixth Schedule shall apply to the administration and control of Scheduled Areas and Scheduled Tribes in any state other than Assam, Meghalaya, Tripura and Mizoram.

Article 275(1) states that 'there shall be paid out of the consolidated fund (All receipts) of India as grant-in-aid for the welfare of STs.

Educational and Cultural Safeguards

Article 15(4) empowers the state to make special provision for the advancement of any socially and educationally backward classes of citizens or for SCs/STs. This section was added to the constitution through Constitution (First Amendment, Act 1951).

Article 16 (4): 'Nothing in this Article shall prevent the State from making any provision for reservation in matter of promotion to any class or classes of posts in services under the State in favour of Scheduled Castes and Scheduled Tribes which, in the opinion of the State, are not adequately represented in services under the State'.

Article 29 (1) provides that 'any section of the citizen residing in any territory in India or any part thereof having a distinct language, script or culture of its own shall have right to conserve the same'. This article has special significance for STs.

Article 350(A): 'It shall be the endeavour of every local authority within the state to provide adequate facilities for instructions in the mother tongue at the primary stage of education to children belonging linguistic minority groups'. This article has special significance for STs.

Political Safeguards

Article 164 (1) states that there shall be a Minister in-charge for Tribal welfare in Bihar, MP and Odisha who may in addition be in-charge of the welfare of the SCs/OBCs.

Article 330 provides for reservation of seats for SCs/STs in the Lok Sabha. We have now 106 reserved seats against 545 seats. There were 123 members from SCs/STs in the 11th Lok Sabha.

Article 332 provides for reservation of seats for SCs/STs in the state legislative assemblies.

Article 334 lays down extension of reservation every 10 years. It was initially given for 10 years up to 1960, and thereafter extended every 10 years.

Article 243 (D) provides reservation of seats for SCs/STs in PRI from village panchayat to Zila Parishads in proportion of their population. There is also a provision for reservation of one-third of the seats for women (Amendment Act, 1992).

Article 243 (T) provides reservation of seats for SCs/STs in the Municipal Bodies in proportion of their population. There is also a provision for reservation of one-third of the seats for women (Amendment Act, 1992).

Service Safeguards

Article 16(4) – The Supreme Court in its judgment dated 16th November 1992, in the case of *Indra Sawhney and Others vs Union of India and Others*, however, observed that reservation of appointments or posts under Article 16 (4) of the Constitution is confined to initial appointment and cannot extend to reservation in the matter of promotion.

Article 16 (4A) – Seventy-seventh Amendment, Act 1995: 'Nothing in this Article shall prevent the State from making any provision for reservation in matter of promotion to any class or classes of posts in services under the State in favour of the Scheduled Castes and Scheduled Tribes which, in the opinion of the State, are not adequately represented in the services under the State'.

Special Safeguards for STs

Article 244 deals with the economic safeguards, Article 275(1) deals with the economic benefits including the grants-in-aid to State governments, Article 338 deals with special officer to investigate all matters relating to the safeguard of the STs and SCs and Article 338 (9) deals with the role of National Commission.

Inclusion in and Exclusion from SCs and STs

Article 341 (1) and Article 341 (2) deal with the inclusion/exclusion in the list of SCs.
Article 342 (1) and Article 342 (2) deal with the inclusion/exclusion in the list of STs.

Direct Recruitment

Concession to SC/ST Applicants for Employment

1. Age relaxation
2. Fee concession
3. Provision of rail/bus fare

Relaxation of Standards and other Steps for Filling up Reserved Seats

4. Relaxation of standards of suitability
5. Relaxation of experience qualification in direct recruitment

6. Separate interview for SC/ST candidates
7. Association of SC/ST officers with selection board/Departmental Promotion Committee (DPC)
8. Pre-examination training facilities
9. Concession in post filled by promotion
10. Relaxation of standards in departmental examination
11. Age relaxation in promotion

Economic Development for SCs/STs

SC-Sub-Plan and Tribal Sub-Plan

Sub-Plan is financed by four sources, viz.

1. Flow from State Plan
2. Flow from Central Sector and Centrally sponsored scheme
3. Special Central assistance, and
4. Institutional Finance.

Land to the Scheduled Castes

Land is an important productive asset in rural India and the backbone of agriculture. Nearly two-thirds of workforce directly or indirectly depends on agriculture for their livelihood. About one-fifth of the National Income is derived from agricultural sector. Farmers view possession of land as a status symbol as it also provides livelihood for them. Depressed Class people were prohibited from acquiring land. Land reform is one of the regulating mechanisms of agrarian activity which may be classified into: (i) Reforms aimed at changing ownership pattern (redistributive reform), (ii) Reforms dealing with leasing of land (tenancy/tenure reform) in Tamil Nadu.

Grant of Land to the Depressed Classes

1. *Missionaries:* For the first time in India, land right was given to Depressed Class people during the British period. During the latter half of the 19th Century, the European missionaries, viz., Adam Andrew and William Goudie, working in Madras Presidency, studied the pathetic and deplorable conditions of Depressed Class people and submitted a memorandum to the then British Government pleading for the intervention of the Government to assign the land.
2. *The Depressed Class Leaders:* The Depressed Class leaders Pandit Iyothidas and Rettamalai Srinivasan had given representation

to the Colonial government to assign land for the Depressed Class people.

3. *Sri Tremenheere:* The Government of Madras Presidency appointed Sri Tremenheere, the Collector of Chengalpattu District in 1891 to conduct an enquiry into the conditions of Depressed Class people and the report of his study was submitted in 1891. After discussing the prevailing situation of Depressed Class people, the Colonial Government enacted a law in British Parliament in 1892 to assign cultivable land to the Depressed Class people. In pursuance of it, the Government of Madras Presidency issued two important orders, viz., 1010 and 1010A on 30–9–1892 and 1–2–1893 to assign government lands to Depressed Class people
4. *Distribution of Landholdings:* At all-India level, SC population constitutes 16.2 per cent, while the land operated by SC was only 8.2 per cent of the land. Area of land includes owned/operated land. Area of land also includes distribution of ceiling surplus land and land bought in the land market. The data show that there was disparity in the distribution of land-holdings by social groups (Table 1).

Reservation of Jobs

History of Reservation

Reservation is nothing but a means to break the monopoly of handful of castes in getting access to employment, education and power. It is believed that caste based reservation in India started in 2nd Century BC. In *Manusmriti* – the law book of Brahmins, all the laws were based on caste and no merit was ever considered. It divided people into high and low castes on the basis of their birth and not on merit. Wealth, political power, spiritual leadership, education, ownership of land, trade and all lucrative aspects were reserved purely to the higher castes. (Shital Kumar Dige – http://drshitalkumardige.blogspot.in/2010/04/why-reservation.html)

Reservations in favour of Backward Classes (BCs) were introduced long before Independence in a large area, comprising the Presidency areas and the Princely States south of the Vindhyas. Chatrapati Sahu Maharaj, Maharaja of Kolhapur in Maharashtra introduced reservation in favour of backward classes as early as 1902 to eradicate poverty from amongst them and to give them their due share in the State administration. The notification of 1902 created

Table 1

Distribution of Operational Landholdings by Social Groups in India – 2005–06 and 2010–11 (Area in ha.)

Social Groups	*Number*		*Percentage*		*Area*		*Percentage*		*Population 2001*
	2005–06	*2010–11*	*2005–06*	*2010–11*	*2005–06*	*2010–11*	*2005–06*	*2010–11*	
Scheduled Castes	1,60,73,467	1,70,99,000	12.4	12.4	1,33,00,400	1,37,21,000	8.4	8.6	16.2
Scheduled Tribes	1,03,43,149	1,20,05,000	8.0	8.7	1,69,29,480	1,82,21,000	10.7	11.4	8.2
Others	10,25,49,772	10,90,06,087	79.4	78.8	12,63,99,027	12,61,08,183	79.8	79.0	75.6
Institutional	2,55,849	2,38,568	0.2	0.2	16,94,077	15,41,913	1.1	0.1	–
All	12,92,22,237	13,83,48,000	100.0	100.0	15,83,22,983	15,95,92,000	100.0	100.0	100.0

Source: All-India Report on Agricultural Censes, 2005–06, 201011.

50 per cent reservation in services for backward classes/communities in the State of Kolhapur. This is the first official instance (Government Order) providing for reservation for Depressed Classes in India.

'The demand for reservation was started in Mysore Province by Brahmanas against Brahmanas. The movement "Mysore only for Mysoreans" started during 1883 by Brahmanas of Mysore province under the leadership of Venkatakrishnayya, against Ayyar and Ayyangar Brahmanas of Madras and Smartha Brahmanas of Andhra Pradesh. It was continued till 1900, Mysore Brahmanas were successful. This Brahmana movement encouraged OBCs and Muslims to form their own party called "Prajamitra Mandali" in 1917. They also asked Reservation of jobs in Mysore province as all the prestigious jobs were held by Brahmanas. So on 8th of August 1918, a committee for Backward Classes was constituted under the Chief Justice Sir Wesley Miller. Based on the report 75% of the jobs in Mysore province were reserved for OBCs and Muslims' (Avinash Baburao Adanakar – http://adanakar.blogspot.in/2011/08/aarakshanreservation-system-hard.html.)

In August 1933 the then Prime Minister of Britain, Ramsay Macdonald introduced the Communal Award, according to which separate representation was to be provided for the Muslims Sikhs, Indian-Christians Anglo-Indians, Europeans and SCs. Depressed Classes were assigned a number of seats to be filled by election from special constituencies in which only the voters belonging to Depressed Classes could vote.

In 1935, the British passed the Government of India Act, 1935, designed to give Indian provinces greater self-rule and set up a national federal structure. Reservation of seats for Depressed Classes was incorporated into the Act, which came into force in 1937. The Act brought the term 'Scheduled Castes' into use, and defined the group as including 'such castes, races or tribes or parts of groups within castes, races or tribes, which appear to His Majesty in Council to correspond to the classes of persons formerly known as 'Depressed Classes', as His Majesty in Council may prefer. This discretionary definition was clarified in *The Government of India (Scheduled Castes) Order, 1936* which contained a list, or Schedule, of castes throughout the British administered provinces.

The framers of the Constitution understood that due to the erstwhile caste system, SCs and the STs were historically oppressed, denied respect and equal opportunity in Indian society and were thus underrepresented in nation-building activities. The Constitution laid down 15 per cent and 7.5 per cent of vacancies to government aided educational institutes and for jobs in the government/public sector, as reserved quota for SC and ST candidates respectively for a period of ten years, after which the situation was to be reviewed. This period was routinely extended by the succeeding governments.

The people of Depressed Class were denied access to education, employment and dwelling units/house sites. When the colonial government expanded railways, postal and military, they were in need of labour to help them. The upper caste people were not ready to provide their labour.

The Depressed Class labourers were engaged as gardeners, cooks, butlers, etc. Thus, the Officers from the Colonial government played an important role in engaging the Depressed Class people as butler and helper in their household activities and for the government. As result of this, many persons belonging to the Depressed Class people could get a decent salary from their employer/government.

Iyothidas was born on 20 May 1845. His original name was Kaathavarayan. Iyothidas was considered as one of the early leaders among the Depressed Class people in India. His grandfather Kanthappan was a butler to George Harrington. Iyothidases father, Kandasamy, was also working as butler. He was a writer, journalist, social reformer, Buddhist scholar and Siddha physician.

Similarly, Dr Ambedkar's father and grandfather were working as Subedar for British Military. The colonial government had also established separate military exclusively with Mahars of Maharashtra known as 'Mahar regiment'. Similarly 'Madras regiment' was also established in Madras Presidency with *Pariahs*. Madras regiment is also known as *'Pariah* regiment'.

Central Government Employment

As per the Indian Constitution, 15 per cent of jobs/employment is reserved for SCs, 7.5 per cent is for STs and 27 per cent is for OBCs. Remaining 51.50 per cent of employment is reserved for General candidates.

The data presented in Table 2 clearly indicates that employment in the Central Government has declined in 2011 as compared to 2009, both in absolute and in percentage terms. The decline in employment may be attributed to recruitment policies of the Government after the introduction of the New Economic Policy in India. The downsizing policy of public employment has been a major contributory factor for this declining trend.

Table 2

Central Government Employment: 2009 and 2011 (in lakh)

Category of Employees	*Number of Employees as on 31st March*		*Increase/Decrease (+) (-)*	
	2009	*2011*	*Absolute*	*Percentage*
Regular	30.99	30.87	–0.12	–0.39
Total	30.99	30.87	–0.12	–0.39

Source: Census of Central Government Employees (As on 31st March 2011), Government of India Ministry of Labour and Employment Directorate General of Employment and Training Survey and Study Division, New Delhi, April 2014.

Of the five major Ministries, the Ministry of Railways has a major share with 43.02 per cent of the employment to the total Central Government Employees followed by Ministries of Home Affairs with 25.95 per cent (Table 3).

Table 3

Regular Central Government Employment in Major Ministries as on 31st March 2011

S. No.	*Ministry*	*Number of Regular Employees*	*Employees Percentage to the Total*
1.	Communications and IT	2,16,490	7.01
2.	Defense (Civilian)	3,75,309	12.16
3.	Finance	1,03,927	3.37
4.	Home Affairs	8,01,092	25.95
5.	Railways	13,28,199	43.02
6.	Others	2,62,261	8.49
	Total	30,87,278	100.00

Source: Same as Table 2.

Women form nearly half of the total population. Their work participation is very low in India due to social and cultural milieu. Women participation has been increasing in the recent past. It may be observed from Table 4 that participation of women was the highest in the Ministry of Communications and IT with 17.30 per cent, whereas participation of women in the Ministry of Railways is quite low with 7.28 per cent as compared to the women participation in other Ministries of the Central Government.

Table 4

Estimated Women Employment in Major Employing Ministries

S.No.	Ministry	Women Employment as on 31st March 2011	
		Number	Number Percentage Share
1.	Communications and IT	37,460	17.30
2.	Railways	96,704	7.28
3.	Defense (Civilian)	42,698	11.38
4.	Other	1,60,577	13.76
	Total	3,37,439	10.93

Source: Same as Table 2.

The Central Government has classified the workforce into four groups, viz., Group 'A' Group 'B', Group 'C' and Group 'D'. Group 'A' posts carry higher administrative and executive responsibilities; Group 'B' constitutes middle management; Group 'C' posts perform supervisory as well as operative tasks and render clerical assistances in Ministries; Group 'D' posts are meant for carrying out routine duties, menials and sub-staff.

The data presented in Table 5 clearly reveal that a bulk of Central Government Employment is in the Group 'C' posts with their share 68.92 per cent share. The employment under group 'D' post constitutes about 16 per cent.

Table 5

Regular Central Government Employees Classified by Group of Posts Held

Group of Posts	As on 31st March 2011	
	No. of Employees	Percentage to Total
A	93,853	3.04
B	3,80,044	12.31
C	21,27,752	68.92
D	4,85,629	15.73
Total	30,87,278	100.00

Source: Same as Table 2.

The data presented in Table 6 clearly indicate that public sector undertakings provide huge employment as compared to private sector undertakings and central government. It is significant to note that public sector employment has gone down, while the employment under private sector has gone up during post-reform period.

Table 6

Employment in Public and Organized Private Sectors (in Lakhs)

Years	Public Sector (March End)		Private Sector (March End)		Total
	Number	Percentage	Number	Percentage	
1991	190.6	71.3	76.8	28.7	267.4
1995	194.7	70.7	80.6	29.3	275.3
2000	193.1	69.1	86.5	30.9	279.6
2002	187.7	69.0	84.3	31.0	272.0
2003	185.8	68.8	84.2	31.2	270.0
2004	181.9	68.8	82.5	31.2	264.4
2005	180.1	68.1	84.5	31.9	264.6
2006	181.9	67.5	87.7	32.5	269.6

Source: Ashutosh Gupta and Krishan Kumar, presentation on Trends Public and Private Sector in India, Tata Institute of Advanced Studies, Rohini, New Delhi.

The Indian Constitution guarantees reservation jobs for SCs/STs based on the proportion of population. 'Only about 4 per cent each of rural Scheduled Tribe and Scheduled Caste households have a member in a government job, according to the findings of the Socio Economic and Caste Census 2011 released earlier this month'[2] (*Indian Express*, 14 July 2015). The data presented in Table 7 clearly indicates that the required quota reservation has not been filled in central government services. The representation was high in Group C and D posts.

Table 7

Representation of SCs/STs in Central Government Services – 2000 (as on 1 January 2001)

	Total	SCs	%	STs	%
Group A	98,066	10,998	11.21	3,382	3.45
Group B	1,44,145	17,915	12.43	5,020	3.48
Group C	23,77,895	3,86,142	16.24	1,54,314	6.49
Group D (Excluding Sweepers)	9,56,947	1,67,947	17.55	64,865	6.78
Sweepers	1,32,102	79,850	60.45	6,456	4.89
Total (Excluding Sweepers)	35,77,053	5,83,002	16.30	2,27,581	6.36

Source: DOPT, as quoted National Commission for Scheduled Castes (NCSC), Seventh Report.

The data presented in Table 8 clearly indicates that the required quota reservation has not been filled in central public sector enterprises (PSE) in all types of posts. The representation was high in Group C and D posts.

Table 8

Representation of SCs/ST in Central Public Sector Enterprises (PSE) – 2000 (as on 1 January 2001)

	Total	*SCs*	*%*	*STs*	*%*
Group A	2,03,329	21,888	10.77	9,167	3.04
Group B	1,91,715	22,090	11.53	8,831	4.61
Group C	9,42,496	1,78,523	18.95	83,051	8.82
Group D (excluding Safai Karamacharis)	3,88,116	88,836	22.89	43,772	11.28
Total	17,25,656	3,11,337	18.05	1,41,821	8.22
Group D (Safai Karamacharis)	21,234	16,107	75.86	726	3.42
Total	17,46,890	3,27,444	18.75	1,42,547	8.16

Source: Department of Public Sector Enterprises, as quoted NCSC, Seventh Report.

Occupational Diversification

Agriculture continues to be the mainstay of Indian population, although some trends show occupational diversification of rural workers from agricultural to non-agricultural sector. Scheduled Castes (SCs) have been denied property rights. Caste system as a system of occupational assignment has relegated them to peripheral occupations and hence, economic immobility. Several welfare programmes have been conceived and implemented by the government to promote the emancipation and economic mobility among SCs. It is worthwhile to evaluate the impact of such policy interventions on the occupational status of SCs in Tamil Nadu.

Rural Labour: Self-employed in agriculture

The data presented in Table 9 reveal the occupational diversification of workers engaged in agriculture. The data indicate that 1. Self-employed in agriculture was low among the SCs; 2. Agricultural labourers was high among SCs. The data further show that the proportion of agricultural workers among SCs was twice that of self-employed in agriculture. Among STs, OBCs and Others, the proportion of self-employed was high as compared to agricultural workers. Thus, the data show the vulnerability of the SCs as compared to other social groups with respect to self-employed in agriculture.

Table 9

Per Thousand Distributions of Households by Social Groups Engaged in Agriculture

Social Groups	*Self-employed in Agriculture*				*Agricultural Labourers (rural labour)*			
	2004–05	*1999–2000*	*1993–94*	*1987–88*	*2004–05*	*1999–2000*	*1993–94*	*1987–88*
STs	393	362	380	377	340	397	378	381
SCs	202	164	201	189	405	514	493	517
Neo-Buddhists		–	–	188	–	–	–	591
OBCs	387	347	–	–	224	292	–	–
Others	433	411	433	433	156	190	232	232
All –India	359	327	378	–	258	322	303	–
	F – ratio = 8.89*				F – ratio = 4.140**			

* Significant at 1 per cent level.

** Significant at 5 per cent level.

Source: NSS Reports on 'Employment and unemployment situation among social groups in India', 1987–88, 1993–94, 199–200 and 2004–05.

Rural Labourers: Self-Employed in Non-agriculture

Self-employed in non-agriculture is an indicator of the economic well-being of people. Self-employed in non-agricultural occupation have some access to capital. The data presented in Table 10 abundantly make it clear that self-employment in non-agricultural occupation was low among STs and SCs. It is also evident from the data that the proportion of households engaged in manual work was the highest among SCs as compared to STs, OBCs and Others. This data again show the vulnerability of SCs and STs in India.

Self-employed: Urban Labour: Urban Areas

Given the limited availability for agricultural land in urban areas, the work-force in urban areas is predominantly engaged in non-agricultural activities. The data on urban workforce by self-employed, regular wages/salaried and casual labourer shows interesting features of urban occupational pattern among social groups.

Table 10

Per Thousand Distributions of Households by Social Groups Engaged in Non-Agriculture

Social Groups	*Self employed in non-agriculture*				*Other labour (Manual workers) (rural labour)*				*Others*			
	04–05	*99–00*	*93–94*	*87–88*	*04–05*	*99–00*	*93–94*	*87–88*	*04–05*	*99–00*	*93–94*	*87–88*
STs	64	52	59	59	113	89	101	116	89	101	82	67
SCs	141	120	107	110	154	100	102	114	98	102	97	69
Neo-Buddhists		–	–	55	–	–	–	54	–	–	–	104
OBCs	176	155	–	–	104	79	–	–	110	127	–	–
Others	181	148	144	138	77	63	69	79	153	187	121	115
All-India	158	134	127	–	109	80	80	–	116	137	112	–
	F – ratio = 5.458*				F – ratio = 8.121*				F – ratio = 4.234**			

* Significant at 1 per cent level

** Significant at 5 per cent level

Sources: Same as above

Table 11

Per Thousand Distributions of Households by Social Groups Engaged as Self-employed: Urban Labour

Social Groups	*2004–05*	*1999–2000*	*1993–94*	*1987–88*
Scheduled Tribes	263	216	216	215
Scheduled Castes	294	273	249	260
Neo-Buddhists	–	–	–	154
Other Backward Classes	403	376	–	–
Others	386	355	355	352
All-India	375	344	337	–
		F – ratio = 4.859**		

** Significant at 5 per cent level.

Sources: Same as above.

Self-employment indicates the economic independence of people. The data presented in Table 11 makes it clear that self-employed in urban areas was low among STs and SCs. The proportion of workers engaged in urban areas as self-employed among SCs was three-fourths, and among STs was about two-thirds as that of Others and OBCs. This data again show the vulnerability of SCs and STs in India.

Regular Wage/Salaried: Urban Areas

Workers employed on regular wage and salaried jobs is an indicator for economic stability of individuals. The data presented in Table 12 clearly illustrates that the rate of workers employed on regular wages and salaried jobs was low among OBCs as compared to Others, STs and SCs. The variation in the workers engaged in regular wage/salaried among social groups shows the positive role of the reservation policy for SCs and STs soon after the independence. This data show the economic independence of SCs and STs in India.

Table 12

Per Thousand Distribution of Households by Social Groups Engaged in Regular Wage/Salaried: Urban Labour

Social Groups	*2004–05*	*1999–2000*	*1993–94*	*1987–88*
Scheduled Tribes	418	380	444	425
Scheduled Castes	411	376	392	394

Cont'd...

...Cont'd

Neo-Buddhists	–	–	–	438
Other Backward Classes	367	363	–	–
Others	448	465	439	450
All-India	413	417	434	–
		F – ratio = 5.059*		

* Significant at 1 per cent level.

Sources: Same as above.

Casual Labourers: Urban Areas

Workforce employed as casual labourers is an indicator for economic instability of the individuals. The data presented in Table 12 show that workers employed as casual labourers were more among SCs as compared to others in social groups. This data again show the economic vulnerability of the SCs in India.

Table 13

Per Thousand Distribution of Households by Social Groups Engaged in Casual Labourers: Urban Labour

Social Groups	*2004–05*	*1999–2000*	*1993–94*	*1987–88*
Scheduled Tribes	173	256	201	220
Scheduled Castes	218	265	276	260
Neo-Buddhists	–	–	–	275
Other Backward Classes	145	174	–	–
Others	62	74	108	103
All-India	118	140	132	–
		F – ratio = 5.014*		

* Significant at 1 per cent level.

Sources: Same as above.

Reservation in Private Sector

Reservation of jobs is necessary for both public and private sectors. Public sector employment has been steadily declining, while the employment opportunity in the private sector has been increasing during the post-reform period. There is a need to introduce caste-based reservation for employment opportunities in private sector also. 'After the economic liberalization, ample employment opportunities were generated in private sector. The number of jobs in the government sector had dwindled owing to outsourcing and disinvestment policies. It is the right time for Dalit organizations to launch a struggle for introduction of reservation for the employment opportunities in private sector' (Mattu, *The Hindu*, 13 June 2016). It is generally stated that employment opportunities are made in the private sector: (i) On the basis of network, (ii) No regular/proper advertisement, (iii) Select candidates based on recommendations.

Arguments Against Reservation of Jobs

The protagonists of the against reservation of jobs in public sector argue that reservation of jobs – legitimizes demerit, causes causality of efficiency, creates elites-creamy layers among SCs and STs, and is against free trade/laissez faire policy.

Quota in Private Sector to Hit Investment and should be Based on Economics

Arun Shourie, the Former Divestment Minister, was of the view that 'Investment will be more uncertain in an increasingly competitive world, if jobs are given on the basis of my birth and not on the basis of my capability'.[3] N.R. Narayana Murthy, Chairman and Chief Mentor, Infosys emphasized the need for economic based reservation policy, 'I am not against reservation, but it should be based on economics and not caste. If a person is hampered by resources, I think those people should be given reservation'.[4] It is significant to note that both of them are against the introduction of caste-based reservation policy.

What is Required?

The Eleventh Five-Year Plan document, Government of India, shows that reservation in private Sector would be brought in, but there was no mention about the reservation in private sector in the Twelfth Five-Year Plan document. The new Government at the Centre has been intensifying the process of liberalization, privatization and globalization (LPG), but has not emerged with the introduction of reservation policy in private sector. The new economic policy consisting of liberalization, privatization and globalization have eroded employment opportunities for SCs, STs and OBCs to retain the gains already achieved. The demand for reservation in private/corporate sector is a legitimate demand to create foundation for the establishment of a society where the opportunities for development are available for all. The Government of

India should come forward to implement reservation in private sectors to open up employment opportunities for SCs, STs and OBCs. In India, private sector enjoys infrastructural development, viz., land, road, power and tax holidays created by the Government. Private sector also takes a lot of money from public sector banks and financial institutions, and there is a huge default in loan repayment and taxes. Hence, private sector in India needs to be a partner to come forward to fulfil the legitimate demand for providing jobs to marginalized people as a matter of social justice for the loss created by the New Education Policy (NEP) in providing employment opportunities. Reservation in private sector will pave way for creating a casteless/class less society.

Conclusion

The results indicate that the land operated by SCs was low; the employment provided by the central government has declined, the representation of SC/ST members in Group A/Grade 1 posts in the Central Government was low, workers engaged as self-employed in agriculture was low among SCs, proportion of agricultural workers was high among the SCs, workers engaged as self-employed in non-agriculture was low among SCs, and proportion of casual labour was high among SCs as compared to other workers in India. There has been an opposition to introduce the caste based reservation policy.

Notes

1. Keer, Dhananjay (2005), *Dr Ambedkar: Life and Mission*, Mumbai: Popular Prakashan Pvt. Ltd., p. 233.
2. *Indian Express*, 14 July 2015.
3. Kaur, Harpreet and R.K. Suri (2009), *Reservation in India: Recent Perspectives in Higher Education*, New Delhi: Pentagon Press, p. 186.
4. People's March (2005), 'Voice of the Indian Revolution', Vol. 6, No. 2, February.

References

Beteille, A. (1996), *Caste, Class and Power: Changing Patterns of Stratification in a Tanjore Village*, Berkeley: University of California Press.

Gupta, Ashutosh and Krishan Kumar (2009), *Presentation on Trends in Public and Private Sector in India*, New Delhi: Tata Institute of Advanced Studies.

http://adanakar.blogspot.in/2011/08/aarakshanreservation-system-hard.html

http://drshitalkumardige.blogspot.in/2010/04/why-reservation.html

Shivamoga (2016), 'Need for Caste-based Reservation for Jobs in Private Sector', *The Hindu*, June 13.

Thangaraj, M. (2014), 'Occupational Pattern', in Sukhadeo Thorat and Nidhi Sadana Sabharwal (eds), *Bridging the Social Gap: Perspectives on Dalit Development*, New Delhi: Sage Publications India Pvt. Ltd.

Index